PENGUIN BOOKS

NELSON MANDELA
THE MAN AND THE MOVEMENT

Mary Benson was born and educated in Pretoria, South Africa. During the Second World War she served as a personal assistant in British headquarters in the Middle East, Algeria, Italy, Greece and Vienna, and subsequently worked among displaced persons in the Ruhr. While she was David Lean's secretary she read *Cry, the Beloved Country* and found her attitude towards South Africa transformed.

From 1950 to 1956 she assisted the Reverend Michael Scott in founding the Africa Bureau in London and in lobbying at the United Nations. She met Walter Sisulu, and then Nelson Mandela, during the early 1950s, and in 1957 became secretary to the Treason Trials Defence Fund in Johannesburg until ill health forced her resignation. She returned to South Africa in 1961 to work on a history of the African National Congress and interviewed Mandela while he was underground. In 1963 she was the first South African to testify before the UN Committee on Apartheid and in 1964 was invited to speak about the men in the Rivonia trial.

Since 1958 she has been a freelance writer. Among her books are biographies of Tshekedi Khama and Albert Lutuli, a history of the ANC *South Africa, the Struggle for a Birthright*, a novel *At the Still Point*, and her autobiography *A Far Cry: the Making of a South African*. She has written radio plays on Nelson Mandela, Robben Island, Rainer Maria Rilke and Thomas Wolfe. She has also edited Athol Fugard's *Notebooks*.

In 1966, after reporting on political trials in the Eastern Cape, she was placed under house arrest. Banned from all writing, she returned to London. Not permitted to return to South Africa until 1990, she recently went home to vote in the country's first democratic election.

NELSON MANDELA

THE MAN AND THE MOVEMENT

Mary Benson

PENGUIN BOOKS

PENGUIN BOOKS

Published by the Penguin Group
Penguin Books Ltd, 27 Wrights Lane, London w8 5tz, England
Penguin Books USA Inc., 375 Hudson Street, New York, New York 10014, USA
Penguin Books Australia Ltd, Ringwood, Victoria, Australia
Penguin Books Canada Ltd, 10 Alcorn Avenue, Toronto, Ontario, Canada m4v 3b2
Penguin Books (NZ) Ltd, 182–190 Wairau Road, Auckland 10, New Zealand

Penguin Books Ltd, Registered Offices: Harmondsworth, Middlesex, England

Published in Penguin Books 1986
Reprinted with revisions and new material 1994
5 7 9 10 8 6 4

Typeset by Datix International Limited, Bungay, Suffolk
Printed in England by Clays Ltd, St Ives plc
Filmset in 10.5/12.5 pt Monophoto Bembo

To those who died for the South Africa
struggling to be born

CONTENTS

LIST OF PLATES

ACKNOWLEDGEMENTS

As my encounters with Nelson Mandela were scattered between 1953, 1956, 1961, 1962, 1990, 1992 and 1994, I have relied also on interviews with his family, friends and comrades – among them fellow prisoners on Robben Island, including Mac Maharaj and Walter Sisulu.

I am grateful to Nicholas Bethell and to the *Mail on Sunday* for permission to quote from his report of a visit to Mr Mandela; to Joel Joffe for access to his writings on the Rivonia trial; and to Peter Davis for a record of interviews with Winnie Mandela and with members of the Mandela family in the Transkei.

To Winnie Mandela and to Ismail Ayob, my thanks for permission to quote extracts from Nelson Mandela's letters while he was in prison, and to Zindzi Mandela for permission to quote her poem 'A tree was chopped down' from *Black As I Am* (Guild of Tutors Press of International College, Los Angeles).

I

'A REASONABLE MAN,
NOT A VIOLENT MAN'

How is it that a man imprisoned for twenty-seven years – who was not allowed to be quoted by the South African media – became the embodiment of the struggle for liberation in that country and the vital symbol of a new society?

What in their everyday experience on Robben Island led his fellow-prisoners, especially men who were not partisan to his cause but members of rival organizations, to speak of the 'veneration' which Mandela inspired?

The testimony of Eddie Daniels, a member of the disbanded South African Liberal Party, is revealing: 'Mr Mandela is a good man. He can walk with kings and he can walk with beggars. I want to tell P. W. Botha,* if he speaks to Nelson Mandela, he speaks to a reasonable man, not a violent man – one of the kindest, most honest, peace-loving men. Mr Mandela took to violence, like I took to violence, not because he wanted to, but the laws of the land pushed me over the brink.'

Fikile Bam, lawyer and member of the Unity Movement, explained 'Once you've put a man in prison "for life", there's nothing else you can do to him – except kill him, of course. He becomes a power in his own self. The longer Mandela is kept in prison, the more of a focus he becomes for the things we all hope for. He and the African National Congress have never been afraid to go to the negotiating table. If the government do not talk to him, it is at their peril and, unfortunately, at the peril of all South Africans.'

These are South African views. But why, for the world at

* Then President of South Africa.

large, did Mandela become a legend in his own time? Even during his imprisonment honours were heaped on him. He was given the freedom of the cities of Rome and Glasgow, of Olympia and Aberdeen. In Grenoble there is a Place Mandela and in London's Camden Town a Mandela Street. Honorary doctorates of law were conferred on him by universities as far apart as Lesotho and New York. In Venezuela he was honoured with the Simon Bolivar award, along with Juan Carlos, King of Spain, for contributing to freedom and democracy. When the Bordeaux Bar Association's first international human rights award was given to him, his name was linked with that of Dreyfus who, found guilty of 'treason', had also been imprisoned on an island, Devil's Island.

Mandela's estranged wife, Winnie, once spoke prophetically of her husband and the men imprisoned with him: 'They are totally liberated; a government in exile.'

2

'THE PRIDE OF THE AFRICAN NATION'

1918–40

Nelson Rolihlahla Mandela spent his childhood in a fertile valley among the rolling hills of the Transkei. The family *kraal* of white-washed huts was not far from the Mbashe River which flowed past maize fields and a wattle plantation, past grasslands where cattle grazed and on eastwards to the Indian Ocean.

In that setting Mandela's love for his country and for his people took root. He was born on 18 July 1918 at Qunu near Umtata, the capital village of the Transkei 'reserve'. As one of the royal family of the Thembu, his upbringing was traditional and a sense of responsibility was bred in him. His father, Henry Mgadla Mandela, was chief councillor to their relative, the Paramount Chief of the Thembu, and with him had joined the South African army to fight the Germans in South-West Africa during the First World War. Henry Mandela also sat on the Transkeian Territories General Council, known as the Bunga – a body of Africans and Europeans which advised the Pretoria government on local matters. A polygamist, Mandela had four wives. Nelson's mother, Nonqaphi (commonly known as Nosekeni), was a woman of strong character and dignity. Neither parent had been educated in the western sense and they were surprised when he returned from school one day and announced: 'My name is Nelson!' A school teacher had given him the name. (His Xhosa name Rolihlahla means 'stirring up trouble'.)

Life in their *kraal* at Qunu was sheltered, and Nelson and his older sisters fulfilled certain duties such as herding cattle, tending the sheep or – in his case – helping with the ploughing. But he longed for an adventurous life; at night he listened fascinated to the tribal elders, bearded old men gathered around a huge open

3

fire, telling of the 'good old days, before the arrival of the white man'. He liked to recall those occasions which he saw as the background to his political development:

> Then our people lived peacefully, under the democratic rule of their kings and their councillors, and moved freely and confidently up and down the country without let or hindrance. Then the country was ours . . . we occupied the land, the forests, the rivers; we extracted the mineral wealth beneath the soil and all the riches of this beautiful country. We set up and operated our own government, we controlled our own armies and we organized our own trade and commerce.
>
> The elders would tell tales about the wars fought by our ancestors in defence of the fatherland, as well as the acts of valour performed by generals and soldiers during those epic days. The names of Dingane and Bambata among the Zulus, of Hintsa, Makana, Ndlambe of the AmaXhosa, and Sekukhuni and others in the north, were mentioned as the pride and glory of the entire African nation.

Attending mission school, Nelson was introduced to another world and it was a shock to find the history books recognized only white heroes, describing blacks as savages and cattle thieves, and referring to the wars between the AmaXhosa and the British as the 'Kaffir' Wars.

His sister Mabel, many years later, remembered his having to wear his father's cast-off clothes, with sleeves and trouser-legs shortened; he did not care that he was a laughing-stock, he was so keen to learn.

At home he heard of more recent events not taught in history lessons: of how in 1921 General Smuts, the Prime Minister, had sent an army which massacred 163 men, women and children at nearby Bulhoek in the Eastern Cape; members of an Israelite sect, they had refused to move from the 'common' ground on which they were camping. And of how, soon after, Smuts's planes bombed the Bondelswarts people in the mandated territory of South-West Africa because they had refused to pay a dog tax they could not afford; more than a hundred were killed. 'Bulhoek' and 'Bondelswarts' were names that lodged painfully in his memory just as they had in the wider African consciousness.

In 1930 Henry Mandela became very ill. Realizing he was dying, he sent for the Paramount Chief and presented his son, saying, 'I am giving you this servant, Rolihlahla. This is my only son. I can say from the way he speaks to his sisters and friends that his inclination is to help the nation. I want you to make him what you would like him to be; give him education, he will follow your example.' Mabel, who was present, heard the Chief give his assurance. Aged twelve, Nelson became the ward of David Dalindyebo and after his father's death went to live at the Chief's Great Place, Mqekezweni. 'The Chief bought him clothes and my brother became a human being,' Mabel recalled. At seventeen Nelson was ready for circumcision, spending several weeks in the mountains with young men of his age group, their faces white-painted, their bodies grass-skirted, as tribal elders led them through the ritual initiation and schooling to prepare them for manhood and for participation in tribal councils. By this time, Nelson was studying at Clarkebury, a nearby training college.

During the holidays he listened to the Paramount Chief conduct the court to which minor chiefs submitted cases. Although the South African government had reduced many chiefs to paid functionaries of the white bureaucracy, the Paramount Chief retained certain powers, along with the respect of his people. For Nelson it was a gripping experience: the prosecution followed by the defence, cross-examination of witnesses and, finally, the judgement given by the chief in consultation with his councillors. The youth dreamed of becoming a lawyer, not realizing that he was being groomed for chieftainship.

During the mid-thirties, as Nelson prepared for matriculation at Healdtown, a Methodist high school, politics rather than examinations were uppermost in students' minds: a crisis affecting their people throughout South Africa struck Cape Africans particularly hard.

Since 1854 African property-holders in the Eastern Cape, which included the Transkei and the Ciskei, had been on the common voters' roll; the result of the liberalizing influence of missionaries who had spread western education so that significant numbers of Africans were educated, many in multiracial schools. Mandela's great-grandfather, Ngubengcuka, had donated land for a mission high school. Africans were encouraged to believe that through education they would achieve all the rights of citizenship. But the discovery of diamonds in British-ruled Kimberley in 1867, then of gold in the Boer Republic of the Transvaal in 1886, pitchforked the country into an industrial revolution. As capital and European immigrants poured in, the demand for cheap labour was insatiable, and Africans, who had already lost land through settler invasions, found themselves forced by taxation to labour in the mines. A black proletariat was in the making. Land reserved for Africans, such as the Transkei and the Ciskei, became reservoirs of migrant labour. The Boers (South Africans of Dutch, Huguenot and German descent) who in the 1830s had trekked from British rule in the Cape – outraged by the abolition of slavery – felt newly threatened by British encroachment and, in 1899, the so-called Boer War broke out.

When Mandela came to study the history of this conflict, he learned how bitter a legacy civil war leaves behind. He also learned that, whatever their mutual hostility, the two white groups would unite whenever confronted by the 'native problem', the *'swart gevaar'* (black danger), as they had in 1910 when Britain, overriding widespread protests by African leaders as well as churchmen and liberals, consigned the blacks of South Africa to being ruled by the white minority. (There had been no lack of warnings; perhaps the most moving came from Olive Schreiner, author and feminist, who envisaged the disasters ahead for a South Africa in which the white man, 'blinded by the gain of the moment', after dispossessing the African of his land and depriving him of citizenship, 'forced him permanently in his millions into the locations and compounds and slums of our cities, obtaining his labour cheap'.*)

* Olive Schreiner, *Closer Union*, Fifield, 1909.

Now again in 1936, despite an upsurge of united opposition from African political, social, religious and other groups under an All-African Convention, the last door to common citizenship was slammed in their faces. The all-white parliament in Cape Town voted by 169 votes to eleven to remove black voters from the common roll. Thus the Africans living in the Cape – the only enfranchised blacks in the whole of South Africa – were now disenfranchised and confined to a separate roll to vote for three 'Native Representatives' (all white) and four members of the Senate (all white). They were also to have a Natives' Representative Council and urban boards, all purely advisory bodies.

And the pass laws were to be applied in the Cape as in the Transvaal, Natal and the Orange Free State. Thirty-six colour bar laws had already been enacted since 1910 – none accepted by the so-called non-European population without protest – but the law most hated, which controlled the movement and daily lives of Africans, was the pass system. An African needed a pass to get a job, to travel and to be out after curfew at night.* Failure to produce it on demand meant a fine or, more usually, imprisonment. Clergy, lawyers, doctors and others of the African middle classes were only partially exempted since they had to carry a certificate proving their exemption. Angry resentment against the system was exacerbated by police brutality in its administration.

The 1936 'Segregation' Bills which were passed by Prime Minister Hertzog – an Afrikaner Nationalist – with the support of his old enemy, General Smuts, were described by a former Chief Justice, Sir James Rose-Innes, as having a 'full-blooded fascist flavour'.

Land, the Africans' only source of security, had been massively plundered under the Native Land Act i 1913. Now, the proportion of land accessible to the eight million Africans was pegged at 12.7 per cent, leaving 87 per cent for the two million whites.

* Such a pass could be issued by any white person, even by children.

The countrywide agitation aroused students, and Nelson Mandela's burgeoning nationalism was further stimulated at Fort Hare College, where he began to study for a Bachelor of Arts degree. Fort Hare, in the village of Alice in the Eastern Cape, had been founded in 1916 and already had a proud record of educating potential leaders not only of South Africa but also of East and Central Africa.

A fellow-student who became a close friend of Nelson's was Oliver Tambo, one year older, also from the Transkei but from Bizana in Pondoland, to the north-east of Thembuland. Son of a peasant farmer, after attending a local Anglican mission school, Oliver had proved a brilliant student at St Peter's in Johannesburg – the secondary school set up by the Community of the Resurrection, known as the African Eton. After matriculating with a first-class pass in 1938, he had been awarded a scholarship to Fort Hare by the Transkeian Bunga and was now studying for a degree in science.

Oliver observed that Nelson, although sensitive and quick to react to insult or patronage, was good-natured and popular. Their friendship was cut short by Nelson's abrupt departure from the college: as a member of the Students' Representative Council, he had joined a protest boycott after the authorities reduced its powers and was among those suspended.

Returning home to Mqekezweni, Nelson was ordered by the Paramount Chief to accept the college ultimatum to abandon the boycott so that he could resume his studies. He would probably have obeyed but an unexpected development saved him from a compromise which could have altered the course of his life. As he later described it: 'My guardian felt it was time for me to get married. He loved me very much and looked after me as diligently as my father had. But he was no democrat and did not think it worth while to consult me about a wife. He selected a girl, fat and dignified; *lobola* (symbol of bride-wealth) was paid, and arrangements were made for the wedding.'

Nelson decided to run away. Accompanied by a cousin, he stole and sold an ox to pay for their rail fares. In retrospect he has said that his rejection of the designated marriage symbolized a deeper rejection, for by this time he had realized he was being prepared for chieftainship and he had made up his mind never to rule over an oppressed people. At the age of twenty-two, he set off for Johannesburg.

3

'WE WILL GALVANIZE THE ANC'

1941–51

In 1941 Mandela, a striking, athletic young man with a natural air of authority, was one among many thousands flocking to Johannesburg. Two years earlier South Africa, under the leadership of General Smuts, had joined Britain and her allies in the war against Hitler's Germany and Mussolini's Italy and there was a massive demand for labour in wartime industries.

Travelling by country bus and then by train – in a carriage labelled NON-EUROPEANS – Mandela headed north through Natal and into the highveld of the Transvaal until yellow-sanded mine dumps marked the outskirts of Egoli, city of gold. He was abruptly thrust into a new world of tall buildings, of fast and confusing traffic, and bustling crowds of all races. Throughout the city and the spacious white suburbs there was evidence of immense prosperity, but Africans – 'natives' – were confined to teeming 'locations' and shantytowns. Overcrowded, insanitary, without electricity, tarred roads or telephones, these urban slums were continually raided by police in search of pass and liquor law offenders. Riots were sparked off, family life disintegrated and crime multiplied. For dispossessed Africans these were the facts of life under the colour bar. Mandela's political education had begun.

Groomed from childhood for respectability, status and sheltered living, he was now thrown into the melting-pot of urban survival. The first thing was to get a job and the best hope was in the mines. Many years later he recalled those events with amusement: he was taken on at Crown Mines as a policeman with the promise that he would soon be promoted to clerk. Armed with *knobkerrie* (a heavy, knobbed stick) and whistle, he guarded the gate to the compound in which black miners were housed. However, within a few days, a representative of the Paramount Chief had tracked him down and again he was on the run.

He found a room in Alexandra, a sprawling township on the north-eastern edge of Johannesburg. There an acquaintance suggested he should meet 'a certain Walter Sisulu', who could be relied on to give useful advice. Sisulu, several years his senior and also from the Transkei, had had a strict and religious upbringing. He knew exceptionally well what it meant to be classified as a 'native': in a mine he had laboured with pick and shovel a mile underground; he had been 'kitchen-boy' in a white household; and he had worked in a succession of factories, clashing with unjust bosses. Meanwhile he had studied for his Junior Certificate by correspondence and stayed with his mother, who took in washing for white families. When Mandela met him, he was running a small estate agency in the city, dealing in such freehold land as still remained accessible to blacks, and he promptly offered the young newcomer a job at £2 a month plus commission.

When Mandela confided his early ambition to study law, Sisulu provided the financial help to enable him to take his BA degree by correspondence course. He also gave Nelson a loan to buy a smart new suit for the graduation ceremony and then introduced him to a firm of white lawyers to whom he could be articled while studying law part-time at the University of the Witwatersrand.

Here Mandela had his first direct encounter with 'Europeans', as whites were then called. In the Transkei they had been magistrates, traders and teachers; now he worked for and with them. On his arrival at the office the senior typist explained, 'Look, Nelson, we have no colour bar here. When the teaboy brings the tea, come and get yours from the tray. We have bought two new cups for you and Gaur. You must use *them*. Tell Gaur. And be careful, he is a bad influence.'

Gaur Radebe, a clerk with the firm, a rather lordly little man, was politically radical and when Mandela told him about the new cups, his response was, 'You watch and do exactly as I do.' As soon as the tea arrived, Radebe avoided the new cups and deliberately chose one of the old ones. Mandela, who had no wish to quarrel with him or with the typist, pretended that he did not drink tea.

Another typist often asked him for work when she had nothing to do. One day while he was dictating to her, a white client came into the office and the girl, obviously embarrassed and wanting to demonstrate that Mandela was not her superior, took sixpence from her purse and commanded, 'Nelson, please go and get me some shampoo from the chemist.'

The humour with which he recounted such incidents was typical of his reaction to white prejudice and ignorance when directed at himself; when directed at defenceless people he was deeply angered.

While still a student, he married Evelyn Ntoko Mase, a pretty, soft-spoken nurse at the City Deep Mine Hospital. She generously contributed to his fees. They set up home in Orlando, one of the expanding townships crammed with uniform match-box houses in a barren landscape about ten miles to the south-west of Johannesburg (an area later named Soweto, an acronym of south-western townships). Near by lived Sisulu and his wife, Albertina, also a nurse. And Oliver Tambo had arrived in Johannesburg to teach science and mathematics at St Peter's School.

Mandela's part-time course at the University of the Witwatersrand was arduous; besides, he lacked proper study facilities and there were the long train journeys and the eleven p.m. curfew. One of the partners in the firm to which he was articled, a Polish Jew to whom he always felt indebted for his kindness, gave him every encouragement and urged him to concentrate on becoming a good lawyer, thus 'earning the respect of all sections of the population'. He should avoid politics.

But Mandela could not agree to such a restraint; he was coming to think of himself as an African nationalist rather than a

Thembu, and was attracted to the African National Congress. Walter Sisulu was already a member and encouraged Tambo and Mandela to make a similar commitment to this most enduring and consistent of black political organizations. However, in 1942, after a period of decline, the ANC had lost members who broke away to form the African Democratic Party. The three friends – as Tambo later put it – thought this was wrong, that their duty was to stay in the ANC and to push their ideas of what it should be doing. They were to prove a historic team as they worked with other young people to activate Congress.

The ANC (originally known as the SA Native National Congress) had been established on 8 January 1912, two years before Afrikaners formed their National Party. Four young lawyers, led by Pixley ka Izaka Seme, who himself had just returned from studying at Columbia University, at Oxford and the Inns of Court, called a conference in Bloemfontein location. Their object was to unite their people. Tribal divisions, said Seme, were an aberration which had caused all their woes and backwardness and ignorance. 'We must think in wider political terms,' he insisted, 'for we are one people.'

An extraordinary event took place in this coming together of chiefs and their followers, leaders of political associations, ministers, teachers, journalists and lawyers. Gathered from all parts of South Africa as well as from British Bechuanaland, Basutoland and Swaziland, they overcame divisions of tribe and language, of rural and urban backgrounds. The Reverend John Dube, an educationist, was elected President-General, Seme became Treasurer, and Sol T. Plaatje, a self-educated newspaper editor and novelist, was appointed Secretary-General. The organization was modelled on the American Congress and contained elements of British parliamentary structure and procedure such as a Speaker and an Upper House of Chiefs. Their aims were to agitate for the removal of the colour bar in parliament, in education, in industry and in the administration. 'We were dreaming of change,' one of the delegates recalled half a century later, 'of the day when Africans would sit in parliament and would be able to buy land.'

They were indeed African nationalists, but they were not anti-white. Nor was it simply that their education had geared them towards seeking a share in the whites' political structures: opposition to white racialism contained within itself a refusal to react with black racialism. Over the succeeding decades, the ANC never deviated from its repudiation of racialism.

That first dignified gathering had opened with a prayer and a hymn by a Xhosa composer, Enoch Sontonga: 'Nkosi Sikelel' iAfrika' (Lord Bless Africa), which became the national anthem of the ANC and of the blacks of South Africa. (In the 1960s it was adopted by a number of independent African states.) In 1925 the ANC acquired a flag: black for the people, green for the land and gold for the resources.

There followed long years of protest against one injustice after another – protest expressed by demonstrations and meetings, by deputations and petitions – non-violent protest to which the only response was intensified repression and police violence. By the 1930s the ANC had declined into a virtual talking-shop, as one critic put it. It was then that an Anglican minister, James Calata from Cradock in the Eastern Cape, despite serious illness and poverty, doggedly began to revive the organization. He had been appointed Secretary-General and the recruitment of a new President-General, Dr A. B. Xuma, set the seal on that revival. Xuma, widely travelled and sophisticated, with a busy medical practice in Johannesburg, was joined by other impressive intellectuals, among them Z. K. Matthews, lecturer in social anthropology and native law and administration at Fort Hare, who had already made a name for himself in educational circles abroad. Politically aroused by the Hertzog Segregation Bills in 1936, Matthews was to play a significant role in the ANC, just as able young men like Mandela and Tambo who had been involved in student politics at Fort Hare were also making their mark.

It was a time of ferment when immense industrial expansion had brought a rapid increase of foreign investment which depended for its high profits on cheap labour. Wages for black workers were usually below subsistence level and African trade unions were becoming more militant. When workers challenged the system, however, employers and state combined to tighten the screws: a rash of strikes during 1942 had been countered by Smuts's War Measure 145, which outlawed all strikes by Africans. Nevertheless, strikes continued illegally and, in Alexandra, people struck against a rise in bus fares they were too poor to pay. In the bitter cold of a highveld winter thousands of men and women walked the ten miles to and from work. After nine days the bus company capitulated. And when, a year later in 1944, fares were again increased, the boycott was renewed. This time the people walked for seven weeks until victory was theirs.

The war against Nazism and Fascism stimulated ideas of freedom and self-determination. Afrikaner extremists might be pro-Nazi but African leaders in South Africa felt themselves part of a wider world, a world in which the colonized peoples of Asia and Africa struggled for their independence. The ANC under Xuma and Matthews produced a document of 'Africans' Claims', desiring to see 'all forms of racial domination in all lands completely destroyed' and 'self-government for colonial people' actively pursued. In addition to other demands such as abolition of the pass laws and the industrial colour bar, and the introduction of free, compulsory education, they wanted full citizenship rights, including the vote.

All these events and influences, and government failure to fulfil promises of reforms, incited the new mood of defiance in Mandela and other young nationalists. 'We were never really young,' Oliver Tambo has said of those days. 'There were no dances, hardly a cinema, but meetings, discussions, every night, every weekend.' (Mandela, however, maintained his physical fitness and had become a fine boxer.) They met in each other's houses or offices as they formulated their political philosophy.

This was most clearly expressed by the scholarly, magnetic Anton Muziwakhe Lembede, son of Zulu farm labourers so poor that they wore sacks for clothing, and so determined that their child be educated that somehow they had scraped together the fees for a primary school. By his own efforts he had then become a teacher and later a lawyer. Lembede and A. P. Mda, also a teacher who was to turn lawyer, with Mandela, Sisulu, Tambo and others, formed a Youth League. They set out to 'galvanize' the ANC which, they recognized, was 'the symbol and embodiment of the African's will to present a united front against all forms of oppression', but which had been organizationally weak, 'regarding itself as a body of gentlemen with clean hands', and failing to give a positive lead. The Youth League would be an assurance to the critics that the 'struggle and sacrifices of their fathers' had not been in vain. It must be 'the brains-trust and power-station of the spirit of African nationalism' and must arouse popular political consciousness. 'Foreign leadership' was firmly rejected as was the 'wholesale importation of foreign ideologies', though such ideologies – if useful – could be borrowed.

Lembede, Sisulu, Mandela and Tambo approached Dr Xuma, who warily embraced their proposal that the Youth League should become a part of the ANC. He was right to be wary; their 'galvanizing' would radically transform the organization.

In April 1944 Lembede was elected President of the League, and Tambo its Secretary. Mandela, who had taken part in the final drafting of a basic policy document drawn up by Mda, said they felt the ANC leadership had paid no attention to the question of organizing Congress into a mass movement. They aimed, through the Youth League, to stimulate development of a powerful national liberation movement; African nationalism would be its creed. Their goal was 'true democracy' and to achieve this the League would struggle for the removal of discriminatory laws and the admission of Africans to 'full citizenship' so that they would have 'direct representation in parliament'. Land would be redivided among farmers and peasants of all nationalities in proportion to their numbers. Trade union rights would be unhampered; free compulsory education for children would be supplemented by mass adult education, and

African culture would assimilate the best elements in European and other cultures. They wanted to create conditions to enable Africa 'to make her own contribution to human progress and happiness'.

Meanwhile, Dr Xuma had formed a united front with leaders of the Communist Party and the South African Indian Congress to campaign against the pass laws. (The Communist Party had been founded in 1921; the Indian Congress in 1894 by Mohandas Gandhi.) This campaign was precipitated after the government had rejected a move in parliament for repeal of the pass laws, and had ordered mass arrests of pass offenders. A flood of protest swept the country: an Anglican Bishop declared that the laws were 'Hitler's methods in a so-called democratic country'. But marches, petitions and deputations – every possible constitutional form of protest – achieved nothing.

All the same, optimism was the mood of the moment, for surely change was inevitable after a war in which the Nazis were defeated – a war in which Africans as well as Coloured people had played a role? The ANC, in cooperation with other organizations, celebrated in May 1945 with a Victory march. The parade was the biggest ever seen in Johannesburg; twenty thousand Africans and a few people of other races followed the brass bands and the ANC's black, green and gold flag. The slogan was 'Let's finish the job!' But the war, in opening the country to greater industrialization and foreign investment, had reinforced the wealth and power of the whites.

In 1946 came a sharp reminder that not only Africans were oppressed: the Indians moved to the forefront of the struggle and two fellow-students of Mandela's at Wits Law School – Ismail Meer and J. N. Singh – played a leading role as the Transvaal and Natal Indian Congresses launched a passive resistance campaign against Smuts's 'Ghetto' Bill, which was designed to restrict Indians permanently to certain areas. Although the actual resistance took place in Durban, much of the organizing was done in Johannesburg.

Mandela sometimes stayed with Meer, whose sparsely furnished flat in Kholvad House in Market Street was a meeting place, a focal point for animated discussion and argument far into the night with friends and students and activists, such as the Reverend Michael Scott, an Anglican priest who later joined the passive resistance, and Ruth First, a brilliant eighteen-year-old whose parents – like many Jewish immigrants from Lithuania and Latvia – were among the Communist Party's bravest campaigners.

Mandela was interested to learn about the Indian people and their struggle in South Africa from Meer, whose family were Muslim. The British had brought Indians to Natal in 1860 to labour in the sugar plantations. Gandhi, as a young lawyer, had settled in Durban and, in the face of repeated injustices, had initiated passive resistance – *satyagraha* or soul-force – in 1907. Now the senior leaders were two doctors in their late thirties: Monty Naicker, a Gandhian, in Natal, and Yusuf Dadoo, a communist, in the Transvaal. Powerful moral and diplomatic support came from the Indian government as that country led Asia in the sweep towards independence.

Mandela, watching the young Indian volunteers set off from Johannesburg to drive the five hundred miles to Durban, there to court imprisonment, was much impressed but politically he remained aloof. Meer and Singh were among many Indians who felt that the Communist Party provided a relevant political and economic philosophy. Bitterly dismayed by their community's representatives – conservative merchants and businessmen who believed in conciliation with the white authorities – they had been stimulated by a remarkable old Englishwoman, Dr Mabel Palmer, a Fabian and friend of George Bernard Shaw, who taught all races on a variety of subjects, including socialism and Marxism. Despite the Communist Party's small numbers it had played a significant role in organizing, particularly on labour issues, and, as a party, it alone offered racial equality.

Mandela was intensely anti-communist, not only because of his strongly traditional background but because his religious upbringing had taught him that communists were anti-Christ.

His hostility was shared by most members of the Youth League and when Ruth First, as Secretary of the Progressive Youth Council, approached them, inviting their affiliation, their reply was a firm refusal.

Bram Fischer, an Afrikaner who was a communist and who, as an advocate, had assisted Xuma in drawing up a more democratic constitution for the ANC, found Mandela and Sisulu – 'young Turks' as he called them – not only anti-communist but against cooperation with whites. He was later to defend them in two historic trials.

The Youth League believed that such cooperation would undermine their struggle; besides, white communists regarded their nationalism as 'chauvinistic'. Furthermore, communist emphasis on division between working class and capitalists clouded the main issue of uniting all Africans. Lembede, Mandela, Sisulu and Tambo tried to force African communists to resign from the Party if they were to remain in the ANC and introduced a motion to this effect at an annual conference. But among the Congress's most respected and active members were the communists J. B. Marks, Moses Kotane and Gaur Radebe, and it was moderates who defeated the Youth League motion.

As for the League's attitude towards whites in general, Mandela said that a great deal of controversy centred on the suggestion that one of its aims should be 'to drive the white man into the sea'. He and his co-workers drafting their Basic Policy had discussed this at many meetings and eventually agreed that they must take account of the concrete situation in South Africa, and 'realize that the different racial groups' had come to stay. 'But we insist,' they added, 'that a condition for inter-racial peace and progress is the abandonment of white domination, and such a change in the basic structure of South African society that those relations which breed exploitation and human misery will disappear. Therefore our goal is the winning of national freedom for African people, and the inauguration of a people's free society where racial oppression and persecution will be outlawed.'

The League conceded that some Europeans loved justice and

condemned racial oppression, 'but their voice is negligible, and in the last analysis counts for nothing'. As for Indians, who were also oppressed and exploited, they differed from Africans in historical and cultural background but should not be regarded as intruders or enemies as long as they did not impede the Africans' liberation struggle. Coloured people, whose suffering differed in degree, should struggle for their own freedom.

But when it came to action, Mandela and the other young intellectuals in the League were not yet ready. It was a revelation to them that migrant workers challenged the system, when, in 1946, African miners came out on strike. Their leaders, Marks and Radebe, had long been warning the Chamber of Mines of the growing unrest. The situation of the 308,000 black miners was common knowledge: the most important workers in the country, they were also the most exploited. Their average cash earning was £3 11s. 8d. per month, on the assumption that, as migrant labourers, they could subsidize wages by a peasant income which was estimated at £2 10s. a month. But in the Transkei and the Ciskei their families lived in abject poverty; malnutrition and disease were rife. Their strike call was for a minimum wage of 10s. a day 'in accordance with the new world's principles for an approved standard of living subscribed to by our government at UNO'.

Seventy thousand men struck. The police, with rifles, bayonets and batons, began driving them back to work.

At this time, the Natives' Representative Council, the advisory body set up when blacks were disenfranchised, was meeting in Pretoria, forty miles to the north of Johannesburg. Z. K. Matthews was Chairman and a newly elected member was Chief Albert Lutuli from Natal. As the casualties on the mines increased, the councillors made powerful but ineffectual protests to the government. 'They treat us like children,' declared Dr James Moroka, a highly respected physician. 'You can do what you like,' another councillor told the government, 'you can shoot us, arrest us, imprison us, but you are not going to break our spirit.' They demanded to see for themselves what was happening on the mines; they were supposed to represent the eight million Africans, to advise the government on their interests. But the request was refused; their protests were ignored. One member said the Council was nothing more than 'a toy telephone'.

Within a week the mine strike was broken, defeated not only by the state and its endorsement of police brutality but by the Chamber of Mines which destroyed the African Mine Workers' Union and – after strengthening the police force on each mine – split miners into compounds according to their tribes. At least nine miners had been killed and 1,248 injured.

Meanwhile Prime Minister Smuts, a much revered elder states-man abroad, had been at the United Nations. A year earlier he had helped draft the Preamble to the Charter: affirming 'faith in fundamental human rights, in the dignity of the human person, in the equal rights of men and women'. Dr Xuma, who was lobby-ing at the UN, remarked: 'When we ask for bread, we get lead.'

Smuts's deputy, Jan Hofmeyr, South Africa's most liberal white politician and a brilliant scholar, had dealt with the Native Representative Councillors' protests. He expressed surprise at what he called their 'violent and exaggerated' statements and he spoke of government goodwill and desire for Native advance-ment. Smuts and Hofmeyr were the leaders of the moderate, mainly English-speaking United Party. Not surprisingly, to Man-dela, as to most blacks, the policies of both main parties were pretty much the same.

In notes for a speech Mandela wrote:

> Since 1912 and year after year thereafter, in their homes and local areas, in provincial and national gatherings, on trains and buses, in the factories and on the farms, in cities, villages, shantytowns, schools and prisons, the African people have discussed the shameful misdeeds of those who rule the country.
>
> Year after year, they have raised their voices in condemnation of the grinding poverty, the low wages, the acute shortage of land, the inhuman exploitation and the whole policy of white domination. But instead of more freedom, repression began to grow in volume and intensity.

In other parts of Africa, the goal of colonies or protectorates or mandated territories was independence. South Africa, however, was already an independent country, a sovereign state, organized and controlled by a locally entrenched, white ruling minority which had accumulated power over many generations of settler incursions, backed by European capital, arms and technology. What Mandela called 'a formidable apparatus of force and co-ercion' was steadily built up: an elaborate system of administrative and economic controls to subjugate the black majority.

In 1948 white domination and segregation were codified into a statutory system: apartheid.* The Afrikaner National Party came to power with a small majority and began to enact their policy of apartheid. Their pro-Nazi and anti-Semitic tendencies were played down as they claimed to be a 'bastion of western Christian civilization' against the 'red menace'. They believed themselves chosen by God to rule, an illusion which steeled them against the outside world and against such ideas as freedom, equality and justice. Not only the government but their Dutch Reformed Church and universities, the police force, army and civil service, were soon permeated by a secret society, the Broederbond (Band of Brothers). Within a few years, despite massive protests from white voters, they were to ride roughshod over the Constitution; by abrogating entrenched clauses they ensured that they could not be defeated by constitutional means.

Apartheid – 'this insane policy' as Mandela called it – was diametrically opposed to every concept of human rights. No-where, except in Hitler's policy towards the Jews, had such a 'philosophy' existed. The Second World War had just been fought against such a doctrine. In the years to come, the govern-ments of Britain, America and other western nations would repeatedly express their abhorrence of apartheid while increasing their investments in South Africa.†

---

* Apartheid is pronounced apart-hate.

† British investment would rise from £4 billion to £11 billion between 1975 and 1981.

More than a hundred thousand Africans were now jammed into the townships and shantytowns surrounding Johannesburg. Enforced removals, police raids, unemployment and other grievances continually sparked off riots but the worst explosion occurred in Durban in January 1949 when a violent quarrel between a young Zulu and an Indian provoked a crowd of Africans. Years of suppressed rage at their oppression and poverty inflamed the Zulu people, who turned on the nearest target, the traders and 'foreigners' they had resented as 'exploiters'. Arson, death, looting: of the 147 people killed, fifty-three were Indians and, mainly as a result of police action, eighty-seven were Africans and one was white. Oliver Tambo and other ANC leaders joined Dr Naicker, Ismail Meer and J. N. Singh in hurrying to the distressed areas to calm the people and to discover their underlying grievances.

Mandela was to remember this coming together of African and Indian leaders as an unforgettable experience. At the same time he and other members of the Youth League remained opposed to the thought of uniting with the Indian Congress. When Xuma, Dadoo and Naicker made a 'Doctors' Pact' for the ANC and the SAIC to work together for full franchise rights, the young nationalists were set in their determination to 'go it alone'. Much had still to be done in building up African self-confidence.

Mda was the League's new President and Tambo the Vice-President. Anton Lembede had died after a long illness in 1947, an incalculable loss; his ideas were to inspire and divide colleagues and followers in years to come. Mandela was elected Secretary; he was neglecting his law studies in his growing political involvement.

The League had prepared a Programme of Action and was now ready to confront Dr Xuma with their dissatisfaction at his cautious leadership, although they had to concede that through his organizing capacity and integrity, the ANC now had membership of several thousand with £3,000 in its bank account. Though joining in the criticism, Mandela had a high regard for

Xuma personally. Shortly before the ANC's annual conference was due to open, he, with Tambo and Sisulu, was deputed to call on Xuma. It was a difficult meeting; Xuma was determined to keep control, while they were more than ever convinced that the people were ripe for action. Besides, the lesson of the mine strike had confirmed their belief that without the workers – the 'masses' – there could be no effective political action. They delivered an ultimatum: if Xuma refused to support their Programme of Action, they would not support him at the coming election for President-General. He gave them short shrift.

At the last moment they settled on Dr Moroka, who had expressed approval for the Programme. The old guard, almost to a man, voted for Xuma and the young for Moroka. The Youth League by this time had majority support – their *coup* had come off.

The appointment to Secretary-General of Walter Sisulu, elected by a majority of one, was significant: for the first time the ANC would have a full-time Secretary who would be paid a salary – £5 a month – and who would occupy an office, a shabby one to be sure, but well-situated in the business district of Johannesburg. Sisulu's wife, Albertina, would support them on her earnings as a nurse.

Mandela was among the new members elected to the national executive, along with moderates, communists and other Youth League representatives. They were sworn to vigorous execution of the Programme of Action which had been enthusiastically adopted by conference.

The Programme became a watershed in the struggle. It aimed at 'national freedom' and self-determination, and rejected apartheid and white leadership motivated by the idea of white domination. New 'weapons' must be employed: boycott, strike, civil disobedience, non-cooperation and such other means as might bring about the accomplishment of their aspirations. But first, a national stoppage of work must be organized, one day of protest against the government's reactionary policy.

Thus the ANC was committed to a wholly new strategy

based on mass action. Mandela pointed out that whereas previously ANC leaders had acted 'in the apparent hope that by pleading their cause they would persuade the authorities to change their hearts and extend to them all the rights they were demanding', now pressure would be exerted 'to compel the authorities to grant their demands'. But he recognized, as he wrote in the Youth League journal *Lodestar*, the immense problem of maintaining 'full dynamic contact with the masses'. 'We have a powerful ideology capable of capturing the imaginations of the masses,' he added. 'Our duty is now to carry that ideology fully to them.'

Before the Youth League could organize the 'national stoppage of work' for May Day 1950, an ad hoc group of communists, Indian Congress and Transvaal ANC called for a stoppage on the same day in the Johannesburg area to protest against the banning of Kotane, Marks and Dadoo. Furious, Mandela and the other young nationalists clashed with the organizers, broke up meetings and, in their journal, attacked the Communist Party in extravagant terms. Since the workers were Africans and were oppressed primarily because they were black, and only secondarily because they were workers, it was clear – this article said – that the 'exotic plant' of communism could not flourish on African soil. Mandela's reputation for being hot-tempered no doubt sprang from those clashes.

Despite the Youth League's opposition to the Johannesburg protest and a government ban on demonstrations, as well as the deployment of two thousand police in the area on May Day, the strike was a considerable success and more than half the workforce stayed at home. But the day had a tragic ending as police attacked gatherings; organizers and 'scabs' brawled and police shootings provoked riots. Mandela and Sisulu hurried around Orlando, trying to calm people, urging them to disperse and to take shelter. Eighteen Africans were killed and more than thirty, including three children, injured.

For the young intellectuals in the Youth League, the grassroots backing given to the strike was an eye-opener. 'That day,' said

Mandela, 'was a turning-point in my life, both in understanding through first-hand experience the ruthlessness of the police, and in being deeply impressed by the support African workers had given to the May Day call.'

He was also impressed by how hard the organizers had worked: he and Sisulu had observed two young Indians, Paul Joseph, a factory worker, and Ahmed Kathrada, a student, setting out very early each morning and again each evening to distribute leaflets. Now they all shook hands and Paul and Kathy found themselves congratulated by the two Youth League men – the first intimation of what became lifelong friendships.

Apartheid laws intended to separate people were driving them together: the Population Registration Act classified each individual by race, causing immense personal suffering; the Group Areas Act divided races and tribes in urban and rural areas, particularly dispossessing Indian traders and presaging massive forced removals for all 'Non-Europeans' – Africans were now to be called Bantu and under the Bantu Authorities Act were to be retribalized.

The Suppression of Communism Act had the severest political impact, directed as it was against a far wider target than the two thousand communists: 1,600 Africans, 250 Indians and 150 whites. During the 1940s communists had been elected as Native Representatives to parliament and also as members of Johannesburg and Cape Town City Councils; now the Cold War spread. McCarthy was chilling the American scene and in South Africa the Minister of Justice, C. R. Swart, announced that he had investigated the growth of communism in Africa in company with Sir Percy Sillitoe, Chief of Britain's Secret Service. (Africans saw this as a further act of collaboration between the British government and the Afrikaner Nationalists at a time when Britain consistently voted with South Africa in UN debates on the mandated territory of South-West Africa.)

The new Act had a uniquely South African twist: as the ANC executive pointed out, it was 'primarily directed against the Africans and other oppressed people'.

'Communism' included any doctrine which aimed at 'bringing about any political, industrial, social or economic change within the Union by the promotion of disturbance or disorder, by unlawful acts or omissions or by the threat of such acts or omissions', and the Minister of Justice was empowered to 'name' any persons whom he considered to be communists and to ban them from organizations; the penalty for 'furthering the aims' of a banned organization was up to ten years' imprisonment.

A national demonstration of protest was planned for 26 June 1950. ANC, Youth League, the Indian Congress and Communist Party joined in a coordinating committee which began work in an atmosphere of mutual suspicion. However, Moses Kotane, arriving from Cape Town to be Secretary of the CP in Johannesburg, helped to dispel that uneasy mood. Mandela came to know him as 'really a nationalist' and they soon became friends.

This was to be the ANC's first nationwide call on people to 'refrain from going to work'; the beginning of confrontation between urban people and the state. 'The protest,' declared the Youth League in rallying support, 'is to us a manifestation of all those divine stirrings of discontent of the African people since the sixth of April 1652', the day when Jan van Riebeeck had arrived at the Cape of Good Hope to establish a base for the Dutch East India Company. Mandela's memory of listening to the tribal elders was clearly evident in the statement as it continued: '... on through the period of the so-called Kaffir Wars, through the days of Dingana, through the days of Moshoeshoe, through the days of Sekukhuni ... through the days of the White Union Pact of 1910'. The government was warned: 'No physical might in the world can crush the invincible spirit of a nation'; the African people had pledged themselves to liberate South Africa, 'black, white and yellow'.

While Dr Moroka, Sisulu, Tambo and Indian leaders visited provincial centres to win support, Mandela's role was to coordinate such activities. The Minister of Justice announced in parliament, with 'a feeling of trepidation', that 'under communist leaders ... a secret organization among the natives' would 'poison the people's water supplies' and 'teach people how to murder'.

On 26 June there was a complete stoppage of work in Port Elizabeth, Durban, Alexandra township and one or two other areas; a partial stoppage in Johannesburg, in Cape Town and small centres. But in parts of the Transvaal the response was poor and the ANC admitted that fieldworkers had not come up to expectation. Indians had given impressive support, particularly in Durban where people had suffered most: a thousand workers were sacked, but were provided with maintenance grants by the organizers.

The ANC was gaining from the organizational experience of Indians and from their fund-raising ability, while the Indian Congress gained obvious advantages from closer cooperation with the African majority. Indians had also rallied diplomatic support at the UN, this at a time when only fourteen of the UN's fifty-four members were Afro-Asian.

Towards the end of 1950 Mandela was elected National President of the Youth League and he and Walter Sisulu discussed the next stage in the Programme of Action: the call for civil disobedience. What form should it take? Mandela, remembering the disciplined enthusiasm of the Indian volunteers setting out for Durban in 1946, spoke of 'passive resistance'. Sisulu wanted it to be 'typically South African and militant'. They could look back to occasions in the ANC's history of protest when passive resistance had been spontaneously used. In the Orange Free State in 1913 black women had protested against the pass laws. After they had dumped sacks of passes at municipal offices, hundreds had chosen to go to gaol rather than pay fines. In *dorp* (village) after *dorp* they had been crammed into police cells. Consequently, that local attempt to impose passes on women had failed and out of the activity had come a women's section of Congress. Later, in 1919, the ANC had organized massive non-violent demonstrations against the pass laws in Johannesburg and on the Rand.

Despite violent attacks from police and white civilians, the protests had continued for weeks and had resulted in a departmental committee recommending abolition of the pass laws. (They were not abolished.)

Sisulu now thought all races should be invited to take part in the campaign however much Mandela still feared that Africans might be dominated by the other races. Mandela thought back to the May Day demonstration when 'the people' had supported something he himself had opposed. Gradually, he gave in and, having reviewed his stand, there was no turning back from his willingness to accept cooperation with other races, as well as from the communists. Africans 'going it alone', he now saw, reflected political naïvety, a lack of maturity.

The CP, for its part, had condemned the Programme of Action for crudity and lack of vision of a socialist revolution, but was optimistic that Africans would learn to develop a consciousness of class interests, and that white workers could be led to overcome racial prejudice. The Party, in recognizing that South Africa was not simply an example of class exploitation but that racial oppression was inherent in the system, had decided that the ANC's national struggle should be supported and guided towards concentrating on the interests of workers and peasants. It believed that opposition to racial discrimination would thus develop into opposition to capitalism. Before being declared illegal, the Party had dissolved itself; its members would work through other organizations or, in time, from underground.

Sisulu, Mandela and other members of the Youth League continued their intense arguments: passive resistance would hardly appeal to the people; but non-violence was the only viable method against a heavily armed, violent state. Then how to restrain people who were daily on the receiving end of that violence? Essential to instil discipline, to train them in non-violent methods, to convey to volunteers that non-violence often took more courage and determination than overtly aggressive action.

In December 1951 their proposal was put to the ANC's annual conference in Bloemfontein: mass protests on 6 April 1952 when white South Africans would celebrate three hundred years of rule; the government to be told that unless six particular unjust laws were repealed there would be countrywide non-violent defiance of those laws. The conference roared its approval. Dr Moroka gave the Congress salute and slogan: '*Mayibuye!*' The reply came: '*Afrika!*' (Let Africa return!) Delegates stood to sing 'Nkosi Sikelel' iAfrika'.

The press overseas observed that the ANC had emphasized that their struggle was not directed against any race but against unjust laws 'which kept in perpetual subjection and misery vast sections of the population'; that the Africans were fighting for the transformation of conditions, and to restore 'human dignity, equality and freedom to every South African'; and that their deliberate intention was to remain non-violent.

In South Africa, the government was banning communists and trade unionists, withdrawing passports from its critics, and preparing to remove the Coloured people from their 'privileged' status on the voters' roll. White liberals and Mahatma Gandhi's son, Manilal, who lived in Natal, expressed doubt that Africans could sustain non-violence; they found support for their misgivings when riots broke out along the Rand between law-abiding blacks and gangs, and between tribal groups; forty-one died and hundreds were injured.

The state was cracking down hard: could the ANC attract sufficient volunteers, and could it lead them in a prolonged campaign of non-violent struggle?

4

'OPEN THE GAOL DOORS,
WE WANT TO ENTER'

1952

Nelson Mandela was appointed national volunteer-in-chief of the Defiance Campaign; his deputy was Maulvi Cachalia, whose father had been one of the bravest resisters alongside Gandhi in 1907. Mandela toured the Cape, Natal and the Transvaal, visiting houses in the townships, explaining the plan, sometimes talking through the night. His task was to inspire people with confidence in their ability to overcome oppression through a direct non-violent challenge to the government. Oliver Tambo sometimes accompanied him. As always, there were the problems of being black in small towns and *dorps* catering only for whites. Perhaps the one available train arrived late at night: there would be no hotel or taxis for Africans, nor were there telephones in township homes. This meant walking miles to the location and knocking on a likely looking door. Sometimes they were welcomed by an enthusiastic stranger; sometimes rebuffed by the cautious.

Dr Moroka had practically abandoned his busy practice in Thaba 'Nchu, while Sisulu bore the brunt of the work at the ANC office in Johannesburg. On 21 January 1952 they wrote to Prime Minister Malan, pointing to the long history of the ANC's endeavour by constitutional methods to achieve the legitimate demands of the African people. The government had never responded to requests for cooperation, and across the years had continually intensified repression to the point where it was now 'a matter of life and death to the people'. For the ANC to remain quiet would be a betrayal of trust. Among laws which had aggravated the tense situation were the pass laws, the Group Areas Act and the Suppression of Communism Act. If the

government did not repeal these, Congress would hold demonstrations on 6 April as a prelude to defying them.

The arid reply came from the Prime Minister's secretary, who
rebuked Sisulu for not addressing the Minister of Native Affairs,
and questioned his claim to speak on behalf of the ANC. It was
self-contradictory, he said, to claim that Bantu should be regarded as no different from Europeans, 'especially when it is
borne in mind that these differences are permanent and not man-
made'. The government had no intention of repealing the laws;
in any event they were not 'oppressive and degrading', they
were 'protective'. If the ANC pursued the course indicated, the
government would make full use of the machinery at its disposal
to quell any disturbances and thereafter 'deal adequately with
those responsible for initiating subversive activity'.

Moroka and Sisulu replied that the ANC had never accepted
the Native Affairs Department as the 'correct channel'. The
point at issue, they added, was not 'a biological one' but one of
'citizenship rights'; 'the African people yield to no one as far as
pride of race is concerned'. Precisely for this reason they were
striving for 'the attainment of fundamental human rights in the
land of their birth'. They concluded that the people were left
with no alternative but to embark on the campaign of mass
action. 'We desire to state emphatically that it is our intention to
conduct this campaign in a peaceful manner, and that any
disturbances, if they should occur, will not be of our making.'

On 6 April, while whites celebrated the tercentenary of the
Dutch landing at the Cape, Africans came together in the main
centres: in the Eastern Cape tens of thousands met to pray for
freedom; in Johannesburg Dr Moroka addressed a great crowd
at Freedom Square, and called for 'a solemn oath that we will
muster all our forces of mind, body and soul to see that these
crushing conditions under which we live, shall not continue any
longer'. He appealed for ten thousand volunteers to defy the
laws.

In a mood of deep seriousness Mandela and Cachalia proceeded
to enrol volunteers. Mandela spoke to some two hundred Afri-

cans and Indians and a few Coloured people in the Garment Workers' Union hall, instructing and advising, pointing out that the authorities would attempt to intimidate people and would be particularly harsh with the first volunteers. No matter what the provocation, they must not retaliate. It was a fundamental principle that discipline must be observed, there must be no rowdiness or any semblance of drunkenness; volunteers must be dignified, erect, alert and clean. He had, said one of the Indians, instant rapport with volunteers; and he himself had learned to control anger.

Mandela went on to Cape Town. A white South African, accustomed to the norm in that country, that blacks were invisible to whites, described his impact: 'I noticed people turning and staring at the opposite pavement and I saw this magnificent figure of a man, immaculately dressed. Not just blacks but whites, including white women, were turning to admire him.'

In Durban, on a 'Day of Volunteers', Mandela addressed a meeting of many thousands; Indians as well as Africans signed pledges. There was a personal significance in his statement: 'We can now say unity between the non-European people in this country has become a living reality.'

The President of the Natal ANC was Chief Lutuli, a relative newcomer to Congress leadership. He and Dr Naicker committed themselves to the Campaign. There was a profound sense that history was about to be made, and Indians were especially moved by the new experience of joining Africans in the freedom songs which accompanied each volunteer coming forward.

The government's first retaliatory act was to list five hundred men and women under the Suppression of Communism Act, making it illegal for them to organize or address meetings. Marks, Kotane and Dadoo, as an act of defiance, addressed meetings and were promptly arrested and imprisoned for several weeks.

On 26 June, the anniversary of the ANC's 1950 call for a national strike, the Campaign began. Very early that winter morning a batch of high-spirited volunteers, women and men, set out from New Brighton township in Port Elizabeth, wearing ANC armbands and chanting '*Mayibuye! Afrika!*' They marched cheerfully through the 'EUROPEANS ONLY' entrance to the railway station, were arrested by waiting police and escorted to the other side of the station which, they noted with satisfaction, meant using the 'EUROPEANS ONLY' bridge. A trainload of Africans shouted encouragement. The group's leader was sentenced to thirty days', the others to fifteen days' imprisonment.

In the Transvaal, 750 miles away, Nana Sita, a veteran Gandhian, with Sisulu, led fifty-two defiers into a location without the permits legally required of non-residents. All were arrested.

That night in Johannesburg, Mandela addressed a meeting which went on until eleven p.m.: curfew time for Africans after which 'special' passes were necessary. He had intended to avoid arrest in order to continue organizing, but found himself hauled in by the police, who had already arrested volunteers. Singing their national anthem, they clambered into the police pick-up vans and were driven off to the cells.

This was Mandela's first experience of police cells. He later described it:

> As we were being jostled into the drill yard, one of us was pushed so violently by a young European constable that he fell down some steps and broke his ankle. I protested, whereupon the young warrior kicked me on the leg in true cowboy style. We were all indignant and I started a demonstration. We drew their attention to the injured man and demanded medical attention. We were curtly told that we could repeat the request next day. And so it was that this man, Samuel Makae, spent a frightful night in the cell, reeling and groaning with pain. Only next day was he taken to hospital.

After he had been released, he observed the spread — 'like wild fire' — of the Campaign, as factory and office workers, doctors, lawyers, teachers, students and clergymen defied apartheid regulations. Older defiers who recalled the early days of the ANC, when their aim was to prove themselves responsible citizens, were exhilarated as they now confronted white authority in the hope of bringing about radical change. Freedom songs had become a feature of the Campaign. One began: '*Thina sizwe! Thina sizwe esinsundu . . .*' ('We Africans! We Africans! We cry for our land. They took it. They took it. Europeans. They must let our country go . . .'). And another: 'Hey Malan! Open the gaol doors, we want to enter, we volunteers . . . '

Walter Sisulu spoke for the fifteen hundred who defied during July, when he was brought to court: 'As long as I enjoy the confidence of my people, and as long as there is a spark of life and energy in me, I shall fight with courage and determination for the abolition of discriminatory laws and for the freedom of all South Africans.' He was among those who chose to spend a week in gaol rather than to pay a fine.

On 30 July police raided homes and offices throughout the country and arrested Moroka, Mandela, Sisulu, Dadoo and Cachalia with thirty others, charging them with furthering the aims of communism. The case was adjourned but the arrests spurred recruitment. By early October several thousand more volunteers had gone to gaol.

Meanwhile, Chief Lutuli had been given an ultimatum: resign from the ANC or from chieftainship of the Groutville area of Zululand. His reply was to address an ANC conference where he was cheered to the echo.

After four months the final stage of the Campaign was imminent: a call to the masses to join the defiance. Mandela believed that if this could be achieved, the government would not be able to administer certain laws. Of course it would not capitulate easily, only as a result of greatly stepped-up pressure. Africans had the initiative and only one thing could rob them of that: violence.

On 18 October at New Brighton railway station a white policeman shot two Africans who were alleged to have stolen a pot of paint and resisted arrest. In the ensuing mêlée the policeman fired more than twenty shots, then escaped, leaving an enraged crowd attacking the station, setting off a riot. Seven Africans were killed and four Europeans (none of them police), while twenty-seven people were injured.

Sisulu rushed to the scene to investigate. The ANC condemned the violence and demanded a judicial inquiry. Government reaction was to step up police activity, to ban meetings throughout the Cape and to enforce the pass laws more strictly. An ANC protest strike was met by employers dismissing thousands of workers. Riots broke out in Kimberley and in East London; at least twenty-five Africans were shot dead by police and many more wounded. In East London the crowd turned on the first whites they saw, a nun coming to aid the wounded and an insurance agent, and killed them both.

The government's repeated refusal to appoint a commission of inquiry, as the ANC repeatedly demanded, and its blaming of the disorders on the Defiance Campaign, strengthened the belief that *agents provocateurs* had precipitated the New Brighton and Kimberley riots to provide a pretext for suppressing the Campaign. An academic observer, Professor Leo Kuper, concluded that there was 'no evidence to connect the resistance movement with the disturbances, nor was violence at any time advocated by the resisters'.

Nevertheless, the Campaign continued and the October total of arrests was 2,354. The discipline and humour of the volunteers had won admiration abroad and the United Nations set up a commission to inquire into apartheid, the first formal expression of international disapproval and, as such, a fresh encouragement to the ANC and its allies. And, in South Africa, white liberals, including the newly arrived Bishop of Johannesburg, Ambrose Reeves, called for 'equal rights for all civilized people', while a handful of whites joined the Campaign, courting imprisonment in Johannesburg and Cape Town.

The government's banning for life of fifty-two leaders and organizers brought the Campaign grinding to a halt. Of the ten thousand volunteers called for, 8,577 had responded. But none of the laws was repealed, indeed the government relentlessly extended apartheid. As the ANC admitted, there had been grave weaknesses in the organizing: defective administration and fund-raising, and the lack of a Congress newspaper. But many thousands of Africans had been politicized and the ANC reckoned that membership soared from seven thousand to a hundred thousand.

At the end of November, Moroka, Mandela, Sisulu and the other leaders were brought to trial. An incidental point the state attempted to make was that the Campaign's songs and the women's ululations threatened violence, a claim refuted by Professor Hugh Tracey, an eminent musicologist, who pointed out that ululating was a typical African expression of joy or sorrow. The judgement which followed was a dramatic repudiation of government propaganda: Judge Rumpff declared the leaders guilty only of 'statutory communism' which had 'nothing to do with communism as it is commonly known'. They had envisaged a range of acts from 'open non-compliance with laws' to something that equalled 'high treason', but the Judge accepted the evidence that they had consistently advised their followers to maintain 'a peaceful course of action and to avoid violence in any shape or form'. Their sentence of nine months' imprisonment was suspended for two years on condition they did not repeat the offence.

Mandela was elected President of the Transvaal ANC, to replace the recently banned J. B. Marks. It was an important role and much was expected of his leadership. He was not ambitious for office, his friend Tambo observed, and loyally served others, content to be one of a team. But he was a born mass leader who could not help magnetizing people. He praised those who had made sacrifices in the Campaign: workers who'd lost their jobs, teachers expelled, professional men whose practices had been neglected. The Campaign had shown how the masses could function politically and provide a powerful method of voicing indignation against government policies. It had inspired and aroused people 'from a conquered and servile community of yesmen to a militant and uncompromising band of comrades-in-arms'.

He was later to point out that the Campaign had led directly to the formation of the Congress of Democrats (a radical white group) and had helped to inspire liberals to establish a multiracial Liberal Party. As for its impact on government, instead of continuing to propagate *baasskap* (bosshood), there was talk of 'self-government' for Africans in Bantustans. A deception of course but, he said, it revealed acknowledgement of the power of the Campaign and of the ANC.

In December 1952 Chief Albert Lutuli* was elected President-General of the ANC, with Mandela as his deputy. Lutuli was a former teacher, a chief of seventeen years' experience, unusually close to his people, and a deeply convinced Christian. His first act as President was to visit Port Elizabeth, where a crowd of thirty-five thousand welcomed him. On his arrival in the Orange Free State, an area much in need of political education, he was met by police who served banning orders on him.

Mandela, too, was placed under bans, as were more than a hundred ANC, Indian Congress, and trade union leaders and organizers.

The South African government's system of bans under the Suppression of Communism Act was a unique form of repression: from the page or two of restrictions issued in those early years, banning orders were to grow to eight or ten pages in length. No charges made, no proof required, no appeal allowed: simply the arbitrary declaration by the Minister of Justice that he considered the recipient of the order guilty of 'furthering the aims of communism'; with a potential sentence of up to ten years for contravention.

Mandela was prohibited from attending gatherings and was confined to Johannesburg for the period of six months. 'I was issued with the order,' he said, 'not as a result of a trial before the court and a conviction, but as a result of prejudice, or perhaps Star Chamber procedure behind closed doors in the halls of government.'

Severe additional laws were enacted: anyone committing any offence 'by way of protest or in support of any campaign against

* Lutuli preferred this modern spelling to Luthuli.

any law' could be sentenced to three years' imprisonment, a £300 fine, a whipping of ten strokes, or a combination of two of these penalties. For those whose words or actions encouraged another to commit an offence as a means of protest, these penalties were increased by an additional £200 or two years.

'The Congresses realize,' Mandela declared, 'that these measures create a new situation . . . We have to analyse the dangers that face us, formulate plans to overcome them and evolve new plans of political struggle . . . Our immediate task is to preserve our organizations and to muster our forces for the resumption of the offensive.'

His public voice might be silenced but he, like most of the banned people, continued to function behind the scenes.

5

'THE WHOLE LIFE OF ANY
THINKING AFRICAN'

1953–6

Nelson and Evelyn Mandela had two sons, Thembekile (Thembi) and Makgatho, and a daughter, Makaziwe. Mandela was devoted to his family. By the early fifties the boys were at primary school in Orlando and he enjoyed their companionship. Six-year-old Makgatho was with him one day when he gave a lift to Adelaide Tsukudu, Oliver Tambo's fiancée. Driving along, they approached a horse-drawn wagon and Mandela slowed down, wanting Makgatho to watch the horses, explaining about the animals in the countryside of his own boyhood. Adelaide thought the incident revealed an intense longing for that other rural world, a feeling he desired to impart to his children, existing as they did in Orlando's bleak landscape of regimented little block houses, under a permanent pall of smoke from the innumerable cooking fires.

Qualified as an attorney, in 1952 Mandela had established a partnership with Tambo, who had switched from teaching to law: MANDELA & TAMBO read the brass plate on the door of their office on the second floor of Chancellor House, near the Magistrates' Court in Johannesburg. An unprepossessing building owned by Indians, it was one of the few in which Africans could hire offices.

Although African lawyers were not unknown – after all, there had been several among the founders of the ANC – their partnership stirred people not only locally but in the Transkei: 'Lawyers from our soil,' exclaimed one of the Thembu, 'we were very excited.'

At law as in politics, Mandela and Tambo were complementary personalities: Mandela a passionate man with a great zest for life, Tambo more reflective and deliberate. Both men were angered by injustice but Mandela was more assertive in expressing that anger.

'For years we worked side by side,' wrote Tambo in an introduction to a collection of Mandela's writings and speeches.*

To reach our desks each morning Nelson and I ran the gauntlet of patient queues of people overflowing from the chairs in the waiting-room into the corridors.

South Africa has the dubious reputation of boasting one of the highest prison populations in the world. Gaols are jam-packed with Africans imprisoned for serious offences – and crimes of violence are ever on the increase in apartheid society – but also for petty infringements of statutory law that no really civilized society would punish with imprisonment. To be unemployed is a crime because no African can for long evade arrest if his passbook does not carry the stamp of authorized and approved employment.

To be landless can be a crime, and weekly we interviewed the delegations of grizzled, weather-worn peasants from the countryside who came to tell us how many generations their families had worked a little piece of land from which they were now being ejected. To brew African beer, to drink it or to use the proceeds to supplement the meagre family income is a crime, and women who do so face heavy fines and gaol terms. To cheek a white man can be a crime. To live in the 'wrong' area – an area declared white or Indian or Coloured – can be a crime for Africans. South African apartheid laws turn innumerable innocent people into 'criminals'.

Apartheid stirs hatred and frustration among people. Young people who should be in school or learning a trade roam the streets, join gangs and wreak their revenge on the society that confronts them with only the dead-end alley of crime or poverty. Our buff office files carried thousands of these stories and if, when we started our law partnership, we had not been rebels against apartheid, our experiences in our offices would have remedied the deficiency. We had risen to professional status in our community, but every case in court, every visit to the prisons to interview clients, reminded us of the humiliation and suffering burning into our people.

* Ruth First (ed.), *No Easy Walk to Freedom*, Heinemann, 1965.

'I would say,' Mandela was to tell the court when he was on trial in 1962, 'that the whole life of any thinking African in this country drives him continuously to a conflict between his conscience on the one hand and the law on the other ... a law which, in our view, is immoral, unjust and intolerable.'

At times Mandela and Tambo dealt with seven cases a day. The nature of apartheid made many of these political but they also took on civil and divorce cases. Mandela added:

> In the courts, we were treated courteously by many officials but we were very often discriminated against by some and treated with resentment and hostility by others. We were constantly aware that no matter how well, how correctly, how adequately we pursued our career of law, we could not become a prosecutor, or a magistrate, or a judge. We became aware of the fact that as attorneys we often dealt with officials whose competence and attainments were no higher than ours, but whose superior position was maintained and protected by a white skin.

Among the advocates briefed by Mandela and Tambo were Joe Slovo and Harold Wolpe, who had been fellow-students of Mandela's at Wits Law School and who, as Marxists, were also politically active. (Slovo found Mandela fiercely anti-communist.) In the office he proved a hard taskmaster. In court Africans filled the gallery, delighting in this black lawyer who could be cuttingly aggressive with magistrate and police. But his sense of humour was evident too, as when he defended an African servant accused of stealing her 'madam's' clothes. After glancing at the garments produced as evidence, he picked up a pair of panties. While displaying them to the court, he asked the 'madam', 'Are these yours?' 'No,' came the reply from a woman too embarrassed to admit they were hers. The case was dismissed.

In 1954 the Transvaal Law Society petitioned the Supreme Court to have Mandela struck off the roll for having been convicted as a leader of the Defiance Campaign, activity which 'did not conform to the standards of conduct expected from members of an honourable profession'. A distinguished advocate,

Walter Pollock, QC, Chairman of the Johannesburg Bar, appeared *pro amico* for Mandela. The Supreme Court found that he had been within his rights; that there was nothing dishonourable in an attorney identifying himself with his people in their struggle for political rights, even if his activities infringed the laws of the country. The court gave judgement for Mandela; the Law Society was instructed to pay the costs.

Meanwhile ANC work continued, with Mandela illegally lecturing to study groups in the townships. The moment banning orders had expired in June 1953, he and Sisulu joined Father Trevor Huddleston in a large cinema to address a meeting protesting against the forced removal of the inhabitants of Sophiatown. Fifty-eight thousand people were to be moved under the Group Areas Act from this black suburb which, most unusually, had freehold tenure for Africans: they could buy land there. And it was a vital community – even if overcrowding had turned parts of it into a slum – unlike the characterless monotony of the townships. Neighbouring whites, whose suburb was encroaching, wanted the land.

Police armed with sten guns and rifles broke up this legal and peaceful meeting. While Sisulu and Mandela calmed the outraged audience, Huddleston argued with the police, only to be warned not to interfere. As he wrote in *Naught for Your Comfort,*★ that day he felt 'the fierce breath of totalitarianism and tyranny' which triggered off in him the determination to reveal the truth. So disciplined was the audience that boos and hisses soon gave way to singing.

The death of Sophiatown was the first of the spectacular forced removals which were to cause such profound suffering through the years to come, and it is eloquent that the white suburb built on its ruins was named Triomf.

In September 1953 the bans were on again: Mandela was not only restricted from attending gatherings for two years and again confined to Johannesburg, but he was forced to resign

★ Collins, 1956.

from the ANC and all related bodies. 'Again without any hearing,' he pointed out, 'without being faced by any charges.' He had to withdraw from personal action in the continuing Western Areas removal protests although, as a lawyer, he could be consulted about resistance to police action.

Banned from attending the Transvaal ANC's annual conference, he nevertheless was able to communicate with his people: to this end the Transvaal executive read his presidential address. In his message he reviewed recent legislation enabling the government 'to create conditions which would permit of the most ruthless and pitiless methods of suppressing our movement'; and he described a plan formulated by the National Action Committee, devising new tactics, and to be known as the 'M' – for Mandela – Plan.

Since it was increasingly difficult to hold street and other public meetings – Congress had to get permission to do so in townships and urban areas – Mandela envisaged grassroots organizing: street-to-street and house-to-house recruiting in townships, with the people urged to meet in factories, on trains and buses and in their homes. He warned against informers and *agents provocateurs,* even policemen, who infiltrated the ranks of Congress and he declared: 'Here in South Africa, as in many parts of the world, a revolution is maturing; it is the profound desire, the determination and the urge of the overwhelming majority of the country to destroy forever the shackles of oppression.' He concluded with a quotation from Nehru: 'You can see that "there is no easy walk to freedom . . "'

Among Mandela's activities through those years of banning was the writing of a series of articles for *Liberation*, a left-wing journal, and he was on the editorial committee of *Fighting Talk*, a political and literary monthly edited by Ruth First. He expressed awareness of the everyday detail of his people's efforts to survive and in 1953 wrote:

> The living conditions of the people, are steadily worsening and becoming unbearable. Their purchasing power is progressively declining and the cost of living is rocketing. Bread is now dearer than it was two months ago. The cost of milk, meat and vegetables is

beyond the pockets of the average family ... They cannot afford sufficient clothing, housing and medical care. They are denied the right to security in the event of unemployment, sickness, disability, old age, and where allowances are paid they are far too low for survival. Because of lack of proper medical amenities our people are ravaged by such dreaded diseases as tuberculosis, venereal disease, leprosy, pellagra and infantile mortality ...

The Native Labour (Settlement of Disputes) Bill forbids strikes and lockouts, depriving Africans of the one weapon they have to improve their position. The aim of the measure is to destroy the present African trade unions which are controlled by the workers themselves ...*

In 1955 he wrote about the 'influx control' laws and the migrant labour system as it affected both families and rural areas:

The breaking up of African homes and families and the forcible separation of children from mothers, the harsh treatment meted out to African prisoners, and the forcible detention of Africans in farm colonies for spurious statutory offences are a few examples of the actual workings of the hideous and pernicious doctrines of racial inequality ...

To the mining and farming cliques the end justifies the means, and that end is the creation of a vast market of cheap labour for mine magnates and farmers. That is why homes are broken up and people are removed from cities to the countryside to ensure enough labour for the farms. That is why non-European political opponents of the government are treated with such brutality.

In such a set-up, African youths with distinguished scholastic careers are not a credit to the country, but a serious threat to the governing circles, for they may not like to descend to the bowels of the earth and cough their lungs out to enrich the mining magnates, nor will they elect to dig potatoes on farms for wretched rations.†

The Transkei was about to be declared a Bantustan, or 'homeland', despite the findings of the government's Tomlinson Commission that it could support only one fifth of its population in a

* *Liberation*, 1953.
† *Liberation*, 1955.

backward subsistence and peasant economy. Writing from an intimate knowledge, Mandela described the area as 'the greatest single reservoir of cheap labour in the country'. He said:

> According to official estimates, more than one third of the total number of Africans employed on the Witwatersrand gold mines come from the Transkei ... The implementation of the so-called rehabilitation scheme, the enforcement of taxes and the foisting of tribal rule upon the people are resorted to in order to ensure a regular inflow of labour... the real purpose of the scheme is to increase land hunger for the masses of the peasants in the reserves and to impoverish them. The main object is to create a huge army of migrant labourers ... By enclosing them in compounds at the centres of work and housing them in rural locations when they return home, it is hoped to prevent the emergence of a closely knit, powerful, militant and articulate African industrial proletariat who might acquire the rudiments of political agitation and struggle. What is wanted by the ruling circles is a docile, spineless, unorganized and inarticulate army of workers.*

Dr H. F. Verwoerd, Minister of Native Affairs, had conceived the idea of Bantustans as an answer to increasingly vociferous international criticism. Bantu were to 'develop along their own lines' in their own areas. In the 'white' 87 per cent of the country, three million whites would rule over six million Africans, one and a half million Coloured people and half a million Indians. Some five million Africans would be confined to the 160 small and separate rural slums to be called 'homelands' in the other 13 per cent where they would have strictly limited rights.

Verwoerd was also architect of Bantu Education, having declared that Africans 'should stand with both feet in the reserves' and that their education should have its roots 'in the spirit and being of Bantu society'. They would henceforward receive primary education mainly in the vernacular.

The Minister, commented Mandela, 'has been brutally clear in explaining the objects . . . to teach our children that Africans are

* *Liberation*, 1956.

46

inferior to Europeans'. The policy meant 'perpetual servitude in a *baasskap* society'. African education was to be taken out of the hands of people (missionaries) who taught equality between black and white. Verwoerd had declared that the churches and missionaries were to be ousted because 'they created wrong expectations on the part of the Native'.

During the early fifties expenditure on education was £44 for each white student, £19 for Asian and Coloured pupils and less than £8 for each African. Bantu Education was forced through, despite outraged protests at home and abroad in which eminent academics played a significant role. However, the ANC's call for parents to withdraw children from schools met with the inquiry: 'If we boycott, what alternative are you offering? We know Bantu Education will dwarf the minds of our children, but are they to run wild in the streets?' The Bishop of Johannesburg, Ambrose Reeves, and Father Huddleston and his Community of the Resurrection took a lonely stand among churchmen in closing schools rather than have the government take them over.

Mandela had suggested 'community schools'; if that became dangerous or impossible, every home, every shack should be made a centre for learning for children. But the cultural clubs set up by ANC and a handful of volunteers soon faded out: under the new law it was an offence punishable by fine or imprisonment to offer education; besides, there was always a shortage of funds. Where the boycott had been sustained, police moved in to make arrests which predictably set off arson attacks, which equally predictably met with fresh police raids.

Bantu Education was soon extended to university colleges. 'Non-Europeans who are trained at mixed universities,' said Mandela, 'are considered a menace to the racial policies of the government. The friendship and inter-racial harmony that are forged . . . constitute a direct threat to the policy of apartheid . . .' The tribal colleges would be used by the government to enforce its political ideology; the education they would give would not be directed towards 'the unleashing of the creative potentialities of the people but towards preparing them for perpetual mental and spiritual servitude to the whites'.*

More forms of banning were continually being thought up. Mandela described what it meant to an individual:

> In the name of the law I found myself restricted and isolated from my fellow men, from people who think like me and believe like me. I found myself trailed by officers of the Security Branch of the police force wherever I went. In short, I found myself treated as a criminal – an unconvicted criminal. I was not allowed to pick my company, to frequent the company of others, to participate in their political activities, to join their organizations ... I was made, by the law, a criminal, not because of what I had done, but because of what I stood for, because of what I thought, because of my conscience.

With first- and second-rank leaders banned, and then the third rank, the ANC struggled on, frankly recognizing such failures as its inability to prevent the Western Areas removals: too much rhetoric, too little carefully planned and organized action. With membership fees adjusted to the general impoverishment of the people, Congress never had resources to sustain its own organization adequately, much less protests and strikes.

As those who had been banned continued to work on, in an enforcedly clandestine manner, Tambo observed their anxiety – the prison sentences could be heavy – but Mandela remained calm, and his wit and confidence helped to dissipate fear. 'The people,' he said, 'are increasingly becoming alive to the necessity of the solidarity of all democratic forces regardless of race, party affiliation, religious belief and ideological conviction.'

Chief Lutuli, after a one-year ban had expired, was even more heavily restricted, confined to the rural backwater of his home for two years. And he fell gravely ill for some months, but as soon as he had recovered he became involved in one of the secret committees planning a new form of protest.

Professor Z. K. Matthews, newly returned from a year as

* *Liberation*, 1957.

48

visiting professor at the Union Theological Seminary in New York, had proposed a 'Congress of the People' when he addressed the Cape ANC's annual conference in 1953: 'I wonder whether the time has not come for the ANC to consider the question of convening a National Convention representing all the people of this country, irrespective of race or colour, to draw up a Freedom Charter for the democratic South Africa of the future.' Lutuli saw it as a practical demonstration of what the National Convention of 1909 should have been: a means of thinking creatively about the country, of defining more clearly what the liberation movement was aiming at.

By 1955 that movement had been formalized: the ANC had been joined by several organizations as a Congress Alliance. Along with the Indian Congress and the SA Congress of Trade Unions (SACTU), there was a newly formed Coloured Peoples' Organization and a Congress of Democrats (COD). COD consisted of a few hundred members, representing the commitment of a group of whites of whom Mandela was to say: 'They were prepared to treat Africans as human beings and equals; to eat with us, talk with us, live with us and work with us for the attainment of political rights and a stake in society.' The formation of SACTU, consisting of eight African unions, three Coloured and one white (laundry workers), marked a revival after legislation had severely restricted African trade unions.

Sisulu, who had recently visited China and the Soviet Union, after passing through Israel and London, was touring the Transkei and the Ciskei to arouse support for the Congress of the People.

Circulars were sent to towns, villages and locations, asking: IF YOU COULD MAKE THE LAWS ... WHAT WOULD YOU DO? HOW WOULD YOU SET ABOUT MAKING SOUTH AFRICA A HAPPY PLACE FOR ALL THE PEOPLE WHO LIVE IN IT? A typical reply came from the Rustenburg Inter-Tribal Farmers' Association condemning Bantu Education, the pass laws and the Bantu Authorities Act, and asking for more facilities for cultivation and grazing, to be more directly represented in parliament and to be given equal education.

'Adequate' wages, better houses and food were also popular demands. When all these had been sifted through, a Freedom Charter was drafted by a committee. Mandela and Sisulu were among the banned members who approved the draft in the days before the Congress took place.

A wide range of organizations and white political parties had been invited to take part. The United Party did not trouble to reply; the Liberal and Labour Parties agreed to send observers, and a handful of independent Christians, among them Father Huddleston, readily accepted. Surprisingly, the authorities did not ban the Congress though there were harassments such as the withdrawal of buses bringing delegates from distant parts.

The Alliance's circulars included a poetic invitation:

WE CALL THE FARMERS OF THE
RESERVES AND TRUST LANDS!
Let us speak of the wide lands and the narrow strips
on which we toil.
Let us speak of the brothers without land and the
children without schooling.
Let us speak of taxes and of cattle and of famine.
LET US SPEAK OF FREEDOM!
WE CALL THE MINERS OF COAL, GOLD
AND DIAMONDS!
Let us speak of the dark shafts and the cold
compounds far from our families.

On Saturday, 25 June 1955, on a patch of veld in Kliptown – a village inhabited by Africans, Coloured people and Indians some miles to the south-west of Johannesburg – about three thousand delegates responded to this 'call'. Banners carried slogans such as: FREEDOM IN OUR LIFETIME; LONG LIVE THE STRUGGLE. It was South Africa in microcosm: Africans, Indians, Coloured and white people, many in national garb; doctors, peasants, labourers, ministers, housewives, servants, trade unionists and lawyers. They were an excited, good-humoured, expectant crowd. At the entrance to the wired-in enclosure stood hefty men in lounge suits: the Special Branch, ubiquitous as always and taking photographs, especially of the white delegates. The ANC colours of black, green and gold dominated the scene.

Inspiring leaders were absent under bans when the Isitwalandwe, an award symbolizing the highest distinction in African society, was announced for Chief Lutuli, Dr Dadoo and Father Huddleston. Only the latter was free to be present, to hear the people's cheers.

Delegates listened to a Freedom Charter read in English, Sesotho and Xhosa, which began: 'We the people of South Africa declare for all our country and the world to know, that South Africa belongs to all who live in it, black and white, and that no government can justly claim authority unless it is based on the will of all the people.'

Its aims were: 'The people shall govern; all national groups shall have equal rights; the people shall share in the country's wealth; the land shall be shared among those who work it; all shall be equal before the law; all shall enjoy equal human rights; there shall be work and security; the doors of learning and of culture shall be opened; there shall be houses, security and comfort; there shall be peace and friendship.'

Some aims arose out of daily experience, for instance: 'the privacy of the house from police raids shall be protected by the law' and 'all shall be free to travel without restriction'. Some were typical of the desire for a social welfare state: 'the aged, the orphans, the disabled and the sick shall be cared for by the state'; some were socialist: 'the mineral wealth . . . the banks and monopoly industry shall be transferred to the ownership of the people as a whole'. The crowd approved each section with shouts of *'Afrika!'* and *'Mayibuye!'*

On the Sunday afternoon came the sound of tramping feet. Police, armed with sten guns, marched towards the seated delegates. A shout went up. The crowd rose, hands raised in the Congress salute, and, as the Chairman urged them to keep calm, they burst into singing *'Mayibuye!'* to its cheerful tune of 'Clementine'.

Special Branch detectives and armed police searched speakers and audience, confiscating every document. Even posters and banners were taken, including two notices from the foodstall: SOUP WITH MEAT and SOUP WITHOUT MEAT. It was announced that 'treason' was suspected.

The meeting continued in a mood that was almost triumphant. At the end all stood and sang 'Nkosi Sikelel' iAfrika'. As darkness fell and delegates began to disperse, the ANC band played freedom songs.

Mandela was not alone in thinking the Congress a 'spectacular and moving demonstration'. The people, he said, had demonstrated that they had 'the ability and the power to triumph over every obstacle and win the future of their dreams'.

He regarded the adoption of the Freedom Charter as an event of major political significance, and indeed the Charter was to become the cornerstone of policy for the United Democratic Front, thirty years later. 'Never before,' he said, 'has any document or conference been so widely acclaimed and discussed by the democratic movement in South Africa. The Charter is more than a mere list of demands for democratic reforms; it is a revolutionary document precisely because the changes it envisages cannot be won without breaking up the economic and political set-up of present South Africa.'

Three months later the biggest police raid in South African history took place at dawn. More than a thousand police searched hundreds of men and women in their homes and offices, seizing anything that might be evidence of treason, sedition or violation of the Suppression of Communism or Riotous Assemblies Act.

Mandela's bans ran out towards the end of 1955. Special Branch detectives promptly arrived at his office to impose new ones: this time the banning orders were for five years. Meanwhile friends had observed that the pressures of political activity were undermining his marriage and that Mandela had grown impatient with Evelyn's religious dedication – she was a Jehovah's Witness. The crisis came when Evelyn, after a year studying midwifery in Natal, returned home to find her husband in the thick of an affair. Her recriminations enraged him and she fled to her brother's house, abandoning husband and home. Eventually their separation became formal. Not only Evelyn suffered deep pain at the break-up of the marriage but Thembi, as the eldest child, would become irrevocably alienated from his father. For the time being, however, Mandela saw as much as possible of the children.

The new Prime Minister, J. G. Strijdom, was pursuing the extension of the police state with the Criminal Procedure and Evidence Amendment Act, the Native Administration Amendment Act, the Natives' Urban Areas Amendment Act and the Group Areas Further Amendment Act. These Acts symbolized the inefficiency of a massive bureaucracy, which year after year required amending legislation to correct mistakes or to close loopholes. Banishment to remote areas was an additional new punishment for those who resisted.

The government announced that from 1956 African women were to carry passes – the *verdomde* (accursed) *dompas* – which more than any other law tormented Africans. Since 1952 boys between the ages of sixteen and eighteen had been obliged to carry them. As in the Orange Free State in 1913, women rose in protest. Many wives of ANC leaders who were in the Women's League were joined by women of other races. Among them was Helen Joseph, British-born social and trade-union worker. The dynamic President of the League, Lilian Ngoyi, explained their driving force: 'Men are born into the system, and it is as if it has become a life tradition that they carry passes. We as women have seen the treatment our men have. When they leave home in the mornings, you are not sure they will come back. We are taking it very, very seriously. If the husband is to be arrested *and* the mother, what about the child?'

In October 1955 two thousand women converged from all over the country to protest to the government in Pretoria. A year later twenty thousand women arrived there. Forbidden to march through the streets, they went in twos and threes to the Prime Minister's office, some wearing ANC blouses, some in saris, some carrying babies or baskets of food. They delivered a huge bundle of protests and then stood, silent, in the amphitheatre of the Union Buildings. At a gesture from Lilian Ngoyi they burst into song, a warrior's song with words for the occasion: 'Strijdom, you have struck a rock once you have touched a woman.' 'Nkosi Sikelel' iAfrika' followed before they dispersed.

Since the Congress of the People, the police had made over a thousand raids, seizing countless documents, among them, naturally, Mandela's writings. On 5 December 1956 came the knock on the door at dawn. Mandela was awakened in his house in Orlando, just as scores of men and nineteen women were similarly roused in all parts of the country. They were arrested and charged with high treason.

6

'CAN THIS BE TREASON?'

1956–9

While Mandela, Sisulu and Tambo were being driven by police to the Fort, Johannesburg's old prison, from all over the country military aircraft were transporting men and women of every race to be incarcerated there: Chief Lutuli, Dr Naicker and Ismail Meer among those from Natal, Professor Matthews among the Eastern Cape contingent. Apart from the leaders, the majority of the 156 accused were drivers, clerks, factory workers, labourers, teachers and housewives.

Loyal Congress leaders from the past, such as Canon James Calata, composer of many freedom songs, had been arrested, and Ruth First, Transvaal editor of *New Age*, the pro-Congress newspaper, along with her husband, advocate Joe Slovo, as well as Lilian Ngoyi and Helen Joseph. The prisoners were a cross-section of South African society: 105 Africans, twenty-three whites, twenty-one Indians and seven Coloured people. They were at once segregated in 'European' and 'non-European' sections of the gaol.

Mandela and others who had long been separated by bans confining them to local areas now found themselves together in two huge cells, able to confer, as Lutuli put it, *sine die*. Paul Joseph, who as a school student had first met Mandela, now came to know him better and was impressed by his attentiveness. He never talked down to others and not only was it a pleasure to be with him, but one felt secure in his company. He seemed to draw strength from people, then return it with abundance.

A 'Stand by our Leaders' movement developed and a Treason Trials Defence Fund was formed by Bishop Reeves, Alex Hepple, MP and Alan Paton (leaders of the Labour and Liberal

Parties), with international support provided by a fund set up in London under Canon John Collins of Christian Action.

While Afrikaner diehards approved their government's vigilance 'in face of a dangerous plot', American scholars – Professors Gwendolen Carter and Thomas Karis – commented that the depth of the conflict between Africans and whites 'was commensurate with the majestic charge of high treason'. But when the Trial's preparatory examination opened two weeks later, on 19 December 1956, the atmosphere was celebratory rather than solemn. Vast crowds singing Congress songs had gathered in the streets surrounding the Drill Hall where the court was to be held, and the prisoners, also singing lustily, were driven up in *kwela-kwelas* (police vans). In the hall, a draughty iron-roofed relic of the colonial past, accused, public and press mingled freely to the consternation of the police. When order was called, the 156 accused were seated on row after row of chairs, as if they were delegates at a conference. No sooner had the magistrate begun to speak than it was discovered the microphone was defective and not a word could be heard. Court was adjourned amid laughter.

The next day a new disposition in the courtroom had the accused contained within a wire cage. The distinguished defence lawyers refused to act for people 'treated like wild animals'. While the cage was being removed, shots were heard: outside the Drill Hall police had panicked and fired into the good-humoured crowd. Twenty-two people were injured. In an explosive atmosphere, the Bishop of Johannesburg and Alex Hepple, both small men, moved into the straining throng, calming them; while the colonel in charge of police angrily reprimanded his men.

In due course the accused were granted bail. Each day Mandela drove several of his fellows from the township to the Drill Hall. They found much to mock in the state's presentation of its case and in the often ludicrously incoherent evidence of its witnesses. The prosecutor said he would prove that the accused were members of the national liberation movement whose speakers had propagated the Marxist-Leninist account of society and the state; the Youth League's Programme of Action and Mandela's speeches and writings were among key documents. The state would also show that the Freedom Charter envisaged steps in the direction of a communist state and was to be a prelude to revolution. The defence repudiated this charge and positively declared the aims of the Congress Alliance as expressed in the Charter, contending that not only 156 individuals were on trial, 'but the ideas that they and thousands of others in our land have openly espoused and expressed'.

As the examination monotonously dragged on, most of the accused, a long way from home, suffered great hardship, and their families were supported by the Defence Fund. Mandela and Tambo were among the few who could live at home and carry on part-time with their work. Thousands of sequestered documents were sworn into the record, among them the signs: SOUP WITH MEAT and SOUP WITHOUT MEAT.

During the lunchbreaks the Eastern Cape choir practised Calata's freedom songs at the back of the hall, while Transvaal leaders were engaged in urgent consultation with organizers of a bus boycott from Alexandra township. As in the 1940s a rise in fares had provoked people: for nearly four months more than fifty thousand men and women walked the long distances to and from work, achieving a rare victory. Not only did the government pass a law requiring employers to subsidize certain transport expenses for employees but fares reverted to the pre-boycott level.

Lutuli and the other ANC leaders, wanting to test the organization's strength while they were handicapped by the Trial, called for a stay-at-home on 26 June 1957. With SACTU support in calling for a £1-a-day minimum wage, the strike was remarkably successful, especially in the Johannesburg and Port Elizabeth areas. Mandela explained the significance of the term 'stay-at-home'. Since a strike necessitated having pickets to prevent people from working in industries which were boycotted, and pickets attracted police violence, Congress had decided to use this alternative, asking people to remain in their houses, thus avoiding violence.

In September there was a long adjournment in the preparatory examination. The excitement of the accused at going home was tempered by news of riots in Johannesburg townships: more than forty Africans were killed and scores injured. The government, as usual, refused to appoint a commission of inquiry. An inquiry set up by the City Council found that among the root causes of the unrest were apartheid's system of ethnic grouping, the migrant labour system, poverty, lack of educational and vocational training, lack of recreational facilities, and the 'utmost discomfort' on trains in which Africans were crammed when travelling to and from work. The Minister of Justice rejected the findings as of no practical value.

Soon after, people's opposition to the imposition of Bantu Authorities, and the ever-present suffering caused by the pass laws, set off violent upheavals in various parts of the Transvaal. Government reaction was to move armed police into these rural areas. Mandela, working with Tambo on the defence of a number of related cases, was prevented by bans from visiting the troublespots. With great difficulty they had maintained their practice, working early each morning and, after wearisome days in the dock, returning to the office in the evenings. At weekends Mandela held a legal 'clinic' in Orlando.

Tambo had intended to become an Anglican priest and in 1956 Bishop Ambrose Reeves had accepted him as a candidate for ordination; charged with treason, however, he had abandoned that hope.

It was through Tambo and Adelaide Tsukudu, the young nurse he was about to marry, that Mandela met Winnie Nomzamo Madikizela. During an adjournment in the preparatory examination, he happened to be buying food in a delicatessen in Johannesburg when the Tambos drove up. With them was an exceptionally pretty and lively young woman. Surely Nelson knew of her, said Oliver, her picture had featured in magazines when she had been appointed the first black medical social worker at Baragwanath African Hospital; and, he added, she came from his home village: 'Winnie from Bizana' he called her.

A few days later Mandela telephoned Winnie, inviting her to lunch. In her early twenties, she felt overawed by this commanding man and his friends but accepted. It was a Sunday and he broke off from his legal work to take her to a popular Indian restaurant, where he watched with affectionate amusement her discomfort at tasting hot curry for the first time. Even there he could not escape people wanting his advice or simply a friendly word or two. Although some of his comrades might find him aloof he was wholly accessible, giving generously of his time and knowledge.

He drove Winnie to open country where they walked. All she recalls of their conversation was his asking her to raise money for the Treason Trials Defence Fund. Perhaps the space of veld and sky reminded them of the landscape of their childhood. Like Nelson, Winnie had herded cattle and goats and loved the countryside of the Transkei. There, her father, Columbus Madikizela, had been principal of a school. A rebellious tomboy, Winnie often came in for beatings from her mother. Nine years old at her mother's death, she helped care for her young brother and sisters before attending boarding-school. 'Going through trials; one who strives' is roughly the meaning of her name, Nomzamo.

What followed could not be called a courtship. 'If you are looking for some kind of romance, you won't find it,' Winnie has said of the developing friendship over the ensuing months. Some days Nelson's friends collected her from the hospital and took her to the gym to watch him 'sweat it out', or she accompanied him on visits to his friends in the townships and suburbs. And she attended ANC meetings although she was not yet a member: at school the Unity Movement had attracted her and now Mandela teased her, telling friends how he had saved her from this rival organization, how thankful she should be. Deeply in love, she yet remained in awe of him. She had no idea his divorce had taken place until one day he suddenly asked her to visit a friend, Ray Harmel, who would make her wedding-dress. 'How many bridesmaids would you like?' he inquired. Winnie's response was the question: when was the wedding to be?

Her father was intensely proud of his daughter's engagement to so important and highly regarded a man, but there were grave anxieties: divorce was frowned on in African society – not only in the Transkei but in the townships – especially the divorce of someone in the royal family who must set an example. Could Winnie cope with the criticism which would inevitably be directed partly at her? And there was the question of Nelson's three children. Although they were living with their mother, they would naturally visit their father and step-mother and she was so young. Furthermore, Mandela was on trial for treason.

Winnie found reassurance in Mandela's nature: he inspired confidence, faith and courage. She knew that he loved her but she had already realized that if you became involved in the cause you could no longer think in personal terms, that he could not be separated from the people, from the struggle. Only long after did she speak wistfully of the 'young bride's life' which she never experienced.

In June 1958 they were married at Winnie's home in Pondoland. Mandela had been granted four days' leave from his order restricting him to Johannesburg. Lilian Ngoyi was among ANC leaders who accompanied them. Columbus Madikizela, in speaking the father's 'words of wisdom' to his daughter, told her that she must remember that she was marrying the struggle and not the man; that by bringing such a man to him as a son-in-law, she was introducing the African National Congress to that part of the country.

Custom required that the wedding ceremony take place in both family homes but there was no time to include Nelson's home in Qunu. Traditionally, their marriage was not completed and, for that occasion, Winnie kept part of the wedding-cake. She was waiting for the day when her husband would be free of restrictions.

Back in Johnannesburg, she began to transform the small house, 8115 Orlando, by adding two rooms, bringing colour and style to the interior, and making a garden in the restricted piece of ground allocated to such featureless ghetto houses. Across the rough dirt road was a barren hill. The Mandelas' stock of books would be continually depleted by police raids in the years to come.

When the Treason Trial proper opened on 1 August 1958 in Pretoria, in what had once been a synagogue, the defence could claim partial victory: the charges against Lutuli, Tambo and fifty-nine others were withdrawn. Mandela and Sisulu were among the ninety-one now formally charged with high treason; the alternative charge under the Suppression of Communism Act was thrown out by the court.

Three judges were trying the case; the prosecutor was Oswald Pirow, QC who had led the 'Under the Swastika' movement in the thirties. He had been a particularly vicious Minister of Justice in 1929. The defence was led by a brilliant team of advocates, among them Israel Maisels, QC, Bram Fischer, QC and Sydney Kentridge. For the accused there was an impressive link with the outside world in the presence of observers from the International Commission of Jurists, one of whom remarked that not since the Reichstag trial, with the exception of the Nuremberg trials, had such worldwide attention been attracted.

Mandela's equanimity and good humour were notable throughout, but all these men and women were so spirited it was hard to believe they were on trial for their lives. Helen Joseph recalls driving from Johannesburg to Pretoria with Mandela and three other men – forty miles each way – discussing the Trial, their lawyers and their fellow-accused; telling jokes, reminiscing about their childhood; stopping to buy peaches along the roadside. Each day at lunchtime many of them repaired to the large garden of a neighbouring vicarage for a meal provided by the Indian community, occasions which resembled garden parties. For Mandela and others who carried on organizing despite the Trial, it was an opportunity to discuss critical events and to advise those directly concerned.

Meanwhile Winnie Mandela had joined the ANC Women's League and the multiracial Federation of South African Women, and soon was on their executive committees. With Albertina Sisulu, she was among hundreds who marched in protest against the pass laws being extended to women. Many carried babies on their backs. The overseas press reported on the good humour of these redoubtable women; as they were arrested they climbed cheerfully into the police pick-up vans, some calling out, 'Tell our madams we won't be at work tomorrow!' They were sentenced to a month's imprisonment in the Fort: Winnie's first experience of prison, of the sisal mat on the floor and the filthy blankets for bedding, and she was pregnant. She knew her conviction would cost her her job at Baragwanath Hospital but that was just one of the risks that must be taken. She and the other women realized that while their protests might delay legislation, they were unlikely to succeed in their ultimate aim. Mandela was immensely proud of her, although they seldom discussed political issues. Walter Sisulu and his wife, and Lilian Ngoyi, were among the individuals who influenced and inspired her.

In the months to come family involvement in the growing conflict in Pondoland would tear Winnie apart. The South African government was imposing Bantu Authorities – the first ploy in preparing for Bantustans – and leaders of the resistance in Pondoland came secretly to the Mandelas' house to consult Nelson. But Winnie's father supported the government and when the conflict in his area deteriorated into a minor civil war, he was attacked as a collaborator. 'To see the anger,' she said long after, 'to see and feel the anger of the people my father in his own twisted way had tried to sacrifice so much for. It was tragic that politically my father and I did not see eye to eye. It left terrible scars in my heart.'

When Mandela's relative, Chief Kaiser Matanzima, was subsequently elevated by the South African government to rule over the Transkei Bantustan, Winnie's father became Minister of Lands and Agriculture. Furious clashes divided father and daughter and only towards the end of his life were they reconciled.

'Politically the talk about self-government for the reserves is a swindle,' Mandela warned in a remarkably prophetic article in May 1959. 'Economically, it is an absurdity.' There would be forcible uprooting and mass removals of millions of people from urban areas to these Bantustans; areas already intolerably overcrowded.

Attempts to impose apartheid had met, time after time, with resistance which often turned to violence. 'Chief after chief,' Mandela pointed out, 'has been deposed or deported for resisting "Bantu Authorities" plans . . . The Bantustans are not intended to voice the aspirations of the African people; they are instruments for their subjection.'*

During 1959 a serious dispute in the ANC came to a head. Weakened by bannings and the virtual immobilization of Mandela and other senior leaders on trial, the organization, particularly in the Transvaal, had been carried on by men who acted dictatorially, setting off petty squabbles and brawls. A group of dissidents calling themselves Africanists attacked the Congress Alliance, charging that white communists and Indians were using it to propagate their own ideology and demanding a return to 'Africa for the Africans'. Their rhetoric resembled that of the Youth League ten years earlier. Lutuli and Tambo failed to heal the breach and the group broke away to form the Pan Africanist Congress (PAC) under the leadership of Robert Sobukwe. An influential member of the Fort Hare Youth League, who had become a lecturer at the University of the Witwatersrand, Sobukwe was admired for his integrity and intellectual vigour. The PAC adopted the slogan emanating from an All-African People's Conference in Accra: 'Independence in 1963'.

Mandela recognized that their 'go-it-alone' nationalism had

* *Liberation*, 1959.

appeal, just as it had had for him and Sisulu and others in the 1940s, but the ANC, as he put it, took account of the 'concrete situation' in South Africa: it was the *system*, not whites as such, they were attacking. It would be tempting to pander to popular resentment against non-Africans, but the ANC chose to educate the masses to accept a more enlightened concept of the struggle.

White liberals were attracted by the Africanists' anti-communist line but, remarked Mandela, it was white communists' record of sacrifice in the interests of African freedom which had reinforced what had always been ANC policy: an absolute rejection of racialism, white or black. Many Africans felt sceptical when warned of the dangers of communism, since government spokesmen labelled all militant opposition 'communist'.

At the very time when the state was quoting anti-imperialist speeches as evidence against Mandela and others in the Treason Trial, he was describing what imperialism meant to the people of Africa and Asia in the journal *Liberation*: the exploitation of mineral and agricultural wealth without the consent of the people and without compensation; the destruction of the economic power of the indigenous populations; low wages and long hours of work; above all, the denial of political rights, and the perpetual subjugation of the people by a foreign power.

While the influence of the old European powers had sharply declined, he saw 'American imperialism' as a threat to the newly won independence of people in Asia and Africa:

> It masquerades as the leader of the so-called free world in the campaign against communism . . . It maintains that the huge sums of dollars invested in Africa are not for the exploitation of the people . . . but for the purpose of developing their countries and in order to raise their living standards. Now it is true that the new self-governing territories in Africa require capital to develop the countries . . . But the idea of making quick and high profits which underlies all developmental plans launched in Africa by the USA, completely effaces the value of such plans insofar as the masses of the people are concerned. The big and powerful American trade monopolies that are springing up in various parts of the continent and which are

destroying the small trader; the low wages paid the ordinary man, the resulting poverty and misery, his illiteracy and the squalid tenements in which he dwells, are the simplest and most eloquent exposition of the falsity of the argument that American investments in Africa will raise the living standards of the people in the continent.*

A highly significant influence on African opinion when it came to international affairs was the voting at the United Nations. Mandela pointed out that whereas the Soviet Union, India and several other nations had 'consistently identified themselves unconditionally with the struggle of the oppressed people for freedom', the United States had often 'allied itself with those who stand for the enslavement of others'.

Nevertheless, at the 1958 UN session, the United States for the first time supported a resolution criticizing South Africa's racial policy and, mild though it was, this shift in direction disturbed the South African government more than all the condemnation from communist powers. Britain, however, continued to abstain.

During 1959 the ANC showed a remarkable upsurge of confidence: not only had the hiving off of the dissident Africanists resulted in a determined unity but Lutuli and Tambo were at last free of bans.

Lutuli took off on a nationwide speaking tour which began with packed meetings of all races in the Cape. To the government, he was more dangerous than an extremist; he, more than any other black leader in the country's history, had profoundly impressed whites. Before he could move on to the Transvaal, the clamp-down came. This time the bans and the exile to his rural home were for five years. Tambo, deputy President-General, was re-banned from gatherings for five years. The government took no such action against PAC leaders who were touring the country, recruiting.

While Winnie Mandela was giving birth to a daughter,

* *Liberation*, 1958.

Zenani, her husband was forced to spend most days in the Treason Trial court. Fragments of family life were all they had together: he would return from his early morning jog to be greeted by Winnie with a glass of orange juice and no sooner was breakfast over than he must set off on the long drive to Pretoria. The Minister of Justice had declared that the Trial would be proceeded with 'no matter how many millions of pounds it costs'. 'What does it matter,' he asked, 'how long it takes?' It was already well into its third year.

On 19 January 1959 the defence team had won a further victory when the indictment against sixty-one of the accused was quashed. Only thirty of the original 156 defendants remained on trial, among them Lilian Ngoyi and Helen Joseph, Walter Sisulu and Nelson Mandela.

Meanwhile, under the Group Areas Act, Mandela and Tambo had been ordered to leave their law office in the city of Johannesburg and practise in a township 'at the back of beyond', as Mandela put it, 'which was tantamount to asking us to abandon our practice, to give up the legal service of our people for which we had spent many years training. No attorney worth his salt would agree easily to do so.' Disregarding the threat of prosecution and eviction, they defied the order. Whenever possible at night and weekends, Mandela joined his partner in keeping the practice alive.

7

'VIOLENCE WILL NOT COME
FROM OUR SIDE'

1960–61

'Africa Year' in 1960 and the independence won by many states to the north of South Africa gave powerful incentive to the struggle in the south. A sense of crisis was in the air: in Natal, where two thousand people had been arrested and black police-men had been killed, vast ANC meetings demanded 'action'; in the Transkei where the Pondo uprising raged on, a state of emergency had been declared; in South-West Africa a crowd protesting against forced removals from Windhoek location had been fired on by police, who killed eleven people and wounded forty-four; and in Cape Town on 3 February the British Prime Minister, Harold Macmillan, shocked the South African govern-ment and its supporters by declaring that a 'wind of change' was sweeping Africa.

Chief Lutuli called for an economic boycott of South African goods, and the ANC, in a unique alliance with thirteen other organizations of all races, planned demonstrations against the pass laws, under which nearly half a million African men and women were convicted each year.

This campaign was to start on 31 March. Ten days earlier the Pan Africanist Congress, under Robert Sobukwe, launched wide-spread protests against the pass laws. At the 'model' township of Sharpeville, outside Vereeniging in the southern Transvaal, PAC volunteers presented themselves, passless, at the police station. The crowd, greatly enlarged by curious residents, was seen by journalists as 'amiable' but by police as 'menacing'. Seventy-five policemen fired more than seven hundred shots into the crowd, killing sixty-nine Africans and wounding at least

180 – mostly shot in the back – including women and children.

In the Treason Trial the prosecutor was making much of a warning Mandela had given in 1952: 'The day of reckoning between the forces of freedom and those of reaction is not very far off.'

A few hours after the Sharpeville killings, far away to the south at Langa, outside Cape Town, some ten thousand demonstrators gathered outside the so-called 'bachelor' zones, where thousands of men lived cramped together, separated from wives and families. Only a handful heard the police order to disperse within three minutes. As so often before, there followed a baton charge by the police, stone-throwing by the crowd, then the order to fire. Two Africans were killed and forty-nine injured. The people went berserk.

SHARPEVILLE, LANGA, the names flashed round the world. The accumulated abhorrence felt for apartheid and the South African government's record of repression, set against the sustained non-violence of the ANC and now of the PAC demonstrations, stirred a profound response. The government was confronted by a political crisis of unprecedented magnitude as riots swept the country.

In Johannesburg Sisulu, Mandela, Duma Nokwe – Secretary-General of the ANC – and Joe Slovo, in a frantic series of all-night meetings, considered what the ANC's response to the crisis should be. On 26 March, Nokwe conveyed their immediate recommendation to Chief Lutuli, who was staying in Pretoria while he gave evidence in the Treason Trial. He agreed and that night he publicly burned his pass, calling on others to follow suit; an action which coincided with government suspension of the pass laws. And Lutuli followed up with a second call, for a national day of mourning, a strike which was almost wholly successful in Johannesburg, Port Elizabeth and Durban. As continuing strikes, mass funerals, protest marches and rioting gripped the country, the government declared a State of Emergency. Police brutality in Langa township provoked a great march of thirty thousand Africans determined to protest to the police in

Cape Town, but the young PAC organizer, Philip Kgosana, who had spontaneously slipped into the leadership, was tricked by a high-ranking police officer into quietly dispersing the crowd; he was arrested and imprisoned.

Meanwhile white South Africa felt its prosperity gravely threatened; a wave of massive selling hit the Johannesburg Stock Exchange. The Minister of Justice called for calm; the Minister of Finance called for immigrants; the Minister of Native Affairs declared that apartheid was a model for the world; and a white man attempted to assassinate Prime Minister Verwoerd.

For the first time the UN Security Council intervened in South Africa's affairs: by nine votes to none, with Britain and France abstaining, a resolution blamed the South African government for the shootings. By this time eighty-three African civilians and three African policemen had been killed; no whites were killed, sixty were injured.

On 7 April the pass laws were reinstated. Leading South African capitalists who had flown to London and New York re-established the infusion of investment.

Under the State of Emergency Mandela and the other twenty-nine accused in the Treason Trial, as well as Lutuli and other defence witnesses, were imprisoned in Pretoria, isolated from their people, impotent to intervene further at this most crucial time. In all, some two thousand activists were detained and thousands of so-called vagrants were rounded up.

On 8 April the government outlawed the ANC and the PAC: in parliament, by 128 votes to sixteen (the four 'Native' representatives and the newly formed Progressive Party), they were declared unlawful organizations under the Suppression of Communism Act; the penalty for furthering their aims was imprisonment for up to ten years. (Newspaper headlines were henceforward to label those being tried for alleged ANC and PAC membership, 'Red'.) The ANC's last 'legal' action was to call for a National Convention to lay the foundation for a new Union of *all* South Africans. Oliver Tambo had already left the country for Britain and Tanzania to set up ANC offices in exile.

The Treason Trial took on new importance. The defence team had withdrawn, protesting that it was impossible to function in a political trial during a State of Emergency. They agreed that Mandela and Duma Nokwe, an advocate, should in the meantime take over the defence.

Conditions in Pretoria prison were intolerable: the African defendants were herded five to a cell, six foot by twelve, with one covered bucket for a toilet and, next to it, another for drinking water; blankets and sleeping mats were lice-ridden; food consisted of maize and *mealiepap* (maize porridge), and only occasional scraps of meat. After ten days they were allowed a shower and ten minutes a day in the exercise yard. Mandela, elected spokesman, was threatened with punishment under the emergency regulations after complaining about the conditions to a particularly harsh warder. Mandela's response was to quote from prison regulations. 'That's a lie!' the warder shouted. 'And government regulations don't require you prisoners to read books!' At which Mandela lost his temper. Towering over the man, he demanded to see a senior officer. And he complained about the food to the Judge-President in the Trial: 'Speaking with the greatest moderation it is no exaggeration to say that the food which is furnished to us in gaol, My Lord, with due respect, is completely unfit for human consumption.' Soon after the Superintendent of Prisons visited the detainees and conditions were improved.

Within a few weeks Mandela was provoked by a new hindrance into formal protest to the court: he and Nokwe were entitled to have consultations with the other defendants and with Professor Z. K. Matthews, who was due to give evidence on their behalf but, for these meetings, the prison authorities had provided a small cell without chairs, dominated by the presence of a full sanitary bucket.

There were more relaxed times when they studied – Mandela thought it useful to learn Afrikaans, Sisulu shorthand and Nokwe French – and then they played Scrabble.

Mandela was feeling his separation from Winnie and their

baby daughter, Zenani, but the other defendants, while aware of this, remarked on his capacity to keep their spirits up. Ironically, in the Trial, ANC members – at the invitation of the state – were daily expounding the organization's policies and activities, literally 'furthering the aims' of a banned organization.

In the last resort the state case depended on proving the ANC had a policy of violence, but attempts to discover such violence in campaigns against the Western Areas removals and Bantu Education had failed, as had an attempt to link Congress with the riots during the Defiance Campaign. The state fell back on trying to prove that the accused 'must have known that the course of action pursued . . . would inevitably result in a violent collision with the state, resulting in its subversion'.

Lutuli, ill and strained after being arrested for burning his pass, and suffering from the prolonged detention, was questioned on another basic element in the state case: that the liberation movement was part of an international communist-inspired conspiracy pledged to overthrow governments where people did not have equal political and economic rights. He said that when it came to 'East' or 'West' the ANC tendency was to judge nations by their attitude to apartheid at the UN.

Early in August 1960 Mandela gave evidence; 441 pages of the official record are taken up by his evidence-in-chief and subsequent cross-examination. Winnie was present in court.

Four years earlier when the Trial had begun, he had given casual observers the impression of being an able lawyer and a delightful man. Now his political maturity was noted: the articulate attack of his evidence, as one of the defence team put it; but there was something more profound: a question of growth under challenge. His stature was a measure of the calibre of the ANC's top leadership.

The defence lawyers noted another strength in the Congress: its continuity and the fact that it included Africans of every political viewpoint, among them peasant leaders who understood their people. Political maturity was common both to these men and the intellectuals such as Matthews and Mandela. One mystery was how the ANC could on occasion appear moribund, then suddenly hundreds and thousands would be stirred to action. Its weakness was in everyday organization, communicating with branches, collecting subscriptions, ensuring that resolutions were followed through. The 'tedious house-to-house work', as the ANC itself said, had not been implemented because the 'easy way' was preferred, 'of street-corner meetings, mass meetings and conferences'.

Much of the state's cross-examination of Mandela was based on his speeches and articles. The three judges intervened from time to time. He described the formation and policy of the Youth League: 'We felt that the time had arrived for the Congress to consider the adoption of more militant forms of political action,' and he gave his view of the achievements of the Defiance Campaign.

'Isn't your freedom a direct threat to the Europeans?' asked one judge.

'We are not anti-white,' he replied, 'we are against white supremacy, and in struggling against white supremacy, we have the support of some sections of the European population . . . It is quite clear that the Congress has consistently preached a policy of race harmony and we have condemned racialism no matter by whom it is professed.'

Questioned about whether the 'People's Democracy' he had written of could be achieved through a series of concessions from the 'ruling class', he said that Congress had not sat down to discuss the question but: 'We demand universal adult franchise and we are prepared to exert economic pressure to attain our demands; we will launch defiance campaigns, stay-at-homes, either singly or together, until the government should say, "Gentlemen, we cannot have this state of affairs, laws being defied and this whole situation created by stay-at-homes. Let's talk." In my own view, I would say, Yes, let us talk.'

At that time he was prepared to envisage a concession of sixty seats in a parliament for Africans which, in his view, would be a victory, a significant step towards attaining universal suffrage.

They would then suspend protest for an agreed limited period while educating the white electorate 'to see that changes can be brought about . . . better racial understanding, better racial harmony in the country'. But, of course, he added, the demand for universal franchise would never be abandoned and eventually they would have their 'People's Democracy'.

But what plans did he have if, as the evidence suggested, the government did not soften in its views?

'The Congress,' he replied, 'of course, does not expect that one single push to coerce the government to change its policy would succeed.' He explained that over a period, as a result of repetition of these pressures, together with world opinion – notwithstanding the government's attitude of ruling Africans with an iron hand – the methods which they were using would bring about a realization of their aspirations.

On the question of violence the prosecution put to him that the ANC propagated the view that the government would not hesitate to use armed force in retaliation against Congress pressure. He agreed. 'But as far as we are concerned we took the precautions to ensure that violence will not come from our side.' And if the ANC grew more powerful? Was the possibility of government violence therefore increased? 'Oh, yes. We felt that the government will not hesitate to massacre hundreds of Africans in order to intimidate them not to oppose its reactionary policy.'

Even when he was cutting the prosecutor down to size, Mandela was unfailingly conscious that he himself was an 'officer of the court'.

His speech, 'No Easy Walk to Freedom', was subjected to detailed examination. For instance, his reference to 'revolutionary eruptions' in other parts of Africa. What had he meant? 'A serious political struggle for democratic changes,' he answered. 'A militant struggle.'

A point frequently raised by the prosecution concerned Congress documents referring to the struggle in other countries, without condemning their use of violence. Mandela explained:

'Look, let us take the example of Kenya. We were concerned there with the fact that there was a colonial war. We condemned, we regarded Britain as an aggressor. We had never heard of the Kikuyu invading Great Britain, bombing their cities, bringing death and destruction to thousands of people by robbing their best land and breaking up their political organizations. These things Great Britain did in Kenya, and our concern was that Britain must leave Kenya. We were not concerned with the methods which the Kikuyu used.'

'They were irrelevant?' asked the prosecutor.

'They were absolutely irrelevant to us,' Mandela replied. 'Our own method here is non-violent; and they are the best judges of what method they should employ, it is not our concern.'

What about the one-party system of government? a judge asked.

'It is not a question of form, it is a question of democracy,' Mandela answered. 'If democracy would be best expressed by a one-party system then I would examine the proposition very carefully. But if democracy could best be expressed by a multi-party system then I would examine that carefully. In this country, for example, we have a multi-party system at present, but so far as the non-Europeans are concerned this is the most vicious despotism you can think of.'

'Are you attracted by the idea of a classless society?'

'Yes, very much so, My Lord,' was his reply. 'I think that a lot of evils arise out of the existence of classes, one class exploiting the others [but] . . . the ANC has no policy in any shape or form on this matter.'

Only once did indignation break through. The Judge-President questioned the wisdom of universal franchise: would this not be dangerous? Mandela replied that every person should have the right to vote. But, insisted the Judge, what was the value of 'people who know nothing' participating in the government? Would they not be subject to the influence of election leaders 'as children would be'?

'No,' Mandela replied, his voice rising, 'this is what happens.

A man stands up to contest a seat in a particular area. He draws up a manifesto; he says, "these are the things for which I stand": if it is a rural area he says, "I am against stock limitation". Then, listening to the policy of this person, you decide whether this man will advance your interests if you return him to parliament; on that basis you vote for a candidate. It has *nothing* to do with education.'

'He only looks to his own interests?' asked the Judge.

'No,' said Mandela. 'I am being practical. A man looks for a man who will be able to present his point of view and he votes for that man.'

Counsel for the defence, Sydney Kentridge, in re-examination, questioned Mandela about his father, who had not been formally educated; how would he have exercised the vote? He would, said Mandela, have had the ability and the sense to vote responsibly.

Defence counsel went on to ask about Mandela's early hostility to communists and his attempt to have them expelled from the ANC before, in 1950, he had for the first time worked with them. Had they then appeared loyal to ANC policy? 'That is correct,' he replied.

'Did you become a communist?'

'Well,' he said, 'I don't know if I did become a communist. If by communist you mean a member of the Communist Party and a person who believes in the theory of Marx, Engels, Lenin and Stalin, and who adheres strictly to the discipline of the party, I did not become a communist.' He had read Marx and was impressed by the absence of a colour bar in the Soviet Union, by the fact that it had no colonies in Africa, and by its strides in industry and science. He added that he was very much attracted to socialism but had not studied it deeply.

On the issue of imperialism, raised by the defence, he had this to say: 'In our experience the most important thing about imperialism today is that it has gone all over the world subjugating people and exploiting them, bringing death and destruction to millions of people. That is the central thing and we want to know whether we should support and perpetuate this institution which has brought so much suffering.'

On 9 August Mandela completed his evidence. Helen Joseph, in wanting to applaud, wondered what had been in the minds of those judges as they listened to this great leader, to this man the Nationalist government had forbidden ever again to be a member of the ANC.

In prison Mandela and other leaders were evolving new ways of working. 'My colleagues and I,' he later revealed, 'after careful consideration, decided that we would not obey the decree outlawing Congress.' The movement was to have a new plan based on the 'M' Plan, reorganizing it to function underground. They had formed a 'caretaker committee'. 'We believed it was our duty to preserve this organization which had been built up with almost fifty years of unremitting toil.'

The Emergency was lifted at the end of August and detainees were released. Immediately ANC slogans and leaflets appeared in various parts of the country. Mandela could return home to his family but as the defence team prepared for the final stages of the Trial he frequently had to stay late in Pretoria for consultations. His wife has described how, in this abnormal life, he hardly had time for meals: he would start, the phone would ring and he would be called on to bail someone out at a police station or to dash to an emergency meeting. Winnie was pregnant at the time and many years later Mandela, from his prison cell on Robben Island, recalled her patience, 'the loving remarks which came daily', and 'the blind eye' which she always turned towards 'those numerous irritations that would have frustrated another woman'. He felt a sense of shame at his failure to be helpful. 'My only consolation,' he added, 'is the knowledge that then I led a life where I'd hardly enough time even to think.'

During the Christmas adjournment he devoted himself to his family. Makgatho fell ill in the Transkei and Mandela, disregarding his banning orders, hurried down to be with the boy; while there his second daughter, Zindziswa, was born, and he returned at once to Johannesburg, to find mother and baby in the 'non-

European' section of a hospital where, clearly, they were not getting adequate attention. Furious, he gathered them up and took them home where they could be properly nursed and cared for. Their spell of normal family life was all too brief.

In the Treason Trial Professor Z. K. Matthews concluded the evidence of witnesses for the defence. Counsel put to him the state's allegation that the bulk of the 'non-European' population was likely to respond 'more quickly, more irresponsibly and more violently to illegal agitation than would be the case with a group whose general standard of civilization was higher'.

'I'm a little sceptical about the use of the word civilization being higher,' replied the Professor. 'I don't know in what sense the word "higher" is used . . . but my own impression would be that even the so-called more highly civilized groups, subject to the conditions to which the Africans are subject in this country, would I think react more violently.'

With regard to the state's allegation that on occasion the accused had 'deliberately created an explosive situation', Matthews retorted that an explosive situation had been created by the authorities and had 'existed, I should say, since the state was created in 1910'.

Replying to one of the Judges, he agreed that the ANC's aim of universal franchise would mean the end of white supremacy, and said that it had been realized that the white supremacists would not readily concede this, but even they would not be impervious to political and economic pressures. Up to now the ANC's campaigns had not been on a sufficiently wide scale nor were they sustained, but if the ANC were stronger, even the white supremacists would talk.

Congress, Matthews added, was optimistic. 'Our optimism was based upon the fact that this is not the only government that has been relentless in the history of political struggle.' Others had been determined not to give in to attempts made by their oppressed subjects, and they had subsequently done so. He mentioned the British in India, and pointed out that 'governments usually act as a result of pressure'.

After more than four years the Trial was drawing to a close. The state's argument concluded in March 1961. The defence opened their argument by denying a 'conspiracy motivated by hostile intent' and disputing the state's contention that no middle ground existed between the ballot box and treason. With weeks of argument still to come, Advocate Bram Fischer, QC suddenly found himself cut short by the senior Judge who adjourned the Trial for a week. Did this mean the court was already convinced that the accused were guilty?

Winnie Mandela described to me how later that day her husband suddenly appeared at their house, accompanied by Sisulu, Nokwe and Joe Modise, another of the accused.

> They all stood outside in the driveway of the garage and he sent a child to call me. On my arrival he simply said, 'Darling, just pack some of my clothes in a suitcase with my toiletries. I will be going away for a long time. You're not to worry, my friends here will look after you. They'll give you news of me from time to time. Look well after the children. I know you'll have the strength and courage to do so without me, I now know you are capable of that.'
>
> I quickly packed his clothes. I was in tears but I had been conditioned in the few months we had together not to ask any questions. I only wished him well before we parted and asked that the gods of Africa take care of him wherever he would be, and that he would have a chance to spare the children and me a few minutes sometimes. He scolded me for reminding him of his duties.

She had no idea of the dangerous days and the anguish that lay ahead. All she had noticed was that during the previous few weeks he had seemed to be meditating a great deal. At times he hadn't heard when she was talking to him. She had asked what was wrong and he had assured her that it was nothing. But he had paid their rent six months in advance; that was most unusual. It was not until she read in the press that he had been in Pietermaritzburg, hundreds of miles away in Natal, that she realized his banning orders had run out and that the authorities had not imposed new restrictions on him.

On 29 March Mandela, back in Pretoria, joined the other

accused in the dock. The public galleries and the press benches were packed. The atmosphere was tense as the senior Judge, Mr Justice Rumpff, gave certain 'findings of fact':

– the ANC and its allies had been working to replace the government 'with a radically and fundamentally different form of state';

– the Programme of Action 'envisaged the use of illegal means' and illegal means had been used during the Defiance Campaign;

– certain leaders made sporadic speeches inciting violence but the state had failed to prove a policy of violence;

– a strong left-wing tendency had manifested itself in the ANC which frequently revealed 'anti-imperialist, anti-West and pro-Soviet' attitudes, but the state had not proved that the ANC was communist or that the Freedom Charter pictured a communist state. Nor had the prosecution proved that members of the Communist Party, after its banning, had infiltrated the ranks of the ANC and become executive leaders. The ANC allowed both communists and anti-communists freely to become members if they subscribed to its policy. When the CP had dissolved itself 'a small number of executive leaders of the ANC' were already members of the Party.

Nine years earlier Mandela and Sisulu had been in the dock before Judge Rumpff in the trial of Defiance Campaign leaders. Now again he asked them and the others to stand. 'You are found not guilty and discharged,' he said. 'You may go.'

Triumphantly they left the court, carrying their leading counsel, Maisels and Fischer, shoulder high, to be greeted by a cheering, dancing, weeping crowd. Outside they all sang 'Nkosi Sikelel' iAfrika'.

8

'IS IT CORRECT TO CONTINUE
PREACHING PEACE?'

1961

The South African government was doubtless confident that African protest and resistance had been crushed by the banning of the ANC and the PAC and by the massive arrests under the Emergency, but even before they were released from the constraint of the Treason Trial, Mandela and Sisulu had joined other leaders in prison planning a new initiative. With Lutuli's blessing, and assuming that the verdict in the Trial would be 'not guilty', Mandela had been chosen to lead at this hazardous time.

He fully realized the implications: the other organizers were to remain secret as protection against police persecution, while he was to go underground, with the task of surfacing for specific public actions. His family life – already much reduced – would have to be sacrificed, his legal practice abandoned. He must, as he later told the court in 1962, 'take up the life of a man hunted continuously by the police', living separated from those closest to him, continually risking detention and arrest. He said it was infinitely more difficult than serving a prison sentence. No one in his right senses would choose such a life: 'But there comes a time, as it came in my life, when a man is denied the right to live a normal life, when he can only live the life of an outlaw because the government has so decreed to use the law . . .' He could not have acted as he did, he emphasized, without the inspiration, support and courage of his wife.

After leaving Winnie with those devastating words, 'I will he going away for a long time,' he had driven to Pietermaritzburg. There, fourteen hundred delegates, many from Zululand and

Pondoland – a cross-section of political, religious, sporting and cultural groups – came together for an All-In African Conference on 25 March 1961.

Mandela's sudden appearance after ten years of enforced silence was, said one delegate, 'electrifying'. Through the day and night delegates considered the grave political situation resulting from government policies. Mandela was especially moved by one man who had resisted Bantu Authorities and who had found that when the hour of decision came, the people were deserted by leaders they had trusted. At this conference, said the man, he felt refreshed and full of confidence: 'We must win in the end.' Mandela felt he represented the solemnity of the occasion.

The conference demanded a 'National Convention of elected representatives of all adult men and women on an equal basis irrespective of race, colour, creed or other limitation' which must have 'sovereign powers' to determine 'a new non-racial democratic constitution' for South Africa. It was eight years since that demand had first been made; eight years of ever-intensifying oppression.

Under Mandela a National Action Council was elected to communicate the demand to the government. If the government failed to call such a Convention, there would be country-wide demonstrations: a three-day stay-at-home to coincide with the establishment, at the end of May, of the new white Republic of South Africa. Mandela left the conference to report to Lutuli. Back then to the Trial in Pretoria, to hear the judgement: in the only home-movie of that occasion he can be glimpsed, a dark-suited presence, at once commanding and exuberant. From the court, he went underground.

It was difficult for a well-known public figure, especially so tall a man, to disguise himself. As he secretly toured the country, a warrant was issued for his arrest. He surfaced here and there to lead and advise, then disappeared when the hunt got too hot; always there was the danger of informers in a country where for generations police had been intimidating and bribing. He found a new potential for action among people in rural areas and among Cape Muslims from whom ANC leaders had been cut off by bans. A wonderful experience: 'You can't comprehend unless you actually stay with the people,' he said at the time. He loved country life and during the years of restriction had almost forgotten what it was like. He moved through townships; in Soweto, he attended small meetings at night with people returning from work. And he moved through cities, meeting factory workers and also groups of Indians. In Port Elizabeth he stayed with the poet Dennis Brutus and his wife May, at their home in Shell Street, and after organizing sessions in New Brighton township he taught their small sons to box. Back in Johannesburg he visited his own family only late at night. He was sensitive to not putting others at risk. He himself had some narrow escapes and on one occasion was obliged to make a quick get-away from a second-floor flat by sliding down a rope.

As he continued to elude the police, the press named him the 'Black Pimpernel', adapting the name of the daring fictional character who evaded capture during the French Revolution. Not the least of the difficulties was that the only car available to him in Johannesburg when he was disguised as a chauffeur continually broke down.

Mandela worked in close collaboration with Walter Sisulu, a wise, shrewd man, always unassuming yet vital to the planning and organization. Over the years Mandela had learned much from him, and also from his own experience. The ability to bring people together, to emphasize points of agreement were useful for Mandela when he called on white newspaper editors and leaders of the Liberal Party who had expressed hostility to the campaign for a stay-at-home. Secretly he went to see them to explain, to listen to their arguments and to argue back. If criticized, he bore no grudge, his sense of humour always prevailed.

From an Afrikaner newspaper came the warning that 'enemies' of South Africa were precipitating the most serious crisis in the country's history.

Mandela addressed leaflets to black students telling of the

'stirring call to action' from the Pietermaritzburg conference and referring to the 'enslaving' nature of Bantu Education. Recent matric results strikingly illustrated the disastrous effects of this policy, he said, and showed that even more tragic consequences would follow if the Nationalists were not kicked out of power. The students to whom he appealed for support in coming demonstrations were to play a significant role.

He knew his people had no interest in the debate on whether there should be continued association with the British monarchy or the establishment of a Boer republic, but it was a convenient peg for action, for drawing international attention to black demands. 'We are inspired by the idea of bringing into being a democratic republic where all South Africans will enjoy human rights without the slightest discrimination,' he said; as opposed to the system of white supremacy which had brought South Africa into contempt and disrepute throughout the world.

The call for a National Convention was taken up by a multiracial group widely representative of liberal, religious and academic opinion.

At all costs, another Sharpeville must be avoided. On 24 April Mandela wrote to the Prime Minister on behalf of the National Action Council, expressing anxiety that under the proposed republic the government 'already notorious the world over for its obnoxious policies, would continue to make even more savage attacks on the rights and living conditions of the African people'. A dangerous situation could be averted only by the calling of a 'sovereign National Convention'.

He gave notice of the intended demonstrations. 'We have no illusions about the counter-measures your government might take,' he went on. 'During the last twelve months we have gone through a period of grim dictatorship.' Nevertheless, he added, 'We are not deterred by threats of force and violence . . .'

As on previous occasions of confrontation with the government, he could hardly have expected the demands to be met. Indeed, the Prime Minister made no reply, only admitting in parliament that Mandela's letter, which he called 'arrogant' with its 'threats', had been received.

Early in May, Mandela wrote to the leader of the United Party, the main parliamentary opposition, pointing to the widespread support the call for a National Convention was arousing. The alternatives, he stated bluntly, were 'talk it out or shoot it out'. 'It is still not too late,' he appealed. 'A call for a National Convention from you could well be the turning-point in our country's history. It would unite the overwhelming majority of our people . . . It would isolate the Nationalist government and reveal for all time that it is a minority government.'

The United Party, rooted in middle-class white society with its security in mining, commerce and industry, was moribund. Its leader did not reply.

The demonstrations were to take the form of a three-day stay-at-home from 29 May. Late in the month, the police made large-scale raids and arrests, again failing to trap Mandela. They arrested not only leaders and organizers but ten thousand Africans under the pass laws: innocent people, as Mandela pointed out. Meetings were banned thoughout the country, printing presses raided and strike leaflets seized.

Prime Minister Verwoerd himself issued stern warnings to 'agitators', to 'members of the ordinary public' including 'intellectuals', 'pseudo-intellectuals' and 'some newspapers' who were 'playing with fire' by advocating a National Convention. Everyone supporting the proposition was jointly responsible for communists' aims.

Even liberal English-language newspapers swung from objective reporting to warnings against responding to Mandela's call. They ignored his press statement protesting against the ten thousand arrests and complimented the police for the 'courteous' manner of the arrests which, said Mandela, had been made with the purpose of forestalling the demonstrations. He himself had successfully gone through police road blocks, but his people had been rounded up. Was it not important for the country to know what he thought on a matter of such importance?

The *Rand Daily Mail* published a 'secret plan' inciting non-whites to invade cities, doubtless conceived by *agents provocateurs*, while ignoring Mandela's absolute repudiation of any such plan.

Mandela visited industrial areas and last-minute leaflets were issued, reiterating the call to 'stay at home':

PEOPLE OF SOUTH AFRICA!
THE PROTEST GOES ON
ARRESTS CANNOT STOP US . . .
VOTES TO ALL
DECENT WAGES FOR ALL
END PASS LAWS
END MINORITY WHITE DOMINATION
WE ARE NOT GOING TO BE FRIGHTENED BY VERWOERD. WE STAND
FIRM BY OUR DECISION TO STAY AT HOME . . . DO NOT BE
INTIMIDATED . . . FORWARD TO FREEDOM IN OUR LIFETIME . . .

NEWSHOUNDS ARRIVE IN LATEST TROUBLE MISSION announced a headline as foreign correspondents flew in to Johannesburg, anticipating another Sharpeville. The London *Observer*'s correspondent set the scene:

In the country's biggest call-up since the war, scores of citizens' force and commando units were mobilized in the big towns. Camps were established at strategic points; heavy army vehicles carrying equipment and supplies moved in a steady stream along the Reef;* helicopters hovered over African residential areas and trained searchlights on houses, yards, lands and unlit areas. Hundreds of white civilians were sworn in as special constables. Hundreds of white women spent weekends in shooting at targets. Gun shops sold out of their stocks of revolvers and ammunition. All police leave was cancelled throughout the country. Armed guards were posted to protect power stations and other sources of essential services. Saracen armoured cars and troop carriers patrolled townships. Police vans patrolled areas and broadcast statements that Africans who went on strike would be sacked and forced out of the town.

---

* The Witwatersrand complex of Johannesburg and nearby mining towns.

On Monday, 29 May 1961, hundreds of thousands of Africans risked jobs and homes to respond to Mandela's call. In Durban they were joined by Indian workers and in Cape Town for the first time by Coloured workers; this despite police propaganda which had the South African Broadcasting Corporation announcing from early morning that throughout the country workers had ignored the call to stay at home. Later in the day the SABC broadcast that all was 'normal'; next day it announced that all had 'returned to normal'. In Port Elizabeth on the second day there was a 75 per cent strike, and in several areas university and school students demonstrated. (The police were eventually to admit 60 per cent absenteeism in the Johannesburg area.)

Mandela praised the 'magnificent response', the result of hard work and devotion from organizers and activists working at personal risk, 'defying unprecedented intimidation by the state, trailed and hounded by the Special Branch, denied the right to hold meetings, operating in areas heavily patrolled by police and teeming with spies and informers'. It was not the whites' republican celebrations that had attracted the international press to South Africa, he said, but the 'stirring campaign' of the people to mark the rejection of that white republic.

There was no doubt, however, that the overall response was disappointing and, on the second day, Mandela called the strike off. That morning journalists from London met him in a sparsely furnished flat in a white suburb of Johannesburg. Wearing a striped sport-shirt, he was not looking in the least conspiratorial and his welcoming laughter boomed. Did he concede, one correspondent asked, that the strike had been a failure?

'In the light of the steps taken by the government to suppress it,' he replied, 'it was a tremendous success.' He described the courage it had taken for workers to defy police and army and also employers. The government was spoiling for a massacre. People were desperate and desperate people would eventually be provoked into acts of retaliation.

Soberly he added: 'If the government reaction is to crush by

86

naked force our non-violent struggle, we will have to reconsider our tactics. In my mind we are closing a chapter on this question of a non-violent policy.' In the only existing news film of Mandela in an interview given to a London television team later that day, he made the same grave declaration.

With his comrades he was already working on an analysis of the strike. They recognized that the failure was partly due to inexperience of the leadership in working underground. It was less than fourteen months since the ANC had been outlawed and it was still reorganizing and retraining cadres accustomed to working openly. There was a delicate balance between functioning secretly, and announcing that you were in fact so functioning, thus courting arrest.

He considered a criticism often levelled at the ANC: that the strike had not concerned a bread-and-butter question, but he rejected this. The demand for a National Convention, after all, meant 'one man, one vote; the key to our future'. And he returned to the question of non-violence: 'The question being asked up and down the country is this: is it politically correct to continue preaching peace and non-violence when dealing with a government whose barbaric practices have brought so much suffering and misery to Africans?'

In his mind he had answered the question. On 26 June 1961, the annual 'Freedom Day', he issued a statement from underground, forecasting new methods of struggle. All he could specify at the moment was 'non-collaboration'. The African people's millions of friends abroad would be asked to intensify the boycott and the isolation of the South African government, diplomatically, economically and in every other way. He would continue to operate from underground.

'I shall fight the government side by side with you,' he promised his people, 'until victory is won. What are you going to do? Will you come along with us, or are you going to cooperate with the government in its efforts to suppress the claims and aspirations of your own people? ... Remain silent and neutral in a matter of life and death to my people, to our

9

'SABOTAGE OFFERED THE MOST HOPE
FOR FUTURE RACE RELATIONS'

1961–2

After discussions in the outlawed ANC, a small group led by Nelson Mandela was given the task of forming Umkhonto we Sizwe (Spear of the Nation).

The decision to turn to violence had not been easily arrived at: some had reservations about efficacy or timing and Mandela himself, although firmly advocating the need for this change in policy, was distressed that the long struggle – his own experience of twenty years of disciplined non-violence – had been to no avail; furthermore, it was obvious that if non-violent protest had been quelled by massacres, violent tactics would be met with ever more overwhelming force.

The ANC as a mass political organization with an express policy of non-violence would not engage in acts of violence but would no longer disapprove of such acts if 'properly controlled'. Sisulu would remain with the ANC and Mandela would lead Umkhonto (MK). A select few – members of the ANC and of the Communist Party – began to organize.

Through the winter and into the spring the planning went ahead. Mandela missed Winnie and his daughters badly and, to his comrades' consternation, slipped out of his various hiding-places to meet his wife. She worked for Johannesburg's Child Welfare Society, visiting children in townships and suburbs and attending children's courts. His disguises, as a window-cleaner, an errand 'boy', a chauffeur, were improbable but effective: once when Winnie's car was giving trouble, she received a message at her office telling her to drive to a particular corner; there a tall man in blue overalls got into the car, telling her to move over from the driver's seat; he drove her to a garage where he bought her a new car, then drove her back to the centre of the city, stopped at a STOP sign, said goodbye, got out and disappeared into a crowd of commuters. At first she had not recognized him.

When he stayed for a while in a flat in a middle-class white area, his host, Wolfie Kodesh, found him deep in study of books on war: Mao Tse-tung, Che Guevara, Liddell-Hart, Reitz's *Commando*, above all Clausewitz, whose classic he read with especial concentration, heavily underlining passages. A problem arose: how to explain to the Zulu cleaner employed by the landlords, the presence of a black man staying as a guest in this apartment block, a black man who never went out by day? They agreed that Kodesh should tell the cleaner that 'David' was a student preparing to go overseas, and studying in the flat until all the arrangements had been made. Kodesh set off for work and when he returned at lunchtime, found Mandela and the Zulu chatting and laughing. It was not the first time that he'd noted Mandela's way of getting on easily with servants: in another household the cook was only too happy to run errands for this 'David'. Disconcerting though, Kodesh found, to wake at five a.m. and find your clandestine guest in a track-suit, running on the spot – Mandela's customary indoor exercise when he could not go out jogging for two hours every morning.

After October the Mandelas had a semblance of family life. A small farm had been rented for Umkhonto; named Lilliesleaf, it was in Rivonia, a suburb on the outskirts of Johannesburg, and among the outhouses was an apartment ideal for an outlaw who until then had only been able to venture out in disguise. Winnie, with Zeni and Zindzi, was brought there by a sequence of cars and for the first time in many months she could cook meals for Nelson and he could take the children for walks in the wooded garden – Zindzi in her pram, Zeni a toddler. Zeni came away with a dream that this rambling house, where her Daddy lived, was her home. Makgatho and Maki also enjoyed visits.

At Lilliesleaf the Umkhonto conspirators and their ANC advisers could work more efficiently. One major change from past policy was that MK accepted all races, although its cadres were mainly African. In the enforced isolation a deep sense of comradeship arose from risks shared; excitement grew as they made their plans.

Four forms of violence were possible: sabotage, guerrilla warfare, terrorism and open revolution. They decided on sabotage, a logical choice in the light of their political background. 'It did not involve loss of life,' Mandela later emphasized, 'and it offered the most hope for future race relations'; bitterness would be kept to a minimum and, if the policy bore fruit, democratic government could become a reality.

This decision to limit the violence arose also from alarm that whites and blacks were drifting towards civil war. If it had taken more than fifty years for the scars of the war between Boer and Briton to disappear, then how much longer, he wondered, would it take to eradicate the scars of inter-racial civil war?

Since South Africa depended to a large extent on foreign capital and trade, they hoped that 'planned destruction of power plants, and interference with rail and telephone communications', would 'scare away capital', and 'make it more difficult for goods from the industrial areas to reach the seaports on schedule'. In the long run, this heavy drain on the economic life of the country would surely compel the voters to reconsider their position.

'Umkhonto,' Mandela said, in summing up, 'was to perform sabotage; and strict instructions were given to its members right from the start, that on no account were they to injure or kill people.' He headed the National High Command which determined the tactics and targets and was in charge of training and finance. Regional commands were set up to direct local sabotage groups.

They faced immense problems. In the teeth of the large and powerful police force, they had to pull their entire organization together, setting up cells, more or less as envisaged in the 'M'

Plan. How much should anyone know? How to ensure that secrets were kept? Historically, Africans had always fought openly; some regarded secrecy as cowardly. How to maintain communication between the different centres, hundreds of miles apart, when telephones were tapped and travel was always difficult for Africans? Even when disguised they risked arbitrary challenges under the pass laws.

Through half a century of open struggle, of raids and arrests, the police had been able to build up formidable records of most, if not all, of the political activists. There were almost as many black policemen as white, while the country was riddled with informers. Not surprising when an informer could get £130 with bonuses for 'scoops'.

As for the actual targets, major installations were closely guarded. Finally, there was the great personal risk, the possibility of the death penalty.

Port Elizabeth, long the most militant area, soon had twenty-one cells established in New Brighton and thirty-three in Kwaza-kele township. The security police there, still smarting from black achievement during the Defiance Campaign, would set out to smash not only the saboteurs but any fragment of political activity for years to come.

Meanwhile, Mandela's survival underground was having an inspiring effect on his people as the wide-flung police net still failed to capture him. But the risks he continually took were little short of foolhardy. During November, after touring Natal and the Cape, he had a narrow escape: wearing chauffeur's coat and cap, he was waiting on a street corner in Johannesburg and the car due to pick him up failed to appear; suddenly he saw one of the black security police approaching and, as the man looked into his eyes, recognizing him, he thought, it's all up; but the man went on by and, as he did so, winked and gave the ANC thumbs-up salute.

That December in 1961 marked an end and a beginning: the ANC's long history of non-violence was acclaimed as Chief Albert Lutuli was awarded the Nobel Prize for Peace. 'The credit is not mine,' he insisted, 'but the ANC's. I inherited policies that go back fifty years which I have been happy to carry out.' Less than a week later, on 16 December – the 'Day of Heroes' on which the ANC had traditionally held its annual conference – Umkhonto we Sizwe struck. Saboteurs exploded bombs at symbolic targets in Johannesburg, Port Elizabeth and Durban. One saboteur was killed in the explosions.

Leaflets announced: UMKHONTO WE SIZWE WILL CARRY ON THE STRUGGLE BY NEW METHODS. The manifesto continued:

> We of Umkhonto have always sought – as the liberation move-ment has sought – to achieve liberation without bloodshed and civil clash. We hope, even at this late hour, that our first actions will awaken everyone to a realization of the disastrous situation to which the Nationalist policy is leading. We hope that we will bring the government and its supporters to their senses before it is too late, so that both the government and its policies can be changed before matters reach the desperate stage of civil war . . . The time comes in the life of any nation when there remain only two choices: submit or fight. That time has now come to South Africa. We shall not submit and we have no choice but to hit back by all means within our power in defence of our people, our future and our freedom.
>
> The government has interpreted the peacefulness of the movement as weakness; the people's non-violent policies have been taken as a green light for government violence . . . We are striking out along a new road for the liberation of the people of this country.*

Early in January 1962 Mandela was smuggled out of the country. He had spent one last night with Winnie in the house of friends he had known for many years, a safe house on the edge of the northern suburbs. His flight to Ethiopia, where Emperor Haile Selassie was hosting a Pan-African Freedom Conference, was the first event in a thrilling experience: for the first time in his life he was a free man. In Addis Ababa he met

* Two months earlier sabotage had been committed by a group of white liberals and socialists who were to call themselves the African Resistance Movement (though African membership was minimal).

Oliver Tambo, who had arranged for him to address the Conference. He was enthusiastically received by delegates from East, Central and Southern Africa. After thanking the states which had enforced sanctions against South Africa and given asylum to refugees and freedom fighters, he spoke of the struggle ahead; it would be long, complicated, hard and bitter and would require the maximum unity of the national movement. 'Naked force and violence,' he said, 'is the weapon openly used by the South African government to beat down the struggles of the African people and to suppress their aspirations.' He described the repressive policies, the persecution of political leaders, the Treason Trial and the massive detentions in the Sharpeville and Transkei Emergencies. He spoke of the widespread unrest and protests in rural areas during the 1950s and the stay-at-home strike of 1961, all crushed by ever more drastic force from police and the military. Yet the people were not deterred. After being outlawed, the ANC had immediately issued a statement announcing that it would defy the government's ban and carry out operations from underground.

'How strong is the freedom struggle in South Africa today?' This, he said, was a question frequently put:

> The view has been expressed in some quarters outside South Africa that, in the special situation obtaining in our country, our people will never win freedom through their own efforts. Those who hold this view point to the formidable apparatus of force and coercion in the hands of the government, to the size of its armies, the fierce suppression of civil liberties, and the persecution of political opponents of the regime. Consequently, in these quarters, we are urged to look for our salvation beyond our borders. Nothing could be further from the truth.

Certainly international condemnation of South African policies had hardened considerably, and the move to ensure effective sanctions against that government was gaining support. South Africa had been expelled from the Commonwealth through the active initiative and collaboration of Ghana, Nigeria and Tanzania. 'This increasing world pressure on South Africa has greatly weakened her international position and given a tremendous impetus to the freedom struggle inside the country.'

He paid tribute to the gallantry of those fighting Portuguese repression in Mozambique and Angola and continued:

> But we believe it would be fatal to create the illusion that external pressures render it unnecessary for us to tackle the enemy from within. The centre and cornerstone of the struggle for freedom and democracy in South Africa lies inside South Africa itself . . . During the last ten years the African people have fought many freedom battles, involving civil disobedience, strikes, protest marches, boycotts and demonstrations of all kinds. In all these campaigns we repeatedly stressed the importance of discipline, peaceful and non-violent struggle. We did so, firstly because we felt that there were still opportunities for peaceful struggle and we sincerely worked for peaceful changes. Secondly, we did not want to expose our people to situations where they might become easy targets for the trigger-happy police of South Africa. But the situation has now radically altered.
>
> South Africa is now a land ruled by the gun. The government is increasing the size of its army, of its navy, of its air force, and the police . . . Armaments factories are being set up . . .
>
> All opportunities for peaceful agitation and struggle have been closed to us. Africans no longer have the freedom even to stay peacefully in their houses in protest against the oppressive policies of the government. During the strike in May last year the police went from house to house, beating up Africans and driving them back to work . . . A crisis is developing in earnest.

No high command announced beforehand what its strategy and tactics would be but, he added, 'a leadership commits a crime against its own people if it hesitates to sharpen its political weapons which have become less effective'. During the previous ten months he had travelled up and down South Africa, 'spoken to peasants in the countryside, to workers in the cities, to students and professional people', and it had dawned on him quite clearly that the situation had become explosive.

He explained that in going underground he had announced that he would not leave South Africa. 'I meant it and I have honoured that undertaking. But when my organization received the invitation to this conference it was decided that I should attempt to come out and furnish the various African leaders, leading sons of our continent, with the most up-to-date information about the situation.'

In concluding, he emphasized that unity was 'as vital as the air we breathe and should be preserved at all costs'. He was confident that in the decisive struggles ahead South Africa's liberation movement would receive the fullest support of African leaders and 'all freedom-loving people throughout the world'.

Accompanied for much of the time by Oliver Tambo, Mandela went on to tour a number of states in North and West Africa to arrange for the military training of recruits, as well as scholarships for the future administrators and technicians who would be needed to run the non-racial state and control the army and police forces.

The sense of freedom he felt for the first time in his life was, he said later, a freedom 'from white oppression, from the idiocy of apartheid and racial arrogance, from police molestation, from humiliation and indignity. Wherever I went,' he added, 'I was treated like a human being.' With Tambo he flew on to London where he met Hugh Gaitskell and Jo Grimond, leaders of the Labour and Liberal Parties. The struggle in South Africa, he emphasized, was multi-targeted. He had chosen the armed struggle but he respected Lutuli's commitment to non-violence. Everyone opposed to apartheid must fight in the area in which they were best able. On Sunday 17 June 1962 he had a day off and toured the sights of Westminster.

Then it was back to Africa, to Algeria, where Colonel Boumedienne, Commander-in-Chief of the Army of National Liberation (later to be President), invited him to inspect – as Mandela put it – 'the cream and flower of the Algerian youth who had fought French imperialism and whose valour had brought freedom and happiness to their country'. While there he took a course in demolition, weaponry and mortar firing. At the Algerian Army HQ he attended lectures; he wanted to be able and ready, if necessary, to stand and fight with his people.

Returning to East Africa, he met Julius Nyerere, future President of Tanzania, Kenneth Kaunda, future President of Zambia, and Oginga Odinga, the opposition leader in Kenya. Everywhere he had been showered with hospitality and assurances of support, although he had also encountered hostility to the ANC's alliance with whites and Indians, hostility which he felt came from ignorance of South Africa's special conditions and a failure to realize that the leadership came from Africans.

He had seen black and white mingling peacefully and happily in hotels and cinemas and residential areas; he had seen them using the same public transport – unimaginable in his own country.

It was time to return there. But before flying south he was able to meet the first batch of recruits who had slipped out of South Africa for military training in Ethiopia. He made the perilous border crossing without incident and was home again. A car driven by an Indian friend awaited him on a dark country road and through the night they drove, hardly talking, until by a devious route they reached Johannesburg, where Mandela was to stay with a family unaware of his identity, who lived opposite a police station: the safest place, his comrades reckoned. Eager to report back, eager to be with Winnie, he was constantly on the move. Somehow he had managed to write to her from abroad, now again they could meet in a friend's house, but all too briefly.

In Johannesburg he reported on his tour to the National High Command of Umkhonto. Some colleagues felt the training of recruits was premature but after long discussion it was agreed to go ahead with the plans because it would take many years to build up a sufficient nucleus of trained soldiers to start a guerrilla campaign. Still exhilarated by all he had experienced, he went to Natal to report to the regional command in Durban. Cecil Williams, a theatre director, had placed a car at his disposal and they drove down, Mandela the chauffeur and Williams the boss.

After the meeting with Umkhonto, Mandela contacted M. B. Yengwa, an old friend and one of Natal's ANC leaders, who was astounded and delighted when the tall chauffeur calling himself 'David' asked to be taken to see 'Chief', as Lutuli was respectfully and affectionately known. Mandela's comrades in Johannesburg had had grave misgivings at his insistence that he must see Lutuli, but had given way in face of his stubborn determination: 'I promised Chief before I left. I must go,' he said. Driving north through sugar plantations to Stanger, Yengwa was regaled with Mandela's stories of his travels. Next morning was a Saturday, and Lutuli joined them at a friend's house at noon.

It was, thought Yengwa, like a meeting between leader and commander, with Lutuli and Mandela embracing, overjoyed to see each other again. Mandela gave a frank and detailed report of his tour. He referred to the uneasiness expressed by a number of African leaders at the ANC's alliance with whites and Indians and at the fact that some were communists. As Yengwa recalled the conversation, Lutuli was even firmer than Mandela on the ANC position: people must understand that this was ANC policy, arrived at over a period and decided in conference.

Then Lutuli raised the question which had long troubled him: Umkhonto's announcement in December 1961 that the policy of non-violence had ended. Aware of Mandela's role, Lutuli criticized the failure to consult himself and the ANC 'grassroots'. He felt they had been compromised. Although apologetic, Mandela said he thought that, tactically, the action had been correct. Besides, they had wanted to protect Lutuli and the ANC from involvement in the drastic change in policy.

They parted with warm good wishes for the future and late that afternoon Yengwa drove Mandela back to Durban, not without qualms that his passenger might be recognized in the slow-moving city traffic. Arrived safely, Mandela asked a favour: could Yengwa take him to see Winnie's sister, a nurse in a TB settlement? After that brief meeting, Yengwa dropped him in a Durban street.

On the Sunday, Mandela and Cecil Williams set off for Johannesburg. Somewhere near the Howick Falls they were stopped by three carloads of police. It was rumoured that a member of the CIA had informed the authorities of Mandela's whereabouts, but Mandela was to deny this and to explain that security in Durban had been extremely lax. So it was that Mandela was captured on 5 August 1962. He had been underground for seventeen months.

The following morning Winnie Mandela was leaving the Child Welfare Office on the way to do fieldwork in Soweto, when one of her husband's comrades suddenly appeared, looking dishevelled and strained. She realized at once that something was wrong: had Nelson been injured, she asked.

No, came the reply, but he would probably be appearing in court within a day or two.

Mandela was imprisoned in the Johannesburg Fort.

10

'A TRIAL OF THE ASPIRATIONS
OF THE AFRICAN PEOPLE'

1962

The corridors of the Magistrates' Court bustled with police. Down below in the cells, Harold Wolpe, attorney, and Joe Slovo, advocate, saw Mandela on his arrival from the Fort. He was smiling, confident and, as always, fully in control of himself. Later 'Verwoerd's most wanted man,' as one journalist put it 'made a slow and dramatic appearance, mounting the steps to the court like a quiet avenging giant.'

The proceedings on 8 August took only a few minutes. Mandela answered to his name and impassively listened to the charges: inciting African workers to strike, and leaving the country without valid travel documents. Whatever the suspicions might be, the state clearly had no evidence to connect him with Umkhonto. Handcuffed, he was led down to the cells. From the public gallery his wife watched him go.

Slogans daubed on township walls demanded FREE MANDELA! Abroad there were widespread calls for his release. The London *Observer* profiled this 'resistance fighter' while, transferred to Pretoria prison, Mandela received a warm message from Robert Sobukwe, the PAC leader, who was serving a three-year sentence for organizing the anti-pass demonstrations of 1960.

In anticipation of Mandela's trial opening in Johannesburg, an escape plan had been worked out by which he could leave the country. The announcement that the trial was to be switched to Pretoria foiled the plot. He set to work on the strategy for the trial. Determined to challenge the court, he told Wolpe and Slovo that he would conduct his own defence.

In Addis Ababa, Mandela had forecast that South Africa's new

Minister of Justice would 'deal out more vicious blows'. Now that Minister, J. B. M. Vorster (who had been interned during the Second World War for pro-Nazi activity), brought in a 'Sabotage' Act. Sabotage covered a wide range: for instance, trespass and the illegal possession of weapons. The minimum sentence was five years; the maximum, the death penalty. In South Africa white and black alike protested vehemently, while the International Commission of Jurists commented that the law reduced the liberty of the citizen to a degree 'not surpassed by the most extreme dictatorships of the left or the right'. And the Minister extended his powers of banning. It was made a criminal offence for one banned person to communicate with another (banned husbands and wives had to apply for dispensation); for a banned person to have visitors; to fail to report regularly to the police; to prepare anything for publication. And it was an offence for anyone to publish the writings or utterances of a banned person. Soon it was made an offence for a banned person to meet with more than one other person at a time. The first list of new bannings included fifty-two whites, thirty-five Africans, nine Coloured people and six Indians.

But the most severe new restriction was house arrest. Helen Joseph, who had recently been publicizing the plight of the banished people, was the first to be placed under house arrest: confined to her home each night and throughout weekends and public holidays. Walter Sisulu was among those placed under twenty-four-hour house arrest.

Police surveillance, harassment and arrests were the order of the day. As the protests against Mandela's imprisonment intensified, the Minister banned any gathering which supported him, in any place, during the time of his trial. Yet crowds gathered outside the old synagogue in Pretoria to await Mandela's appearance on 22 October. Inside, the court was crowded with police and with spectators, including Winnie Mandela wearing Xhosa dress. Only nineteen months earlier, Mandela had stood there with the other accused in the Treason Trial, to hear the Judges acquit them all. Now when he entered, wearing a jackal-skin robe presented by his people, spectators and press rose to their feet. With fist raised, he called *Amandla!* and the answer came *Ngawethu!* (Power! To the People!).

'I hope to be able to indicate,' he told the magistrate, 'that this case is a trial of the aspirations of the African people, and because of that I thought it proper to conduct my own defence.'

He proceeded to apply for the magistrate's recusal not, he explained, in any way reflecting on his honour's integrity but because he challenged the right of the court to hear the case. 'I consider myself neither legally nor morally bound to obey laws made by a parliament in which I have no representation. In a political trial such as this one, which involves a clash of the aspirations of the African people and those of whites, the country's courts, as presently constituted, cannot be impartial and fair.'

His air of authority was such that the police, normally bored or contemptuous, were listening attentively. 'Equality before the law', he said, was a meaningless phrase and he listed other rights and privileges monopolized by whites:

It is fit and proper to raise the question sharply, what is this rigid colour-bar in the administration of justice? Why is it that in this courtroom I face a white magistrate, am confronted by a white prosecutor and escorted into the dock by a white orderly? Can anyone honestly and seriously suggest that in this type of atmosphere the scales of justice are evenly balanced? I feel oppressed by the atmosphere of white domination that lurks all around in this courtroom. Somehow this atmosphere calls to mind the inhuman injustices caused to my people outside this courtroom by this same white domination.

It reminds me that I am voteless because there is a parliament in this country that is white-controlled. I am without land because the white minority has taken a lion's share of my country and forced me to occupy poverty-stricken reserves, over-populated and over-stocked. We are ravaged by starvation and disease.

The magistrate intervened: What had starvation to do with

the case? The prisoner must confine himself to the real reasons for asking for recusal.

Mandela raised the question: 'How can I be expected to believe that this same racial discrimination which has been the cause of so much injustice and suffering right through the years, should now operate here to give me a fair and open trial?'

He was aware that in many cases, South African courts had upheld the right of the African people to work for democratic changes and that judicial officers had even openly criticized discriminatory policies.

> But such exceptions exist in spite of, not because of, the grotesque system of justice that has been built up in this country. These exceptions furnish yet another proof that even among the country's whites there are honest men whose sense of fairness and justice revolts against the cruelty perpetrated by their own white brothers to our people ... However, it would be a hopeless commandant who relied for his victories on the few soldiers in the enemy camp who sympathize with his cause. A competent general pins his faith on the superior striking power he commands and on the justness of his cause which he must pursue uncompromisingly to the bitter end.

'I hate race discrimination most intensely and in all its manifestations,' he went on, and something of the passion of his feeling sounded through the legal challenge he was making: 'I have fought it all my life; I fight it now, and will do so until the end of my days.'

> Even although I now happen to be tried by one whose opinion I hold in high esteem, I detest most violently the set-up that surrounds me here. It makes me feel that I am a black man in a white man's court. This should not be. I should feel perfectly at ease and at home with the assurance that I am being tried by a fellow South African who does not regard me as an inferior, entitled to a special type of justice.

In the further exposition of his argument he pointed out that South African whites regarded it as fair and just to pursue policies which had outraged the conscience of mankind, and of honest and upright men throughout the civilized world.

They suppress our aspirations, bar our way to freedom and deny us opportunities to promote our moral and material progress, to secure ourselves from fear and want. All the good things of life are reserved for the white folk and we blacks are expected to be content to nourish our bodies with such pieces of food as drop from the tables of men with white skins. This is the white man's standard of justice and fairness. Herein lies his conception of ethics . . .

We, on the other hand, regard the struggle against colour discrimination and for the pursuit of freedom and happiness as the highest aspiration of all men. Through bitter experience, we have learnt to regard the white man as a harsh and merciless type of human being whose contempt for our rights, and whose utter indifference to the promotion of our welfare, make his assurances to us absolutely meaningless and hypocritical.

In concluding the application, Mandela expressed confidence that the magistrate would not regard the objection as frivolous. He had spoken frankly and honestly because the injustice he had referred to contained seeds of an extremely dangerous situation.

The prosecutor submitted that Mandela's application had not been based on legal grounds and the magistrate, concurring, dismissed the application. 'Will you now plead to your charges?' he asked Mandela.

'I plead not guilty to both charges, to all the charges.' And Mandela went on to conduct his defence. For the most part the witnesses – policemen, township superintendents, journalists and printers – gave technical evidence of preparations for the May 1961 national strike.

Among them was the private secretary to the Prime Minister, Dr Verwoerd. Mandela's cross-examination focused on the letter which he had sent to the Prime Minister on 24 April 1961. The secretary remembered the letter and agreed that the Prime Minister had not replied to it. Unwillingly he conceded that the letter had raised questions of vital importance to the African people, the rights of freedom and civil liberties.

'Scandalous,' Mandela suggested, that a Prime Minister should ignore a letter raising such vital issues. He had not ignored it, insisted the secretary, and, when Mandela probed further, revealed that it had been referred to the Department of Justice. Why then, asked Mandela, had he not been favoured with the courtesy of an acknowledgement and the explanation that the letter had been thus referred?

'The whole tone of the letter,' was the explanation.

'The tone of the letter demanding a National Convention,' persisted Mandela, 'of all South Africans? That is not the type of thing your Prime Minister could ever respond to?' No clear reply was forthcoming. 'I want to put it to you,' Mandela continued, 'that in failing to respond to this letter, your Prime Minister fell below the standards which one expects from one in such a position.'

A National Convention would save the country from economic dislocation and ruin and from civil strife and bitterness. He had made this point in a further letter to Verwoerd, sent on 26 June 1961. Again the Prime Minister's secretary agreed that there had been no reply.

The police, who at the time of the stay-at-home strike had widely propagated its total failure, now gave evidence of its success. Newspapers were produced by the prosecutor to establish that Mandela had been in Addis Ababa during February, together with evidence that he had gone without a valid travel document.

The state case concluded with the prosecutor pleading for the court to find him guilty on both counts. The persons 'incited' to protest under the first count were divided into three categories: 'employees in essential services, who are not allowed to strike; African mineworkers for whom it is unlawful to desert or absent themselves from employment without lawful cause; servants in general, other than agricultural labourers, for whom it is unlawful to absent themselves from their masters' premises.'

'Have you anything to say?' asked the magistrate.

Mandela declared, 'Your Worship, I submit that I am guilty of no crime.'

'Is that all you have to say?'

'Your Worship, with respect,' he replied, 'if I had something more to say, I would have said it.'

On 25 October, Mandela was found guilty on both counts.

The magistrate had no doubt that he was the 'leader, instigator, figurehead, main mouthpiece and brains' behind the organization which had called the nationwide strike in 1961. His activities were not only unlawful but undemocratic. He showed no remorse but seemed proud of his achievements. He had stated in no uncertain terms that he would continue his activities whatever the sentence passed on him. 'We are living under abnormal and trying conditions,' the magistrate added, and if 'law and order' were not maintained, anarchy would reign; the court was not concerned with politics but with the maintenance of law and order.

There was an air of exhilaration as Mandela prepared to make his address to the court in mitigation of sentence. His aunt and other relatives from the Transkei – all in Xhosa dress – were present with Winnie. Outside, the street swarmed with police keeping back the crowds. One shouted at black spectators leaving the court to go to the toilets, *'Jy kannie hier rond loop nie, dis nie "a bioscope" nie!'* ('You can't walk around here, it's not a cinema!') Again, as on each occasion when he entered the court, Mandela was greeted by spectators rising to their feet and by the exchange of *Amandla! Ngawethu!*

From the dock he made a political testament. Having earlier 'indicted white domination', he was ready to speak of his role in calling the strike:

> It was my duty, as Secretary of the Action Council, to establish the machinery necessary for publicizing the decision of this Pietermaritzburg conference and for directing the campaign of propaganda, publicity and organization which would flow from it. The court is aware that I am an attorney by profession and no doubt the question will be asked why I, as an attorney who is bound, as part of my code of behaviour, to observe the laws of the country and to respect its customs and traditions, should willingly lend myself to a campaign whose ultimate aim was to bring about a strike against the proclaimed policy of the government of this country.

For the court to understand, he explained the background to his political development from the days when, as a boy, he had listened to elders of the tribe telling about the acts of valour performed by their ancestors in defence of the fatherland, when the land had belonged to the whole tribe, when there had been no classes, when all members of the tribe could participate in deliberations. This had been the inspiration which, even today, sustained him and his colleagues in the struggle.

Since joining the ANC in 1944, he had followed its policy and believed in its aims and outlook for eighteen years. Its policy appealed to his deepest inner convictions. 'It sought for the unity of all Africans,' he said, 'overriding tribal differences. It sought the acquisition of political power for Africans in the land of their birth and believed that all people, irrespective of the national groups to which they may belong, and irrespective of the colour of their skins, all people whose home is South Africa and who believe in the principles of democracy and of equality of men, should be treated as Africans.'

He quoted the Freedom Charter, 'the most democratic programme of political principles ever enunciated' in South Africa, principles adopted not only by the African people but by the Indian, Coloured and white Congresses, all of whom supported the demand for one man, one vote.

Reverting to his career as an attorney, he described the difficulties imposed on him as a black man and the effect of the colour bar within the judicial system:

> I regarded it as a duty which I owed, not just to my people but also to my profession, to the practice of law, and to justice for all mankind, to cry out against this discrimination which is essentially unjust and opposed to the whole basis of the attitude towards justice which is part of the tradition of legal training in this country. I believed that in taking up a stand against this injustice I was upholding the dignity of what should be an honourable profession.

The conflict he had experienced as a lawyer, he said, was not peculiar to South Africa. It arose for men of conscience, for men who thought and who felt deeply, in every country. In South

Africa, however, 'The law as it is applied, the law as it has been developed over a long period of history, and especially the law as it is written and designed by the Nationalist government, is a law which in our view is immoral, unjust and intolerable. Our consciences dictate that we must protest against it, that we must oppose it, and that we must attempt to alter it.'

For fifty years the ANC had sought peaceful solutions to the country's ills and problems, only to be treated with contempt, to find their protests ignored.

Mandela went on to spell out government behaviour in crushing the non-violent strike in a passage which speaks for all political prisoners, for all those who continued to be detained without charge, in solitary confinement, at the mercy of their interrogators:

> The government set out . . . not to treat with us, not to heed us, not to talk to us, but rather to present us as wild, dangerous revolutionaries, intent on disorder and riot, incapable of being dealt with in any way save by mustering an overwhelming force against us and the implementation of every possible forcible means, legal and illegal, to suppress us. The government behaved in a way no civilized government should dare behave when faced with a peaceful, disciplined, sensible and democratic expression of the views of its own population . . .
>
> If there was a danger during this period that violence would result from the situation, then the possibility was of the government's making. They set the scene for violence by relying exclusively on violence with which to answer our people and their demands. The counter-measures which they took clearly reflected growing uneasiness which grew out of the knowledge that their policy did not enjoy the support of the majority of the people, while ours did. It was clear that the government was attempting to combat the intensity of our campaign by a reign of terror.
>
> The evidence in this case has shown that [our campaign] was a substantial success . . . In the end, if a strike did not materialize on the scale on which it had been hoped, it was not because the people were not willing, but because the overwhelming strength, violence and force of the government's attack against our campaign had for the

time being achieved its aim of forcing us into submission against our wishes and against our conscience.

He referred to the long record of violence by successive governments: the 1921 massacre at Bulhoek and the 1924 massacre of the Bondelswarts in South-West Africa. 'Government violence,' he said, 'can do only one thing, and that is to breed counter-violence. We have warned repeatedly that ultimately the dispute between the government and my people will finish up by being settled in violence and by force. Already there are indications.'

Elsewhere in the world, a court would have said: 'You should have made representations to the government.' He was confident this court would not say so, nor indeed did it.

Nor would the court say that his people should say nothing and do nothing. 'Men are not capable of doing nothing, of saying nothing, of not reacting to injustice, of not protesting against oppression, of not striving for the good society and the good life in the ways they see it. Nor will they do so in this country.'

And if the court said they should at least stay within the letter of the law, it was the government and its administration of the law which had brought the law into contempt and disrepute. Mandela illustrated this from his repeated experience of being banned, never as a result of a trial and a conviction. 'Can it be wondered that such a man, having been outlawed by the government, should be prepared to lead the life of an outlaw, as I have led for some months, according to the evidence before this court?'

His wife, Winnie, who would soon be repeatedly banned and persecuted, heard him say:

It has not been easy for me during the past period to separate myself from my wife and children, to say goodbye to the good old days when, at the end of a strenuous day at an office, I could look forward to joining my family at the dinner-table, and instead to take up the life of a man hunted continuously by the police, living separated from those who are closest to me, in my own country, facing continually the hazards of detection and of arrest.

This has been a life infinitely more difficult than serving a prison sentence. No man in his right senses would voluntarily choose such a life in preference to the one of normal, family, social life which exists in every civilized country.

But there comes a time, as it came in my life, when a man is denied the right to live a normal life, when he can only live the life of an outlaw because the government has so decreed to use the law to impose a state of outlawry upon him. I was driven to this situation, and I do not regret having taken the decisions that I did take . . .

A lot has been written since the Pietermaritzburg conference, and even more since my arrest, much of which is flattering to my pride and dear to my heart, but much of which is mistaken and incorrect. It has been suggested that the advances, the articulateness of our people, the successes which they are achieving here, and the recognition which they are winning both here and abroad are in some way the result of my work. I must place on record my belief that I have been only one in a large army of people, to all of whom the credit for any success of achievement is due.

Answering to the second count, he briefly described his tour of Africa. He had returned home to report back to his colleagues.

I am prepared to pay the penalty even though I know how bitter and desperate is the situation of an African in the prisons of this country. I have been in these prisons and I know how gross is the discrimination, even behind the prison walls, against Africans, how much worse is the treatment meted out to African prisoners than that accorded to whites.

Nevertheless, these conditions do not sway me from the path that I have taken, nor will they sway others like me. For to men, freedom in their own land is the pinnacle of their ambitions, from which nothing can turn men of conviction aside. More powerful than my fear of the dreadful conditions to which I might be subjected is my hatred for the dreadful conditions to which my people are subjected outside prison throughout this country.

His hatred of racial discrimination was passionately expressed: the systematic inculcation of children with colour prejudice, the racial arrogance which decreed that the good things of life should be retained as the exclusive right of a minority of the population, confining the majority to a position of subservience and inferiority, and maintaining them as voteless chattels to work where they are told and behave as they are told by the ruling minority.

> I am sustained in that hatred by the fact that the overwhelming majority of mankind both in this country and abroad are with me. Nothing that this court can do to me will change in any way that hatred in me, which can only be removed by the removal of the injustice and inhumanity which I have sought to remove from the political, social and economic life of this country.
>
> Whatever sentence Your Worship sees fit to impose upon me for the crime for which I have been convicted before this court, may it rest assured that when my sentence has been completed, I will still be moved, as men are always moved, by their consciences. I will still be moved by my dislike of the race discrimination against my people when I come out from serving my sentence, to take up again, as best I can, the struggle for the removal of those injustices until they are finally abolished once and for all.

On 6 November, the day before Mandela was to be sentenced, the General Assembly of the United Nations voted for the first time in favour of sanctions against South Africa by sixty-seven to sixteen, with twenty-three abstentions; not the mandatory majority of a Security Council vote required before action became significant, but a beginning. That night in the townships of Port Elizabeth acts of sabotage were committed.

On 7 November, Mandela was sentenced to five years imprisonment with hard labour: three years for 'incitement' to strike and two for leaving the country without travel documents.

'I have no doubt that posterity will pronounce that I was innocent,' he said, 'and that the criminals that should have been brought before this court are the members of the Verwoerd Government.'

As he left the court, three times he repeated the cry *Amandla!* and three times came the roar of response, *Ngawethu!* He was driven away in a police van and the crowd, ignoring the ban on demonstrations, half marched, half danced along the streets, singing 'Tshotsholoza Mandela' ('Struggle on, Mandela').

Winnie Mandela had smiled and sung 'Nkosi Sikelel' iAfrika', with other spectators in the court. Afterwards she made a statement to *New Age*, the left-wing newspaper soon to be banned: 'I will continue the fight as I have in all ways done in the past.' Zeni and Zindzi, she said, were too young to understand:

> All the oldest one knows is that her daddy was taken by the police ... I shall certainly live under great strain in the coming years, but this type of life has become part and parcel of my life. I married Nel in 1958 ... He was then a Treason Trial accused and I was aware that even a death sentence was hanging over his head. The greatest honour a people can pay to a man behind bars is to keep the freedom flame burning, to continue the fight. My husband correctly said suffering in gaol is nothing compared to suffering outside gaol. Our people suffer inside and out of the gaols. But suffering is not enough. We must struggle.

In Pretoria Central prison, a crenellated red-brick remnant of colonial times, Mandela began serving his sentence, wearing prison garments of baggy shorts and tunic, with sandals. The small cement-floored cell was furnished by felt mat, sanitary pail, enamel dish and mug. Woken before dawn by alarm bells and commands shouted in Afrikaans, he followed his usual strict routine of exercises. The basic food was *mealiepap*, with lunch at 10.45 a.m. and supper at three p.m. His days were spent sewing mailbags.

II

'RIVONIA IS A NAME TO REMEMBER'

1963–4

Mandela was transferred to the maximum security prison on Robben Island, the penal settlement lying off Cape Town, where he was held in solitary conditions.

On the mainland, sabotage continued and by mid-1963 about two hundred acts had been committed, many by Umkhonto men in the Eastern Cape. In the Western Cape and the Transkei, the murder of a handful of whites and clashes with police marked the emergence of Poqo (We go it alone), an offshoot of the PAC.

On 1 May the 90-Day detention law was passed. Vorster's security police could detain people without trial, in solitary confinement, incommunicado, for periods of up to ninety days, which could be extended – until 'this side of eternity', remarked Vorster – while they interrogated until they received 'satisfactory' answers. Hundreds of men and women vanished into gaols and police cells to undergo what an opposition MP called 'torture by mind-breaking'. Soon came evidence of physical torture – electric shock, near-suffocation, repeated assaults – and, in September, Looksmart Solwandle Ngudle, an ANC member from Cape Town, was the first political detainee to die while under interrogation.

Drastic measures against those suspected of belonging to unlawful organizations were increased: from five years to the death penalty for advocating change by 'violent or forcible' means, for undergoing training or obtaining information of use in 'furthering the aims' of communism or of an unlawful organization. (When Vorster had listed alleged communists a few months earlier, the totals had been 308 'non-whites' and 129 whites.)

Political prisoners who had served their sentences could promptly be detained: a law directed against Robert Sobukwe who, after completing a three-year sentence, was transported to Robben Island where he was detained alone in a small dwelling.

Against these laws extending the police state, the one MP who consistently expressed opposition was Helen Suzman, a symbol of the individual whites – lawyers, churchmen, trade unionists and academics – who strove for a more humane society. The group of young whites, with one or two Coloured allies, who had embarked on sabotage, were soon rounded up and held in 90-Day detention, or they fled the country.

Walter Sisulu was persistently harassed. Arrested six times during 1962, then sentenced to six years' imprisonment for furthering the aims of the ANC and for his part in 'inciting' the 1961 stay-at-home strike, he was granted bail pending an appeal and, on 20 April 1963, went underground. Two months later his wife, Albertina, was detained under the 90-Day law.

On 12 July the security police made their most spectacular *coup*: Sisulu and eight other men were captured in the house in Rivonia, outside Johannesburg, the house where Mandela had stayed when underground. It was assumed that the police had browbeaten and bribed the information out of a man held under 90-Days, but undoubtedly some men in the political collective at Rivonia had become over-confident of their security as, disguised, they functioned from the unreal world of 'underground'. Always referring to the government as 'fascist', they never operated as though it was; a failing that would continue to weaken the liberation movement. An immense haul of incriminating documents was discovered by the police and three other men were subsequently arrested.

Of the six whites detained, two escaped from police cells and one, after agreeing under pressure to become a state witness, also managed to flee the country. A fourth was soon released for lack of evidence. Of the two remaining, Lionel 'Rusty' Bernstein, an architect, had been a defendant in the Treason Trial and Dennis Goldberg, a civil engineer, came from Cape Town.

Among the Africans, Govan Mbeki and Raymond Mhlaba came from the Eastern Cape, and Elias Motsoaledi and Andrew Mlangeni – like Sisulu – from the Transvaal. Ahmed Kathrada, the only Indian, had been active since his schooldays. All disappeared into 90-Day detention, cut off from families and from lawyers; kept in solitary confinement while police pursued their interrogations and investigations. Clearly they did not dare mistreat the leaders, but Motsoaledi and Mlangeni were tortured.

Mandela was suddenly transferred from Robben Island back to Pretoria prison. Cut off from all news of the outside world he could only speculate on what lay ahead.

In the prison all were held in racially segregated sections but every evening came a moment of communication: after the shouts of the warders had ceased for the day, singing reverberated through the cells as African voices were raised in traditional and freedom songs. Just before lights-out the singing would die away and in that silence a voice shouted *Amandla!* – could it be, one of the white detainees wondered, Mandela's voice? In response came the communal response: *Ngawethu!*

Families of the Rivonia detainees appointed lawyers in the hope that the men would in time be brought to trial. Bram Fischer, QC headed the team with Vernon Berrange, who also had played a leading part in the Treason Trial defence, and there were two young advocates, Arthur Chaskalson and George Bizos, who would act for the defence in many subsequent political trials. The attorney was Joel Joffe.

From the start the state handling of the case was bizarre. The government openly proclaimed the guilt of the captives. The defence team were unable to find out who precisely the accused would be or what the charges were. The day before the trial was due to open the prosecutor, Dr Percy Yutar, said that if they went to Pretoria prison they would find out who their clients were.

In an interview room of the prison Fischer, Chaskalson, Bizos and Joffe met the men who had been arrested at Rivonia. A sound of marching feet and Mandela appeared, guarded by warders. Astounded and delighted, prisoners and lawyers gathered round. Mandela and Sisulu hugged, hands reached out to hold Mandela's, and Fischer introduced him to Chaskalson and Joffe. But they were shocked by his appearance: he had lost nearly three stone (40 lb) in weight, the prison uniform of boy's shorts and shirt hung on him, and his face was a sickly yellowish colour. Yet his bearing was proud and as his laughter rang out they observed the same confident, easy-going man they had known.

As the consultations proceeded Joffe found that Mandela emerged naturally as the leader but he never dictated; he would discuss calmly, argue and finally be guided by the opinion of his colleagues. His stature impressed even the prison staff who treated him not quite with deference but as if realizing that he was a 'big' man; not that this mitigated their hatred of all he stood for but there was a strange kind of awe for one whom they regarded as a 'kaffir'. On one occasion when he complained to a white warder, the retort was: 'When you are the government, you will do it to us.'

Although the charges were not yet known, it was clear from what had been leaked to the press that the defence team would have a desperate fight to save the men from being hanged.

On 9 October 1963 the Palace of Justice in Pretoria was surrounded by armed police while inside they were equally ubiquitous. Security police and press outnumbered white spectators in the court, but the 'non-white' section of the public gallery was crammed with families and supporters of the accused. To one side sat diplomats and other distinguished visitors.

Winnie Mandela was not present. On 28 January 1962 she had been banned for two years; her banning order restricted her to Johannesburg; an application for permission to attend the trial had been refused.

The defendants were driven up in a heavily armed convoy to be greeted by the crowd shouting *Amandla* Mandela! *Ngawethu* Sisulu! The dark-panelled court with its high-domed ceiling had a rococo atmosphere reminiscent of the American South. Suspended from the ceiling above the prosecutor's table was an old fan which wobbled and creaked as it slowly turned. Police with satchels of teargas grenades guarded the doors. The galleries were crowded despite security police intimidation: spectators' names and addresses were taken and they were photographed on leaving the court.

Quartus de Wet, Judge-President of the Transvaal, scarlet-robed, sat enthroned under a canopy of carved wood, while before him, Mandela and the other defendants occupied the carved dock which had been awkwardly extended to become a long wooden box.

The men's demeanour was strong but they looked drawn and haggard after months of solitary confinement. Bram Fischer complained of their harsh treatment and successfully argued for an adjournment and better prison conditions.

Several weeks later the change in their physical state was remarkable, particularly in the case of Mandela: companionship with his old friends had transformed him; besides, he no longer looked wasted and was his old elegant self in a three-piece suit.

'*Stilte in die hof! Opstaan!*'('Silence in the court! Stand up!') Again the police, the crowds, the formalities, the Judge's imposing arrival. Bram Fischer led with a blistering attack on the state's indictment, a legally shoddy document, he asserted, which, among other patently absurd allegations, involved Mandela in acts of sabotage committed long after he had been imprisoned. The Judge agreed and quashed the indictment. Under the law, the accused were free.

But before they could react, Lieutenant Swanepoel, the most notorious of security policemen, had thumped each man on the back, declaring, 'I am arresting you on a charge of sabotage!' They were roughly shepherded back to the cells.

On the morning of 3 December the trial resumed: Mandela led his comrades into the dock; court rose; the Judge entered. The amended charges were read out: recruiting persons for training in sabotage and guerrilla warfare for the purpose of violent revolution; conspiring to aid foreign military units when they invaded the Republic, thus furthering the aims of communism; soliciting and receiving funds for these purposes from Algeria, Ethiopia, Liberia, Nigeria, Tunisia and elsewhere.

The Registrar then asked: 'Accused No. I, Nelson Mandela, do you plead guilty or not guilty?'

'The government should be in the dock, not me,' Mandela stated firmly. 'I plead not guilty.'

Each defendant in turn repeated an indictment of the government.

No sooner had they finished than the prosecutor, Percy Yutar, began handing out copies of his opening address: one to the Judge, one to the defence team and eight to the press. Clearing his throat he prepared to read, only to be interrupted by Fischer, who had risen to address the Judge. Indicating a microphone on the table in front of Yutar, he wondered whether the judge was aware that the South African Broadcasting Corporation intended to broadcast the prosecutor's address to the nation – a most extraordinary procedure.

Ordered by the Judge to have the microphone dismantled, Yutar put his case, which culminated in the declaration that Umkhonto we Sizwe's operations were planned to lead 'to confusion, violent insurrection and rebellion, followed at the appropriate juncture by armed invasion of the country by military units of foreign powers. In the midst of the resulting chaos, turmoil and disorder,' he added, 'it was planned to set up a provisional revolutionary government to take over the administration and control of this country.'

He alleged that the defendants had been responsible for 222 acts of sabotage, a number soon reduced to 193. He concluded that the accused had so planned their campaign that 1963 'was to be the year of their liberation from the so-called yoke of the white man's domination'. Clearly he had confused the ANC with the Pan Africanist Congress which had made such a call. Yutar later referred to 26 May 1963 as the day of 'the mass uprising in connection with the launching of guerrilla warfare' –

a choice of date which mystified defendants and their lawyers, since at that time, apart from explosives, Umkhonto possessed only an air rifle with which Mandela had once tried target practice.

Such were the pointers to the prosecutor's handling of the case. Although witnesses for the state testified that Umkhonto leaders had instructed members not to endanger human life, Yutar talked of murder and attempted murder. The defence were outraged; no specific allegations had been made. The Judge agreed that other organizations as well as Umkhonto had been committing sabotage and that only a small number of the 193 acts alleged (none of which had resulted in loss of life) were proved to be the responsibility of Umkhonto.

(Yutar's prose, so appropriate to the baroque architecture of the court, would be quoted two decades later by President P. W. Botha, as if it had been the actual judgement in the trial. And when a group of Canadians expressed concern about the continued imprisonment of Nelson Mandela, a South African diplomat in Toronto once more quoted Yutar as gospel, adding flourishes of his own, to the effect that Mandela's plans for 'a general uprising' in South Africa were to be 'patterned on the communist revolution launched by Fidel Castro in Cuba'.)

From the start Mandela and his comrades made it clear to their counsel that they were not interested in a trial in law, but in a confrontation in politics. They were determined to speak proudly of their ideals, to be defiant in face of the enemy. They readily admitted that most of them had taken part in a political campaign designed to bring down the government; that they had, in varying degree, known about or taken part in preparation for military and para-military action such as sabotage. They welcomed the opportunity to use the court as a platform from which to clarify to the country and to the world their position on the matter they considered at the very forefront of South African politics. But they would not under any circumstances reveal any information about their organizations or about the people involved, where such information could endanger others.

In essence, then, where the state case centred on acts of sabotage, it was not only unassailable, except in respect of the number – the defence conceded only twenty out of the alleged 193 acts – but the accused had no wish to deny it.

The state, not content with this, brought witnesses who blatantly lied. Of the 173 state witnesses the most important was dramatically introduced by Yutar: this man's evidence must be taken in camera because he was 'in mortal danger'. Yutar added that he would not, however, object to the presence of the press, provided they did not identify the man but referred to him as 'Mr X'.

'X' was Bruno Mtolo, a former ANC member and trade unionist from Natal. He appeared in court accompanied by a group of white security police who treated him as a hero. His betrayal shocked Mandela and the ANC men. They had accepted that people could crack under torture and indefinite periods of solitary confinement; what they could not understand was that Mtolo, who had undergone no such treatment, went out of his way to implicate others and actually manufactured evidence. The defence team discovered that Mtolo had indeed been a saboteur for Umkhonto but that, unknown to his comrades, he had thrice been convicted for theft and fraud. His evidence against Mandela, which purported to describe Mandela's report to the Natal Regional Command after his tour of Africa, was a mixture of fact and fiction.

The fiction included the suggestion that Mandela was a communist. Joffe has described Mandela's reaction:

> Nelson instructed us to join issue on this and to cross-examine Mtolo. He told us that we should admit that he addressed a meeting of the Regional Command, but that we should deny that he had ever mentioned anything about communists or that he, Mandela, and Umkhonto were communist. We pointed out to Nelson that cross-examination along these lines was an admission of guilt; that by admitting that he was at that meeting, he must be found guilty on virtually all the charges against him and that, in effect, we might thus be signing his death-warrant. He was unperturbed: he was not a

communist, he never had been and he was not prepared to allow 'Mr X' to give false evidence.

Mandela added that since Umkhonto was on trial, and since he was its leader, he did not intend to get off through legal niceties. He would be most unhappy if he were to be acquitted when his comrades and followers were found guilty. He felt no moral guilt, there had been no alternative but to resort to violence. The only thing he regretted was that their plans had been thwarted.

Through the hot summer of 1963 the state case developed: Yutar introduced the hundreds of documents captured at Rivonia, including maps marked to show police stations, Bantu Administration offices, electric power stations, railways and the homes of African policemen. The cornerstone of the case, which Yutar frequently quoted, was a document called Operation Mayibuye, outlining guerrilla war and foreign intervention. 'An entirely unrealistic brainchild of some youthful and adventurous imagination' was Bram Fischer's description. It had been written after Mandela's arrest and he knew nothing of it. However, he had kept a diary during his tour of Africa; he'd assumed it had been destroyed but, typical of the reckless disregard for security, it too was captured at Rivonia.

As the network of factual evidence accumulated, the morale of the accused fluctuated, but not Mandela's; he rallied the others. They had their laughs at the expense of the police, particularly at Swanepoel, a gross red-haired man in sports coat and flannels, who hovered at the door of the interview room, a brooding presence, while they consulted with their legal team. Knowing the room was bugged, they had a system of writing notes to each other on important points. On one occasion, Bernstein passed a note to Joffe to say that he, Mhlaba and Kathrada intended to dispute their guilt – although politically active they had not been involved with Umkhonto – and Joffe was burning the note over an ashtray when Swanepoel glared from the doorway. Mandela promptly scribbled a note saying

'Isn't Swanepoel a fine-looking chap?', winked at Joffe and passed it to him with exceptional care. Joffe read it attentively, crumpled it and, as he slowly took out matches, Swanepoel made a dash to grab it. 'Ag, man, we've got to be careful of fires in the gaol,' he said as he made for the door. Then, turning in fury after reading the note, he stamped off. Now, said Mandela, they would have some peace.

When the defence demolished a state witness, police took revenge against defendants' families: Sisulu's son, though not yet sixteen, was arrested under the pass laws; and Elias Motsoaledi's wife, Caroline, was detained under 90-Days, separated from their seven children, with defence lawyers powerless to help her. The Judge considered the incident irrelevant; she was held for 113 days.

Five months after the trial had begun on 29 February 1964, the state concluded its case. The defence had just over a month in which to prepare. With limited resources they had a huge task: analysing hundreds of documents and statements, and interviewing witnesses throughout the country, as well as taking statements from each of the accused – difficulties magnified not only by the bugging of consultations which slowed down their work, but by the inconvenience of a new interview room. Instead of sitting freely together, defendants were now separated from lawyers by a partition in the form of a high counter, topped by iron bars; on either side of this were five high stools fixed to the concrete floor.

The lawyers were shown in to their side of the partition by the commissioner of prisons, Colonel Aucamp. On the opposite side Mandela and four men were perched on the stools, while the other four had to stand in a row behind. Smiling politely, Mandela asked, 'What'll it be today, gentlemen, chocolate or vanilla?' His mockery infuriated the colonel, and counsel's protests at the impossibility of consulting satisfactorily in such discomfort made no impression. Nor did their request that they be allowed to consult through the prison two-hour lunch-break: Mandela and Sisulu were convicted prisoners, on no account could they be allowed sandwiches.

Bram Fischer told the men that they had to succeed in proving that guerrilla war was never actually decided on and that it had been established policy that human life should not be sacrificed in the sabotage. 'I must be frank,' he added; 'even if we succeed, the Judge may yet impose the death sentence.' Joffe knew how hard it was for Fischer to discuss this possibility. Molly Fischer had told Joffe how, night after night, she heard her husband cry out in his sleep, 'We must save them!' Joffe, too, dreamt of them stepping on to the scaffold, and often woke in a cold sweat.

The defence team was divided on whether Mandela and the others should give evidence. Joffe especially objected to their being subjected to cross-examination – that men he had grown to admire and respect should be sneered at by a man like Yutar. But George Bizos insisted that unless they gave evidence and convinced the Judge they had not decided on guerrilla warfare, it would mean death. Besides, he felt it would be much harder for the Judge to send them to the gallows after he had heard them in the witness box. Fischer refused to come down on either side and asked the defendants for their opinions.

Sisulu said they certainly had no fear of Yutar's cross-examination and Mbeki felt their case was strong. Mandela addressed himself to Joffe: 'I think, Joel, as a lawyer I can understand your motives. You are concerned with saving our lives. We are also concerned with that, but it's a secondary consideration. Our first concern is the fulfilment of our political beliefs. We have fought for freedom and dignity, as we've said before, and what matters is what is politically right. After all, we are only going to tell the truth.' As he turned to the others, they all assented.

'That's settled then,' said Fischer, who proceeded to pass a note to him; Bizos passed a similar note to the other defendants: this said that the only way in which Mandela could make a political statement in the manner he wanted – loud and clear – was from the dock. He scribbled a reply: he wanted to submit to cross-examination; he felt great bitterness at Yutar's sneers about the 'so-called' grievances of the African people and his efforts to discredit the ANC as communist-controlled. But the others agreed with their counsel: Mandela should put their case strongly from the dock, then they would handle the cross-examination. After much argument on paper, reluctantly he agreed.

Joffe then passed a note to him; as Mandela read it he grinned: it said that the decision must be kept secret, therefore they would pretend he was preparing to give evidence by feeding him with documents which would have the added advantage of keeping the prison authorities busy, not to mention Yutar. 'By the way,' Mandela said loudly to Joffe, 'I'll need the Treason Trial record to prepare my evidence.' And, beaming at the thought of Yutar having to plough through a hundred thick volumes, he burnt Joffe's note.

Joffe proceeded to feed a stream of documents and books into the gaol, marked for Mandela; the books included treatises on economics and Tolstoy's *War and Peace* which Mandela was eager to read. The authorities returned the novel to Joffe with the comment that on no account would the commandant permit communist literature to be sent to a prisoner and most certainly not communist literature dealing with war.

In his cell Mandela worked on his statement through the evenings and weekends, drafting and redrafting. On Monday, 20 April 1964, he joined the other defendants in the prison van and they were driven under heavy escort to the Palace of Justice. In the packed court Winnie Mandela sat with her mother-in-law who had arrived from the Transkei. Dignified and strong despite her age, Mrs Mandela was very proud of her son. Winnie's permit to attend the trial had forbidden her to wear tribal dress which might lead to 'an incident'; she was accompanied by a young relative who was wearing her Thembu dress. Distinguished observers whose presence in court had fluctuated according to the significance or the tedium of the proceedings were there in full force.

Bram Fischer, QC led for the defence: certain parts of state evidence would be conceded; and, equally important, parts would be denied. Most importantly, he said, while admitting that Umkhonto planned sabotage, the defence would deny that a plan had been adopted to embark on guerrilla warfare.

'That will be denied?' asked the Judge.

'That will be denied,' replied Fischer. 'The evidence will show that while preparations for guerrilla warfare were being made, no plan was ever adopted; it was hoped throughout that such a step could he avoided.' Then he added: 'The defence case, My Lord, will commence with a statement from the dock by Accused No. I, who personally took part in the establishment of Umkhonto we Sizwe.'

'My Lord!' Yutar was up with a cry of dismay, appealing to the Judge to warn the accused that what he said from the dock had far less weight than if he submitted to cross-examination.

'I think, Dr Yutar,' was the Judge's reply, 'that counsel for the defence have sufficient experience to advise their clients without your assistance.'

The always courteous Fischer expressed appreciation for the advice. 'Neither we nor our clients are unaware of the provisions of the criminal code,' he told Yutar, and resumed: 'I call on Nelson Mandela.'

Mandela rose slowly, adjusting the spectacles he wore for reading, and with calm deliberation began:

> My Lord, I am the first accused. I hold a Bachelor's degree in Arts and practised as an attorney in Johannesburg for a number of years with Oliver Tambo. At the outset, I want to say that the suggestion made by the state that the struggle in South Africa is under the influence of foreigners or communists is wholly incorrect. I have done whatever I did, both as an individual and as a leader of my people, because of my experience in South Africa and my own proudly felt African background, and not because of what any outsider might have said . . .
>
> I hoped [in his youth] that life might offer me the opportunity to serve my people and make my own humble contribution to their freedom struggle. This is what has motivated me in all that I have done in relation to the charges made against me in this case.
>
> Having said this, I must deal immediately, and at some length,

with the question of violence. Some of the things so far told to the court are true and some are untrue. I do not, however, deny that I planned sabotage. I did not plan it in a spirit of recklessness, nor because I have any love of violence. I planned it as a result of a calm and sober assessment of the political situation that had arisen after many years of tyranny, exploitation and oppression of my people by the whites.

I admit immediately that I was one of the persons who helped to form Umkhonto we Sizwe and that I played a prominent role in its affairs until I was arrested in August 1962.

He proceeded to deal with the relationship between the ANC and Umkhonto, correcting state evidence and describing government violence which, in 1961, had culminated in the decision to answer violence with violence. 'But the violence which we chose to adopt was not terrorism. We who formed Umkhonto were all members of the African National Congress, and had behind us the ANC tradition of non-violence and negotiation as a means of solving political disputes.'

He briefly referred to the founding of the ANC in 1912 and its policies in the long struggle.

But white governments remained unmoved, and the rights of Africans became less instead of becoming greater. In the words of my leader, Chief Lutuli, who became President of the ANC in 1952, and who was later awarded the Nobel Peace Prize: 'Who will deny that thirty years of my life have been spent knocking in vain, patiently, moderately and modestly at a closed and barred door? What have been the fruits of moderation? The past thirty years have seen the greatest number of laws restricting our rights and progress, until today we have reached a stage where we have almost no rights at all.'

Mandela went on to describe the Defiance Campaign of 1952; the increasingly harsh laws that were passed yet failed to deter protest; the Treason Trial in which they were all acquitted on all counts, 'which included a count that the ANC sought to set up a communist state'.

The government had always sought to label its opponents as

communists, as in the present trial, but the ANC had never been a communist organization. After the shooting at Sharpeville, when the ANC had been declared unlawful, he and his colleagues had decided to defy this decree. He had no doubt that no self-respecting white political organization would disband itself if declared illegal by a government in which it had no say.

He spoke of the mood of the people who for a long time had been talking of violence: 'of the day when they would fight the white man and win back their country'.

> We, the leaders of the ANC, had nevertheless always prevailed upon them to avoid violence and to pursue peaceful methods. When some of us discussed this in June of 1961, it could not be denied that our policy to achieve a non-racial state by non-violence had achieved nothing, and that our followers were beginning to lose confidence in this policy, and were developing disturbing ideas of terrorism.

He reminded the court that violence had become a feature of the political scene: 'Small groups had arisen in the urban areas and were spontaneously making plans for violent forms of political struggle. There now arose a danger that these groups would adopt terrorism against Africans, as well as whites, if not properly directed.' Particularly disturbing was the type of violence engendered in rural areas: 'It was increasingly taking the form, not of struggle against the government – though this is what prompted it – but of civil strife against themselves, conducted in such a way that it could not hope to achieve anything other than loss of life and bitterness.'

And so, at the beginning of June 1961, he and other colleagues had come to plan Umkhonto we Sizwe.

The ANC, he stated, had remained a separate, mass political organization. As for Umkhonto, its founders had felt the country was drifting towards a civil war in which blacks and whites would fight each other, a prospect which had to be taken into account in formulating plans: 'We required a plan which was flexible and which permitted us to act in accordance with the needs of the times; above all, the plan had to be one which recognized civil war as the last resort, and left the decision on this question to the future. We did not want to be committed to civil war, but we wanted to be ready if it became inevitable.'

Of the four forms of violence possible, sabotage had been chosen and was to be exhausted before any further decision was taken.

After the first sabotage attacks, he admitted that the whites had failed to respond by suggesting change. Characteristically they had retreated into the laager.

> In contrast, the response of the Africans was one of encouragement. Suddenly there was hope again. Things were happening. People in the townships became eager for political news. A great deal of enthusiasm was generated by the initial success, and people began to speculate on how soon freedom would be obtained.

> We in Umkhonto weighed up the white response with anxiety. The lines were being drawn. The whites and blacks were moving into separate camps, and the prospects of avoiding a civil war were made less. The white newspapers carried reports that sabotage would be punished by death. If this was so how could we continue to keep Africans away from terrorism?

He spoke of the scores of Africans who had died as a result of racial friction. How many more Sharpevilles could the country stand without violence and terror becoming the order of the day?

> Experience convinced us that rebellion would offer the government limitless opportunities for the indiscriminate slaughter of our people. But it was precisely because the soil of South Africa is already drenched with the blood of innocent Africans that we felt it our duty to make preparations as a long-term undertaking to use force in order to defend ourselves against force. If war were inevitable, we wanted the fight to be conducted on terms most favourable to our people. The fight which held out prospects best for us and the least risk of life to both sides was guerrilla warfare.

> All whites undergo compulsory military training, but no such training was given to Africans. It was, in our view, essential to build up a nucleus of trained men who would be able to provide the

leadership which would be required if guerrilla warfare started . . . It was also necessary to build up a nucleus of men trained in civil administration and other professions, so that Africans would be equipped to participate in the government of this country as soon as they were allowed to do so.

He described his tour of Africa, his study of the art of war and the course of training he had undergone. The court had before it copies of notes he had made on these matters, seized at Rivonia.

After repudiating sections of Mtolo's evidence he came to the state's allegation that the aims and objects of the ANC and the South African Communist Party were the same:

> The ideological creed of the ANC is, and always has been, the creed of African nationalism. It is not the concept of African nationalism expressed in the cry: 'Drive the white men into the sea.' The African nationalism for which the ANC stands, is the concept of freedom and fulfilment for the African people in their own land.

> The most important political document ever adopted by the ANC is the Freedom Charter. It is by no means a blueprint for a socialist state. It calls for redistribution, but not nationalization, of land; it provides for nationalization of mines, banks and monopoly industry, because big monopolies are owned by one race only, and without such nationalization racial domination would be perpetuated despite the spread of political power. . . Under the Freedom Charter nationalization would take place in an economy based on private enterprise. The realization of the Freedom Charter would open up fresh fields for a prosperous African population of all classes, including the middle class. The ANC has never at any period of its history advocated a revolutionary change in the economic structure of the country, nor has it, to the best of my recollection, ever condemned capitalist society.

> As far as the Communist Party is concerned, and if I understand its policy correctly, it stands for the establishment of a state based on the principles of Marxism. Although it is prepared to work for the Freedom Charter, as a short-term solution to the problems created by white supremacy, it regards the Freedom Charter as the beginning, and not the end, of its programme.

> The ANC, unlike the Communist Party, admitted Africans only

as members. Its chief goal was, and is, for the African people to win unity and full political rights. The Communist Party's main aim, on the other hand, was to remove the capitalists and to replace them with a working-class government. The Communist Party sought to emphasize class distinctions whilst the ANC seeks to harmonize them. This is a vital distinction.

It is true that there has often been close cooperation between the ANC and the Communist Party. But cooperation is merely proof of a common goal – in this case the removal of white supremacy – and is not proof of a complete community of interests.

The history of the world is full of similar examples. Perhaps the most striking illustration is to be found in the cooperation between Great Britain, the United States of America and the Soviet Union in the fight against Hitler. Nobody but Hitler would have dared to suggest that such cooperation turned Churchill or Roosevelt into communist tools, or that Britain and America were working to bring about a communist world.

Another instance of such cooperation is to be found precisely in Umkhonto. Shortly after MK was constituted, I was informed by some of its members that the Communist Party would support Umkhonto, and this then occurred.

He gave examples of communists' participation in colonial countries' fight for their freedom – in Malaya, Algeria and Indonesia – countries which had not become communist states. And he described how, in the past, African communists could and did become members of the ANC, among them Moses Kotane and J. B. Marks. In his younger days, he recalled, he had been one of a group in the Youth League which wanted communists expelled from the ANC, a proposal heavily defeated – by conservatives among others – on the ground that the ANC from its inception had been built up, not as a political party with one school of thought, but as a parliament of the African people, accommodating various political convictions. He had eventually been won over to this point of view.

It is perhaps difficult for white South Africans, with an ingrained prejudice against communism, to understand why experienced African politicians so readily accept communists as their friends. But to us the reason is obvious. Theoretical differences among those fighting against oppression is a luxury we cannot afford at this stage. What is more, for many decades communists were the only political group in South Africa who were prepared to treat Africans as human beings and their equals; who were prepared to eat with us, talk with us, live with us and work with us. They were the only political group which was prepared to work with the Africans for the attainment of political rights and a stake in society. Because of this, there are many Africans who, today, tend to equate freedom with communism. They are supported in this belief by a legislature which brands all exponents of democratic government and African freedom as communists and bans many of them [who are not communists] under the Suppression of Communism Act. Although I am not a communist and I have never been a member of the Communist Party, I myself have been named under that pernicious Act because of the role I played in the Defiance Campaign. I have also been banned and imprisoned under that Act.

It is not only in internal politics that we count communists as among those who support our cause. In the international field, communist countries have always come to our aid. In the United Nations and other councils of the world, the communist bloc has supported the Afro-Asian struggle against colonialism and often seems to be more sympathetic to our plight than some of the western powers. Although there is a universal condemnation of apartheid, the communist bloc speaks out against it with a louder voice than most of the white world. In these circumstances, it would take a brash young politician, such as I was in 1949, to proclaim that the communists are our enemies.

He turned to his own position. 'I have always regarded myself, in the first place, as an African patriot,' and he described his upbringing in the Transkei, under the guardianship of the acting Paramount Chief of Thembuland. Today he was attracted to the idea of a classless society, an attraction springing partly from Marxist reading and partly from his admiration for the structure and organization of early African societies in Southern Africa, when the land had belonged to the tribe and there had been no exploitation.

It is true that I have been influenced by Marxist thought. But this is also true of many of the leaders of the new independent states. Such widely different persons as Gandhi, Nehru, Nkrumah and Nasser all acknowledge this fact. We all accept the need for some form of socialism to enable our people to catch up with the advanced countries of this world and to overcome their legacy of extreme poverty. But this does not necessarily mean we are Marxists.

Indeed, for my own part, I believe that it is open to debate whether the Communist Party has any specific role to play at this particular stage of our political struggle. The basic task at the present moment is the removal of race discrimination and the attainment of democratic rights on the basis of the Freedom Charter. Insofar as that party furthers this task, I welcome its assistance. I realize that it is one of the means by which people of all races can be drawn into our struggle.

But from my reading of Marxist literature and from conversation with Marxists, I have gained the impression that communists regard the parliamentary system of the West as undemocratic and reactionary. On the contrary, I am an admirer of such a system.

The Magna Carta, the Bill of Rights, were held in veneration by democrats everywhere. He added that he had great respect for British political institutions, for Britain's system of justice, and also for America's Congress and independent judiciary. He had been influenced in his thinking by both West and East. In his search for a political formula he wanted to be absolutely objective.

Mandela then reverted to the question of communism: three exhibits in his handwriting were notes that he once had made and he explained the circumstances: an old friend who was a member of both the ANC and the CP had been trying to persuade him to join the Communist Party. In his repeated refusals, Mandela had criticized communist literature as being obtuse and full of jargon. His friend had asked him to re-draft the material in the simplified form he had in mind. 'I agreed,' Mandela told the court, 'but I never finished the task . . . I never again saw the unfinished manuscript until it was produced at the trial.'

(Two decades later President Botha was to make much of an

extract from one exhibit when he attempted, in his 'manifesto' of August 1985, to portray Mandela as a violent communist: 'We Communist Party members,' read the extract, 'are the most advanced revolutionaries in modern history. . . . The enemy must be completely crushed and wiped from the face of the earth before a communist world can be realized.' Mr Botha failed to mention that Mandela had not composed but had copied it from a Chinese book exhibited at the trial.)

Mandela went on to deal with the financial support received from abroad to supplement their own internal sources of funds. During the Treason Trial such assistance had come from sympathetic individuals and organizations in western countries and they had not felt it necessary to go beyond these sources. But when Umkhonto was formed, realizing that the scale of their activities would be hampered by lack of funds, he had been instructed to raise funds from African states. In discussions with African leaders of political movements he had discovered that almost every one had received assistance from the socialist countries as well as from the West. Some well-known African states, all non-communist and even anti-communist, had received similar assistance. On returning to South Africa, he had strongly recommended to the ANC that they should not confine themselves to seeking help from African and western countries but should try to raise funds from socialist countries as well.

The state had suggested that Umkhonto was the inspiration of the Communist Party which sought to play upon 'imaginary grievances' to 'enrol the African people into an army which ostensibly was to fight for African freedom, but in reality was fighting for a communist state'.

He declared:

> Nothing could be further from the truth. In fact, the suggestion is preposterous. Umkhonto was formed by Africans to further their struggle for freedom in their own land. Communists and others supported the movement, and we only wish that more sections of the community would join us.
>
> Our fight is against real, and not imaginary hardships . . . Basically

we fight against two features which are the hallmarks of African life in South Africa and which are entrenched by legislation which we seek to have repealed. These features are poverty and lack of human dignity, and we do not need communists or so-called 'agitators' to teach us about these things.

South Africa is the richest country in Africa, and could be one of the richest countries in the world. But it is a land of extremes and remarkable contrasts. The whites enjoy what may well be the highest standard of living in the world, whilst Africans live in poverty and misery. Forty per cent of the Africans live in hopelessly overcrowded and, in some cases, drought-stricken reserves . . . Thirty per cent are labourers, labour tenants and squatters on white farms, and work and live under conditions similar to those of the serfs in the Middle Ages. The other 30 per cent live in towns where they have developed economic and social habits which bring them closer in many respects to white standards. Yet many Africans, even in this group, are impoverished by low incomes and high cost of living.

He quoted the poverty datum line for the average African family in Johannesburg, the most prosperous area: 46 per cent did not earn enough to keep them going. Hand in hand with poverty went malnutrition and disease. South Africa's incidence of infant mortality was one of the highest in the world. But poverty was not the African's only complaint. The laws made by the whites were designed to preserve this situation. 'There are two ways to break out of poverty. The first is by formal education, and the second is by the worker acquiring a greater skill at his work and thus higher wages. As far as Africans are concerned, both these avenues of advancement are deliberately curtailed by legislation.'

He quoted the relative amounts spent on white and black education in 1960–61: whites were getting about twelve times as much per child, while Bantu Education restricted Africans to a vastly inferior education. Under the industrial colour bar all the better jobs were reserved for whites; black trade unions were not recognized and strikes were illegal.

Mandela went on:

The lack of human dignity experienced by Africans is the direct result of the policy of white supremacy. White supremacy implies black inferiority ... Whites tend to regard Africans as a separate breed. They do not look upon them as people with families of their own; they do not realize that they have emotions – that they fall in love like white people do; that they want to be with their wives and children like white people want to be with theirs; that they want to earn enough money to support their families properly, to feed and clothe them and send them to school. And what 'house-boy' or 'garden-boy' or labourer can ever hope to do this?

Out of personal experience and out of all he had witnessed as a lawyer and as a political leader, Mandela placed on record precisely what Africans had endured under governments which claimed to represent European Christian civilization; what they had endured and what they wanted:

Pass laws, which to the Africans are among the most hated bits of legislation in South Africa, render any African liable to police surveillance at any time. I doubt whether there is a single African male in South Africa who has not at some stage had a brush with the police over his pass. Hundreds and thousands of Africans are thrown into gaol each year under pass laws. Even worse than this is the fact that pass laws keep husband and wife apart and lead to the breakdown of family life.

This breakdown of family life and poverty led to dreadful social disruption and to the sort of violence that had become endemic in townships. Imprisonment and hanging could not cure the festering sore.

Africans want to be paid a living wage. Africans want to perform work which they are capable of doing, and not work which the government declares them to be capable of. Africans want to live where they obtain work, and not to be chased out of an area because they were not born there. Africans want to own land in places where they work, and not be obliged to live in rented houses which they can never call their own. We want to be part of the general population, and not confined to living in ghettos. African men want to have their wives and children to live with them where they work, and not be forced into an unnatural existence in men's hostels. African women want to be with their menfolk and not be left permanently widowed in the reserves. We want to travel in our own country and to seek work where we want to and not where the Labour Bureau tells us to. We want a just share in the whole of South Africa; we want security and a stake in society.

Above all, we want equal political rights, because without them our disabilities will be permanent. I know this sounds revolutionary to the whites in this country, because the majority of voters will be Africans. This makes the white man fear democracy. But this fear cannot be allowed to stand in the way of the only solution which will guarantee racial harmony and freedom for all. It is not true that the enfranchisement of all will result in racial domination. Political division, based on colour, is entirely artificial and, when it disappears, so will the domination of one colour group by another. The ANC has spent half a century fighting against racialism. When it triumphs it will not change that policy.

This then is what the ANC is fighting for. Their struggle is a truly national one. It is a struggle of the African people, inspired by their own suffering and their own experience. It is a struggle for the right to live.

Mandela ceased reading. The court was very quiet. He looked up at the Judge and when he spoke again, his voice was low:

During my lifetime I have dedicated myself to this struggle of the African people. I have fought against white domination, and I have fought against black domination. I have cherished the ideal of a democratic and free society in which all persons live together in harmony and with equal opportunities. It is an ideal which I hope to live for and to achieve. But if needs be it is an ideal for which I am prepared to die.

He sat down. From the galleries came a deep sigh. Then again, silence, until the Judge addressed Bram Fischer: 'You may call your next witness.'

Mandela had spoken for more than four hours. Now Accused No. 2, Walter Sisulu, as the main defence witness, came under prolonged attack from the prosecutor. But once he had taken the measure of Yutar, it was as if Sisulu forgot he was in the witness-box. It must have been eleven years since he had appeared on a public platform and now he dominated the situation. To him and to Govan Mbeki fell the task of defining the distinction between the ANC and Umkhonto. Mbeki, Kathrada and Bernstein spoke of their long allegiance to the Communist Party. All the defendants strongly denied that guerrilla warfare had been planned.

Dr Yutar prepared to give his closing speech for the state. After handing a set of bound volumes to the Judge, he proceeded to read from the first volume. He was again asserting that guerrilla warfare had not only been agreed upon but that a date had been set, when the Judge interrupted, asking him to concede that he had led no evidence to contradict the defence insistence that such warfare was not decided on. 'As Your Lordship pleases,' Yutar gave way. His address lasted four days, with little attempt to analyse or evaluate evidence.

'On the evidence,' he concluded, 'it is clear that without the action of the police, South Africa would today have found itself embroiled in a bloody and savage civil war. The public owes a great debt of gratitude to the police.'

The defence team presented substantial legal argument, and Bram Fischer drew from Judge de Wet confirmation that no decision or date had been fixed for a change to guerrilla warfare.

Mandela and six others having conceded their guilt on certain counts, two questions mattered: what would the verdict be in the case of Kathrada, Bernstein and Mhlaba, who denied all charges; and would there be death sentences for Mandela and his comrades?

On a Monday and Tuesday early in June 1964, Mandela – in gaol – wrote papers for a London University law examination. (He was to pass.) On the Thursday, 11 June, the court assembled. Winnie Mandela arrived with her mother-in-law and Zeni and Zindzi, aged five and four. The children were not allowed to enter the court and had to remain with friends outside.

In Pretoria's Church Square, the crowds, the heavy police presence; inside the Palace of Justice, the armed police, the galleries humming; the silence that fell as Mandela led the men from the cells below up the stairs and into the dock. *'Stilte in die hof! Opstaan!'*

The Judge-President took three minutes to deliver his findings. Mandela was the prime mover in founding Umkhonto we Sizwe for the purpose of sabotage. The defence contention was accepted that the leaders had given instructions 'that care should be exercised that no person was injured or killed', but they should have contemplated that the saboteurs 'would probably get out of hand'. The plans for guerrilla warfare had not been accepted by the leaders. 'I am not convinced,' he added, 'that the motives of the accused were as altruistic as they wish the court to believe. People who organize a revolution usually take over the government.'

'The verdict,' the Judge concluded, 'will be: Nelson Mandela is found guilty on all four counts; Walter Sisulu is found guilty on all four counts . . .'

Only Lionel Bernstein was acquitted, to be promptly re-arrested by Swanepoel and charged with having broken a ban sometime in the past.

The Judge would pronounce sentence next day. The court adjourned. Mandela waved to his wife and to his mother. As the men were driven away in a police van with its convoy of armed escorts, they thrust their hands through the bars to give the traditional salute to the cheering crowd. Albertina Sisulu led the people in singing 'Nkosi Sikelel' iAfrika'.

Joel Joffe has described what followed:

> Defence counsel and I, on our way back to Johannesburg, stopped at the gaol. The accused were calm, living now in the shadow of death. The only matter they wanted to discuss was how they should behave in court if the death sentence was passed. We said the Judge would first ask Nelson Mandela, 'Have you any reason to advance why the sentence of death should not be passed?' Nelson decided he would have a lot to say. If they thought by sentencing him to death

they would destroy the liberation movement, they were wrong; he was prepared to die, and knew his death would be an inspiration to his people in their struggle. We pointed out that such an address was hardly designed to facilitate an appeal. Nelson's answer was simple: if sentenced to death, he would not appeal. Sisulu and Mbeki felt the same. And all three were insistent that this must not influence the case of the others.

In the townships, at tremendous risk, illegal leaflets were distributed and slogans painted in support of the Rivonia men, while abroad there was a surge of protests, of demonstrations and vigils, generating an atmosphere of extreme tension as the sentences were awaited. Already the United Nations had called for the unconditional release of the Rivonia men and all political prisoners in South Africa, by 106 votes to South Africa's one. Newspaper editorials reflected the mood: 'The essence of the South African tragedy is that men like Mandela find themselves on the wrong side of the law,' remarked the conservative *Sunday Telegraph*; 'To most of the world,' said *The New York Times*, 'these men are heroes and freedom fighters. The George Washingtons and Ben Franklins of South Africa.'

'The verdict of history,' prophesied *The Times*, 'will be that the ultimate guilty party is the government in power – and that already is the verdict of world opinion.'

Intent on saving the men from death, Bram Fischer had approached two distinguished South Africans to argue in mitigation: Harold Hanson, QC compared the African struggle for rights to the Afrikaner struggle for freedom and cited precedents for temperate sentencing, even in cases of rebellion and treason; while Alan Paton, National President of the Liberal Party and a devout Christian, praised the sincerity and courage of Mandela, Sisulu and Mbeki and spoke of their lack of a desire for revenge. He appealed for clemency 'because of the future of this country'.

On 12 June police roadblocks and armed forces spread through the forty miles between the Witwatersrand and Pretoria. For hours a huge crowd waited silently outside the Palace of Justice, with women carrying banners: WE ARE PROUD OF OUR LEADERS and NO TEARS: OUR FUTURE IS BRIGHT.

In court Mandela and the other accused showed no signs of emotion while the Judge pronounced sentence: 'The crime of which the accused have been convicted . . . is in essence one of high treason. The state has decided not to charge the crime in this form. Bearing this in mind and giving the matter very serious consideration, I have decided not to impose the supreme penalty.' There was a gasp of relief but the Judge was continuing: 'Consistent with my duty that is the only leniency which I can show. The sentence in the case of all the accused will be one of life imprisonment.' The men in the dock turned to the public galleries and smiled. Mandela gave the ANC thumbs–up *Afrika!* salute before descending to the cells for the last time.

Junior counsel shook hands silently with Bram Fischer. It had been his responsibility in the first place to save the men's lives and it was his legal victory that they would live.

In the street Winnie together with Zeni and Zindzi waited for a last glimpse of her husband but the crowd was too great. As the men were driven away the shouts rang out, *Amandla! Ngawethu!* Robin Day managed to reach her, to interview her for BBC's 'Panorama' programme – a typically powerful and brave statement. Then climbing into her car, and giving the ANC salute as she did so, she drove off. When she reached her home in Orlando, after putting the children to bed, she broke down and wept.

The Rivonia men, said Albert Lutuli, in a moving appeal to the outside world, represented 'the highest in morality and ethics' in the country's political struggle. He called on 'South Africa's strongest allies, Britain and America . . . to take decisive action for sanctions' to 'precipitate the end of the hateful system of apartheid'.

The extremes of white opinion in South Africa were expressed by two newspaper editorials: 'The Rivonia conspiracy,' said an Afrikaner Nationalist newspaper, 'was a diabolical plan to initiate a black revolution designed to lead to the submission of the free

1   Nelson Mandela at nineteen

2 Mandela with Yusuf Dadoo in the Defiance Campaign, 1952

3 Mandela with Oliver Tambo in the Sudan, 1962

4   Treason Trial defendants, 1956: Mandela (centre, third row)

5   Nelson Rolihlahla Mandela marries Winnie Nomzamo Madikizela, 1958

6 Winnie and Nelson celebrating the end of the Emergency, 1960

7 Mandela outside the Houses of Parliament, London, 1962

8 Mandela on Robben Island, 1966

9 Mandela revisits the lime quarry, 1994

10 Winnie with Zindzi and Zeni, at the time of Mandela's arrest, 1962

11 Winnie with Zeni Dlamini and Zindzi on their way to visit Mandela in Pollsmoor prison, 1985

white way of life.' The *Rand Daily Mail* declared that the case had captured the imagination because it told 'a classic story of the struggle of men for freedom and dignity, with overtones of Grecian tragedy in their failure. Rivonia is a name to remember.'

Dennis Goldberg, as the only white man, was returned to Pretoria Central prison. Mandela, Sisulu, Mbeki, Mhlaba, Motsoaledi, Mlangeni and Kathrada were flown to Robben Island. They all refused to appeal against sentence.

According to South African officials, for political prisoners a life sentence meant exactly that.

12

'PRAY THAT YOUR GOD CAN GET YOU
OUT OF THIS CELL'

1964–70

It was shortly before his forty-sixth birthday that Mandela again found himself on Robben Island, a small rocky windswept outcrop of land surrounded by turbulent seas, some seven miles to the north-west of Cape Town; but this time he had the comradeship of Sisulu and the other Rivonia men. On the Island, among his friends, he was known by his clan name, Madiba.

Mid-winter, the island was dankly cold; on days of dense mist the foghorn from the lighthouse echoed mournfully. Abusive guards – one with a swastika tattooed on the back of his fist – ordered their every move. At first they were held with other 'politicals' in the *Ou Tronk* (old gaol); for showers they were made to strip and run naked to a washroom in the *Zinc Tronk*, some two hundred yards away. Guarded by men with Alsatian dogs on leash, some laboured on the completion of a new maximum security 'isolation' section of eighty-eight cells which they were the first to occupy, as their names inscribed in the cement testified. Separated from the other blocks by a thirty-foot wall, these singled-out politicals occupied one side of a central yard; criminal lifers the other.

Mandela's cell was typical, about seven foot square, lit by a forty-watt bulb, on the floor a mat and a bedroll of two blankets. The regulation shorts and khaki shirt, thin jersey and jacket were no protection against the bitter nights. Woken before sunrise for a cold wash and shave and cleaning out of sanitary pails, he and his companions – about thirty in all – took turns to dish out breakfast: porridge for everyone, but whereas

Indians and Coloureds were allowed a spoonful of sugar and a ration of bread, Africans were restricted to half a spoonful with no bread. Maize, tasteless soup and black coffee were basic to their other meals, with small lumps of meat or vegetables sometimes added.

Resounding through their days, the warders' shouts ordered them to remain in their cells, to be silent: they were in 'isolation'.

The initial struggle, then, was for primitive rights: to be let out of the cells for exercise, to do useful work, to speak to each other, to have more blankets, long pants, and better and more food. *Klagte* (complaints) time on Saturday mornings was evidently regarded by the prison officers as something of a joke but Mandela demanded attention. He was coldly polite and firm, not treating them as enemies but as men who should do their job properly and abide by prison regulations.

After a few weeks came the first, however limited, victory: they were let out into the yard where, seated on blocks of stone, they crushed rocks into small pieces with hammers. If caught talking, they were punished by *drie maaltye* (having to go without three meals); a second offence meant the loss of six meals, but against the din of the hammering they contrived to communicate, even to play word games.

Dennis Brutus, schoolmaster, poet and organizer of the sports boycott, who was serving a short sentence for breaking a banning order, recalls a game: each day a prisoner would pose a question which went round the group, often something to puzzle over when alone in a cell. Mandela asked what was the origin of 'Fabian', the name of the British socialist group to which G. B. Shaw and H. G. Wells had belonged. Brutus came up with the answer: the Roman general, Fabius Maximus, whose masterly tactics gradually wore out Hannibal's army; thus the symbolic use of the name for the gradual introduction and spread of socialism.

During those early months of labouring in the yard, one press photographer was allowed to take pictures of the men breaking stones, and of Mandela and Sisulu together during a break: the only ones to be taken of them through the long years in gaol.

With the imprisonment of the Rivonia men and the subsequent capture of other Umkhonto and ANC leaders and organizers, the ANC-in-exile admitted that 'the enemy had smashed the very heart' of the movement; it was 'a very serious setback'. Through the physical and psychological torture of 90-Days and the work of paid informers, not only ANC but PAC and Poqo, and members of other radical organizations, arrived in a constant stream from the mainland. Only black men – white politicals were held in Pretoria; black women usually in Kroonstad – teachers, peasants, doctors, labourers, accountants, factory workers, trade unionists. Aged from fifteen to seventy they were united as never before on this small island, although leaders in the special section were cut off from blocks where more than a thousand politicals and about three hundred criminals were held, sixty to a cell. Soon, Namibians would arrive – leaders of the South-West African People's Organization (SWAPO) – to be imprisoned in the *Zinc Tronk*. In a house near the village where the white warders lived was Robert Sobukwe, detained under guard.

In mid-summer Mandela and his comrades in the 'isolation' block were ordered out to labour in the lime quarry towards the centre of the Island. Mandela took the lead. *'Hak! Hak!'* ordered the warder from the back of the *span* (work team). Mandela deliberately walked very slowly. 'Faster! Faster!' the warder repeated. Mandela took no notice. And the *span*, now singing freedom songs, followed at his slow pace. In this way he established his leadership. When another *span* from the main block approached, the latter were ordered to halt and turn their backs while the leaders went by. No communication, no glance of mutual encouragement must be exchanged. The authorities could not prevent them enjoying the Island's yellow-blossomed bush and eucalyptus trees, and an occasional deer or ostrich, while, far off to the south-east, across the glittering sea was the panorama of Table Mountain looming over Cape Town.

At the quarry the men dug and cut limestone with pick and shovel, then loaded the slabs on trucks. Trapped in that huge hole, as the day wore on it became an oven with the lime reflecting the sun's glare, so that they were scorched from below as from above, while warders drove them on, '*Werk, man, werk!*' Limbs and backs aching, ankles and hands blistered, eyes gritty and strained, they dug and cut and loaded, hour after hour. In the afternoon, limping back, the men were ghostly white, covered in limedust; they made straight for the showers before dropping exhausted on the mats in their cells. Each evening as soon as the warders had gone off duty, through the cell walls the prisoners' voices joined in prayers and in singing freedom songs.

Seals (*robbe* in Dutch) had first occupied the Island, and penguins and snakes, until the Dutch East India Company, the first Europeans to establish a base at the Cape of Good Hope, realized its suitability for a prison: the sea not only kept prisoners from escaping but kept unwanted visitors out. The Island became part of the history of black resistance to imperialism: in 1658 a Khoi rebel, Autshumayo – Herry, the Dutch called him – was the first to be banished there and was among the few ever to escape; rebellious sheikhs, rajahs and princes of Java and the Moluccas were exiled there by the Dutch; then the British, on occupying the Cape in the nineteenth century, banished to the Island some of those heroes Mandela had revered since childhood – Makana in 1819 and Maqoma in the 1850s – great warrior chiefs of the AmaXhosa who had been defeated by the superior force of the colonists. Makana had escaped and was drowned; some prisoners called it Makana Island. The British had also sent the 'chronic sick, lunatics and paupers' of all races to the Island; among them lepers. Many died there and their bones mingled with those of the black prisoners and exiles whose sentences had been for 'life'. In 1959 Minister of Justice Vorster announced that it would be a maximum security prison for 'non-white' men: with no ship allowed within a mile and strong currents sweeping the ocean, it was said to be impregnable.

Political prisoners were Category D: every six months, one letter of five hundred words and one visit, and they were allowed to discuss family matters only. Winnie has described the 'utter hell' of those early months when she was 'stripped of a man of such formidable stature'. As she 'fumbled along and tried to adjust', she kept rereading his first letter.

When the time for the first visit came, she set off with Albertina Sisulu and Chief Lutuli's daughter, Dr Albertina Ngakane, whose husband was serving a short sentence. They travelled nearly a thousand miles to Cape Town. On arrival at the docks they had to sign the prison visitors' book, agreeing to the regulations: no cameras, no cats, no dogs, no children under sixteen. The journey by ferry took forty-five minutes and, finally, they had reached the Island. But as prison officers marched them from the dock to the waiting-room they saw little of their men's new surroundings. To one side a high wall hid the prison, to the other was the sea. For the first time Winnie Mandela heard the warning she was to be given every time she visited her husband in the years to come: a senior officer told her she was not to speak in Xhosa or say anything about anyone other than the children and 'first-degree relatives'; if she broke that rule, the visit would be ended.

Meanwhile, Mandela and the other men who had been granted a visit would hear their names called and be marched to the visiting section. They had been similarly warned, with the additional order not to discuss prison conditions.

At last husband and wife were together again, each accompanied by two or three warders and able to see each other only dimly through a small window; hear through a telephone controlled by a warder. In that artificial manner they shared what they could of their lives. Zeni was six and Zindzi four-and-a-half; their parents discussed their development and needs. Zindzi had just gone to kindergarten but refused to remain. She wanted to go to a 'proper' school like her sister and her father agreed with Winnie that she could do so. The half hour was abruptly ended by a warder's 'Time up!'

The women loitered at the exit to catch a glimpse of their men being marched back to the cells. Albertina Sisulu could not help exclaiming, 'Oh, our men are shrinking here!' 'But,' she added, 'their spirit is so strong.' Then the women were marched off, back to the ferry, back to the mainland and the long journey home. Later, Mandela and the others fortunate to have had a visit would be eagerly questioned by lonely comrades.

At home in Orlando, Winnie told the children about the father they could not remember. All Zeni recalled of the occasion when last she had seen him was the crowds and the cars outside the Palace of Justice. Now they were separated from their mother, as increasingly stringent banning orders restricted her life. She has described the effect of bans which prohibited her from entering schools and from visiting any African areas apart from Orlando:

> I was never there as a mother to hold my little girls' hands, take them to school and introduce them to their teachers, as is the glory of every mother when her children are starting school. Each mother looks forward so much to that day. I've never entered any of the schools attended by my children. I've never met any of my children's teachers. I couldn't do that because it would have meant violating the terms of my banning order.
>
> I placed the children at a very early age in boarding-schools. The first was a Roman Catholic institution in Swaziland. Ironically, the name was Our Lady of Sorrows . . . So they virtually had to bring themselves up.

However, on occasion, the girls stayed with Helen Joseph, their old family friend, and Winnie's sisters sometimes helped out. Through those years Zeni cherished a memory of her mother singing Xhosa lullabies.

The bans ended Winnie's job with the Child Welfare Department. Police intimidation of employers added to the hazards of her struggle to earn a living: from a furniture shop in the city she went to a dry cleaning business, then to a shoe repair shop.

She had grown from the shy girl to a beautiful young woman, with something of her husband's buoyant vitality. At times the loneliness, the burdens, were intolerable and her natural tendency to be over-trusting was exacerbated by that loneliness. Over the course of several years, two people whom she regarded as reliable friends turned out to be police informers, and when the security police contrived to spread a rumour that she herself was an informer, she suffered an extremely painful period of ostracism from a number of political colleagues. The authorities made sure that Mandela, on Robben Island, came to hear of such gossip; somehow, he succeeded in sending out a message asking that his wife be supported in these difficult times.

The state, not satisfied with this base form of persecution, intensified Winnie's banning orders: in 1966 she was also prohibited from writing or publishing anything. Twice arrested in 1967, she was charged with contravening one ban or another and, after four nights in police cells, was given a suspended sentence of fourteen months.

Many years later she was to describe the impact of such harassment on the family:

> Insofar as the black woman in South Africa is concerned, each black home is a political institution. The black woman finds herself having to explain to the children what is going on in society. When Zindzi was about six years, she asked me questions each and every mother gets faced with. She was playing outside and then she came into the house and said, 'Mummy, you say Daddy is in prison because he is fighting for the black people?' I said, yes. And she said, 'But next door, their father is there at home. Why is my father in gaol, and not the father next door?' Difficult questions like that, at that early age: about police, the state, the position of the father next door.

Meanwhile, George Bizos told of his first visit to the Island. 'Eight guards marched towards me and in the middle was Nelson, wearing sandals, shorts and tunic, at ease among them. "George," he said, "I want to introduce you to my guard of honour," and he introduced all eight of them.'

Year after year Mandela and his comrades laboured on. When not digging lime or breaking rocks, they repaired roads. He was unwell on one occasion and unable to lift heavy rocks on to a lorry. His refusal to obey orders was witnessed by the brigadier in charge of prisons who had accompanied the commandant on an inspection. Charged with laziness and failing to obey a lawful command, Mandela was tried by the Island's judicial officer and sentenced to six days' solitary on spare diet. The solitary cells were ice cold; spare diet was water in which rice had been boiled.

The physical assaults which had been commonplace during the early sixties had given way to attempts to break the men's morale. 'When we went to prison,' said Eddie Daniels, a Liberal Party member and one of the African Resistance Movement saboteurs, 'the government had two aims: to destroy our morale and to get the world to forget us. They failed dismally. Because being in the company of Mandela and Sisulu, instead of being weakened, they lifted you, they made you strong. Mandela,' he added, 'taught me how to survive. When I was ill, he could have asked anybody else to see to me. He came to me personally. He even cleaned my toilet.'*

Through hunger-strikes, go-slows and other forms of protest, and with growing expressions of international concern, the political prisoners had won better treatment: the right to talk to each other, improved food, more blankets, and long pants. Dennis Brutus has described how at night, after the warders had gone, a prisoner might begin to whistle a melody – although whistling was forbidden – and from another cell the harmony would be picked up until it became a small orchestra of whistles.

A recurring complaint was of medical laxity or callousness. And the regular replacement of commanding officers was disconcerting: each newcomer had his whims to which prisoners had to adjust. One, nicknamed '*Staalbaard*' (Man of Steel), fortunately stayed only six months. Later came a man who actually listened to their complaints; but he in turn was replaced.

Despite the hardships Mandela kept up his routine of physical

* *Grassroots*, May 1985.

exercises, and despite the monotony of prison existence he found – as they all did – that even there each day was different, a day of developing friendships and shared experiences, a day of reliving past events and of re-asserting confidence in the future.

He liked to tell about his youth in Thembuland and about his tour of Africa, sometimes embroidering the original anecdote as his sense of humour carried him away. One particular story was told at his own expense, describing his consternation when, in Ghana, he had flown in a plane piloted by Africans. How could *they* possibly pilot a big jet aircraft? His mistrust was quite involuntary, the result of an upbringing in South Africa. But at the time, when the pilots had come back to chat with passengers, he – not knowing that there was such a thing as an automatic pilot – had thought how irresponsible these Africans were!

'However adverse the conditions you will find something to laugh at,' said one of his fellow prisoners, Dr Pascal Ngakane. 'It's one of the protective mechanisms of human nature. Once we were asked, All those who have drivers' licences, stand to one side! So all of us who could drive, we thought we would be driving the lorries, we stood aside. And we were given wheelbarrows to push!'

The right to study meant more than any other privilege, except visits. Mandela, continuing with law degrees, could work until eleven p.m., as could Mbeki and others at university level, but those at matric level had to finish an hour earlier. If anyone was found reading after the permitted hour it meant *drie maaltye*. Fikile Bam, a law student before he was sentenced, appreciated the fact that Mandela tested his memory and understanding of what he had studied by passing on information which, in its turn, led to political discussion. There was a continual process of exchange among the men, learning from each other. The worst punishment was curtailment of studies.

Political prisoners were never allowed newspapers and news from the outside world. Mandela was charged and punished when press clippings were found hidden in his cell, yet somehow the men contrived to pick up information and every scrap was seized on and its implications analysed.

There had been much excitement in 1965 when they learned that Bram Fischer, on trial for leadership of the illegal Communist Party, had gone underground in a bid to revive the struggle. For nearly a year he had evaded capture. The government had passed a new law: 180-Days' detention in solitary confinement of anyone the security police cared to pick up for interrogation. Within weeks they had the information they wanted and Fischer was tracked down, arrested and brought to trial, accused of having conspired with the very men he had defended in the Rivonia Trial. Found guilty, he too was sentenced to life imprisonment and joined other white political prisoners in Pretoria Central prison.

Intimations that important events were happening were often manifested by the behaviour of warders. Mandela and the men on the Island were treated more roughly on such occasions, as, for instance, when the armed struggle broke out in Namibia in 1966. The politicals got the general gist, but the full story only became clear later, when the SWAPO leader, Andimba Ja Toivo, joined them in the section to serve a twenty-year sentence. The African liberation struggle was continually taking on new dimensions: Angola, Mozambique and now Namibia.

J. B. Vorster had become Prime Minister, succeeding Dr Verwoerd, who had been assassinated in September 1966 by a deranged white messenger in the House of Assembly.

The following year several Umkhonto men who had been captured by the Rhodesian army and handed over to the South African police, were brought to the Island to serve long sentences. With Joshua Nkomo's ZAPU (Zimbabwe African Peoples' Union), they had formed a guerrilla contingent attempting to establish bases between Zambia and South Africa. The ill-conceived plan to traverse huge areas of game reserve and bush, short of equipment and of experience, ended in disaster.

In July 1967 Chief Albert Lutuli died. On a habitual walk across a railway bridge near his home, he was run down by a train. Many, including his family, were sceptical of the official inquiry's conclusion that it was an accident resulting from his deafness.

In exile, Oliver Tambo became President-General of the ANC. In 1969 in Tanzania he met fraternal delegates from the Organization of African Unity, from Tanzania, from Mozambique's FRELIMO (Mozambique Liberation Front) and Angola's MPLA (Popular Movement for the Liberation of Angola), who pledged full support for the ANC's struggle for freedom. The 'unholy alliance' of Vorster, Smith and Portugal's Caetano was to be met with an alliance between the liberation movements.

In South Africa, the government passed the 'Terrorism' Act and at two a.m. on 12 May 1969 the first arrests were made. In the Mandela household Zeni and Zindzi were home for the holidays; they and their mother were asleep when the police banged at the door and shone torches through the windows. Winnie was ordered to dress and as the children clung to her skirt, imploring the police to leave her alone, she asked to take them to her sister Nikiwe Xaba, who lived near by. Her appeal was roughly rejected; she had to leave them. Only two days earlier she had seen a specialist who had diagnosed a heart condition – the security police knew of this. When the children contacted their aunt next morning, they could get no information about Winnie's whereabouts or her state of health. On the Island, Mandela soon learned of her arrest.

Later she realized that twenty-one others had also been detained: the four women included a poet and a trade unionist; one of the seventeen men was seventy-three years old. Most of them had been involved with Winnie in organizing aid for families of political prisoners; the police had infiltrated an informer into the group who remained at large. Winnie and the others were held in solitary confinement, incommunicado. Under the new law they could be detained indefinitely. One of the detainees died that night, another died nineteen days later.

At first Winnie was held in a tiny cell. She later recounted:

All I had was a plastic bottle with about five glasses of water, a sanitary bucket, three blankets and a sisal mat. About a week later I was transferred to a 'condemned' cell: a cell which usually holds prisoners who are going to be executed.

The first thing I usually do when I am arrested is to draw my calendar on the wall so that I can keep track of the date. In the condemned cell I think the whole idea was to give one a feeling of eternity, that your political life had come to an end. There were two grille doors besides the prison door and to this day the memory of the bunch of keys – the clicking, the noise they would deliberately make in the stillness and solitude of prison life – you felt they were hitting the inner core of your soul. They never switched off the light. I lost track of time; I didn't know whether it was morning or evening. I could only tell by the plate of food; food which was inedible. In the morning I knew by the coffee, the porridge.

Three white wardresses brought the food. They would then take the sanitary bucket, turn the lid upside-down and put your plate of food on that. So I never ate.

I was not allowed outside, I would just exercise in front of the cell door by going up and down, up and down, for ten to fifteen minutes. The mind finds it very difficult to adjust to such solitude. I could feel my mind was so tortured with lack of communicating with anyone that I found myself talking to the children, as if they were with me in the cell. If I had an ant there, or a fly, I regarded myself as having company for the day.

One day this Swanepoel stood at the cell door and flung the Bible at my face and said very sarcastically, 'There you are, pray that your God can get you out of this cell!'

All this is in preparation for the inevitable hell – interrogation. It is meant to crush your individuality, to change you into a docile being from whom no resistance can arise, to terrorize you.

Two weeks after her arrest, interrogation began, under the direction of the brutal Major Swanepoel. Winnie Mandela was kept sleepless through five days and nights while successive teams of security police fired questions at her. On the third day she appealed to them, showing her blue and swollen hands and feet. She felt dizzy and her heart was palpitating. 'For God's sake,' Swanepoel taunted, 'leave us some inheritance when you decide to pop it. You cannot go with all that information.'

From the next-door room she could hear scuffling noises and the laughter of interrogators. Other detainees were being forced to stand barefoot on bricks day and night until they collapsed, and were then forced up again. Some were hanged by their wrists and beaten. There was a variety of violent assaults and insults meted out according to the whim of the interrogators. Prisoners died as a result of the torture, among them the Imam Haroun, a religious leader detained in Cape Town.

'It was during that experience,' Winnie later said, 'that I realized the extent to which the Afrikaner is frightened of the black man. It was then that I discovered the type of hate I had never encountered before.'

After five months in solitary confinement, the twenty-two prisoners were brought to trial at the old synagogue court in Pretoria. Police armed with sten guns paraded outside. Having been held under the Terrorism Act, they now found themselves charged under the Suppression of Communism Act, with recruiting for the ANC and finding targets for sabotage, with distributing banned literature and using funerals for furthering the ANC's political aims, and with being in touch with guerrillas and encouraging hostility between white and non-white.

Winnie Mandela was accused of getting 'instructions' from her husband on Robben Island. In short, the charges amounted to their having revived the ANC in Johannesburg, the Eastern Cape and Natal. There would be eighty witnesses, most of whom were held in detention. Especially painful for Winnie was the imprisonment of her youngest sister, Nonyaniso 'Princess'. After their mother had died, she had mothered the little girl, carrying her on her back and taking her for long walks.

With extraordinary courage Winnie's friends – among them Shanthie Naidoo, a young woman whose father had been adopted by Gandhi – refused to give evidence for the state and accepted further imprisonment. Twenty witnesses gave evidence of such flimsiness that the state itself asked for an acquittal of all the accused.

On 16 February 1970 the Judge told them: 'I find you not guilty and you are discharged.' Before Winnie and her companions could join families and friends to celebrate, spectators were ordered to leave the court and they were re-detained, again under the Terrorism Act, and taken off back to solitary confinement for further 'interrogation'.

'The prosecution's strategy seems clear,' commented *The New York Times*, 25 February 1970: 'It will simply hold the defendants under the Terrorism Act until more "evidence" can be obtained or concocted by the bestial methods that have become a hallmark of South African "justice".'

Two months after Winnie's arrest, the commandant called Mandela to his office; he was told that his son, Thembi, had been killed in a car crash. Thembi who, as a boy, had been closest to him and who, later – apparently still unforgiving about the divorce – had refused to visit him on the Island. Warders were to describe Mandela's anguish: for nights he was unable to sleep and just stood at the tiny window of his cell, staring out.

In South Africa and abroad protests were mounting at the treatment of Winnie Mandela and her colleagues. In June, after one of the defendants had been withdrawn to face separate charges, she and nineteen others were again brought to trial, this time charged under the Terrorism Act. Again, on 14 September 1970, the court acquitted them all. They had spent 491 days in solitary confinement.

'The most consoling thought right through our ordeal,' she wrote to a friend in London, 'was the knowledge that we are not alone in our struggle for human dignity. It was indeed a brutal test of the durability of one's ideals . . . We are determined to put up the fight at whatever cost if we want our children to be spared the injustices we are suffering.'

In October fresh banning orders, extending for five years, were served on her: not only was she restricted to Orlando, but each night and through weekends and public holidays she was under house arrest, allowed no visitors at any time. When she became ill and was visited by one of her sisters, Winnie was promptly arrested for breaking this latter ban. There seemed no limit to the harassment.

But a month later, with special permission enabling her to leave Orlando, she was at last able to visit her husband, for half an hour. They had not seen each other for two years.

On the Island Mandela had drafted a petition which he and twenty-one others signed, calling for the release of all political prisoners. Pro-German Afrikaner Nationalists, the petition pointed out, had rebelled against the state during the First World War – causing hundreds of casualties – and again at the time of the war against Hitler, and yet had been released after serving only a few years of their sentences. Mandela and the other signatories demanded the same treatment and declared that they had been treated differently because it was the black man in revolt.

Helen Suzman visited the Island to discuss the petition with them and pointed out: 'The difference is that your struggle is ongoing. It's true the rebels of 1915 were released but their struggle had been defeated. Are you prepared to say you will abandon the armed struggle?'

'No,' was Mandela's reply, 'not until our people have won their freedom.'

13

'THE CORNERSTONE OF THE STRUGGLE
LIES INSIDE SOUTH AFRICA'

1971—8

On Robben Island the man referred to in *The Times* as the 'colossus of African nationalism in South Africa', prisoner No. 466/64, spent his days on the beach in a *span* collecting seaweed for fertilizers: back-breaking labour with the added discomfort of walking on sand washed by the icy waters of the south Atlantic. In the distance ships sailed to and from Cape Town harbour.

Mandela had once said that 'South Africa's prisons are intended to cripple us so that we should never again have the strength and courage to pursue our ideals', but the fact that they were treated not just as prisoners but as black men was in the end counter-productive, as it stiffened their resistance.

By the early seventies their stubbornly expressed complaints, combined with international pressure, had gained more modest but always significant improvements: a table and bench in the cell and, in winter, the 'right' to wrap up in a blanket while reading or studying; hot water for washing; and in the yard, a volley-ball court which was later turned into a tennis court. Their request for soccer was turned down because it meant coming out of the segregated section. Indoors they had table-tennis and chess and, once a month, a film show. Canned music was played each evening. But whistling was still a punishable offence and, more importantly, repeated demands for access to news continued to meet with adamant rejection, as did the request for creative activities such as carpentry and basketwork.

Because Mandela had originally been sentenced in 1962, before the flood of political prisoners had brought a change in regulations, he had permission to study for a University of London law degree but it became impossible to get up-to-date books in time to complete the course. Then the authorities banned politicals from post-graduate studies, a serious deprivation of intellectual stimulus. Mandela turned to economics and, since neither French nor German was permitted, to higher levels of Afrikaans.

Suddenly, a heavy blow: he was deprived of all study rights for four years. Prison officers claimed to have found 'memoirs' hidden in his cell and politicals were forbidden to keep diaries or personal notes; paper was strictly limited for study purposes and for the 500-word letters now permitted to the family each month. 'Show me the memoirs,' he demanded, but they were never produced.

After the years of labour in the lime quarry he was not the only man whose eyesight had deteriorated. Certain concessions were made since he suffered from high blood pressure and a bad back: he was given a bed and, instead of the bench, a chair, and was put on a salt-free diet. Like the other Rivonia men who had worked their way up from Category D to C to B, he was allowed more frequent visits, but still limited to half an hour.

Each time a visit was due, Winnie had to go through the same procedure: first get written permission via the local magistrate from the Minister of Justice and from the police, then report to the police both on departure and on arrival. She was no longer allowed to travel by train or by car but must go by air to Cape Town which entailed a far costlier fare. Generous friends at home and abroad contributed. It was always difficult to remember the constraints of censorship: asked what sort of remark might cause warders to cut off her conversation with her husband, she said, 'When he asked about Ruth First, or Ruth Matseoane [his former secretary], or Oliver Tambo; when he discussed the Transkei situation which involved his family – the Matanzima brothers; and mentioning that a book was being written about him.'

Sometimes he persuaded warders to let the visit continue. 'He addresses them like small boys: "Surely you can see I'm in the middle of a sentence and haven't seen my family for some time; I'll continue anyhow, just continue listening, which is what your duty really is."'

Among his visitors was his elder sister, Mabel Notancu Ntimakhwe. His aged mother also made the long journey and the crossing to the Island. After their allotted time together, as he watched her leave for the ferry, he sensed it was to be the last time he would see her. Soon after, he received a letter from his sister to say their mother had died. Winnie and the children attended the funeral in the Transkei.

A relative from the Transkei, who visited Robben Island after the funeral, said how grateful Mandela was to those who had arranged the service: 'He kept asking was so-and-so there, and so-and-so? I could not believe he was so well informed. He asked me to greet and thank all these people for having attended the funeral.'

In December 1973 the Minister of Prisons, Jimmy Kruger, visited the Island and – a reflection of the government's eagerness to sell its policy of 'independent' Bantustans – he indicated to Mandela and to a deputation led by Mac Maharaj, a fellow-prisoner, that if they would recognize the Transkei and settle there, they would be offered remission of sentence. 'The policy of separate development is wholly unacceptable,' was the reply; there could never be compromise on that point. (Nevertheless, the government was to repeat the offer to Mandela on several subsequent occasions; always his reply was 'no'.) Ironically, Kaiser Matanzima, the minor chief who, through South African government support, had led the Transkei to 'independence', according to Thembu custom was Mandela's nephew. Winnie Mandela was also offered 'freedom' by Prime Minister Vorster if she would accept the Transkei as her 'homeland'. 'The audacity of it!' was her response. 'If anybody should leave South Africa it's the settler government.'

She had again been charged with breaking her bans and, during 1974, served six months' imprisonment in Kroonstad prison. It had been an enriching experience, she said. She felt more liberated there, and the physical identification with her beliefs was more satisfying than expressing them in speeches. Besides, the whole country was a prison for the black man. But for the family her imprisonment was upsetting. Zindzi wept when she learned of the sentence. 'You must never cry,' her mother told her, 'you give them satisfaction if you do.' Zeni recalls school holidays, when she and Zindzi were taken by their guardian, Uncle Harry (Dr Nthato Motlana), to visit their mother on Sundays: the half hour they had talking to her through a glass partition about school, about pocket money and who they were staying with. Winnie always looked well. But the girls were beginning to find that friends were scared to visit them at home because security police might pick them up for questioning.

Long after, Mandela recalled his feelings: 'Although I always try to put up a brave face, I never get used to you being in the cooler,' he wrote to his wife. 'Few things disorganize my whole life as much as this particular type of hardship, which seems destined to stalk us for quite some time still. I will never forget the desperately distressing experiences we had from May '69 to September '70 and the six months you spent in Kroonstad.'*

It is difficult to keep track of details of the repeated arrests, charges, convictions, appeals, suspended sentences and periods of imprisonment inflicted on Winnie Mandela. The long-drawn-out resistance on her part exposed the system under which many thousands of men and women were similarly victimized. In brushes with the police she was fearless, aggressively retaliating against their often violent intrusions. However, against a series of sinister assaults when she was physically attacked and her house petrol-bombed, there was nothing she could do and she was given no protection. Zindzi appealed to the United Nations to call on the South African government to ensure her mother's safety. 'We believe that these attacks are politically motivated,' she said.

* Letter of 1 March 1981.

The two girls had been rescued from an unhappy time at the convent by Elinor Birley, who was living in Johannesburg while her husband, Sir Robert Birley – formerly headmaster of Eton – was visiting professor of education at the University of the Witwatersrand. Lady Birley arranged for them to go to Waterford, the multiracial boarding-school in Swaziland.

The time had come when the teenagers would be permitted to meet their father. Winnie understood the trauma: would they break down or would they be strengthened by the experience and emerge proud of this prisoner?

Zeni could hardly recognize Mandela from the pictures she had seen in which he looked 'very big and fat', but what struck her most was how humorous her father was and if there was ever any worry then, or in her later visits, he hid it well.

Zindzi also found his humour and warmth reassuring. 'I was angry and slightly apprehensive beforehand,' she told a journalist, 'but I found him to be a very diplomatic, charming man. He managed to take my mind away from the environment and made me think of more comfortable circumstances. He said, "You know I can imagine you sitting on my lap at home and having a Sunday roast with the family."' Although not allowed to see him standing up – by the time they were led into the cubicle he was already seated on the other side of the glassed-in partition – she managed to watch him walk away afterwards and noticed how fit and strong he looked, how young and brisk was his stride.

When next the girls visited him, they went alone. The friend who drove them to the docks in Cape Town watched them board the ferry along with a group of warders in rugby gear: it was, he thought, a poignant scene; these two young girls and those men singing their Afrikaner songs.

During the half-hour visits, Winnie and her husband had achieved the essence of communication so that each, inspired and invigorated by the other, returned to their separate areas of struggle: Mandela, in his unobtrusive way, to help comrades with their problems regardless of their political affiliations;

Winnie, despite all restrictions, at the heart of the community of Soweto, that ghetto of more than a million people, where a new phase in the struggle had been marked by the rise of Black Consciousness. In her view this 'made the people more aware of their worth, their power, and it developed more self-reliance'. The black man had become prouder of his blackness.

In 1969 Steve Biko and Barney Pityana had led black students in breaking away from the multiracial National Union of South African Students (NUSAS) to form the all-black South African Students' Organization (SASO) and by 1972 the Black Peoples' Convention had been formed. Although influenced by American 'black power' movements and the radical writings of Frantz Fanon, Black Consciousness had developed in response to white racism and its aims were psychological liberation, to free blacks from dependence on whites and to unite all blacks: for the first time Indians and Coloured people grouped themselves with Africans as 'black'. Out of this movement which embraced religious, cultural and educational spheres, as well as political, came a new assertiveness among the youth.

Although closer in philosophy to the PAC than the ANC, these young leaders were at first welcomed by the exiled ANC executive for taking the struggle forward 'in their heroism and discipline' and in their demonstration of the importance of securing the unity 'of the main motive forces of the revolution: the oppressed peoples'. The term 'black' for anyone the government labelled 'non-white' was, said the ANC journal *Sechaba*, an innovation.

'Azania' was the Black Consciousness name for the country. Inherited from the PAC in the sixties, its origin was obscure. Was it the land of barbarians in old British maps or a name for a country of slaves in East Africa? Evelyn Waugh's imaginary African state in *Black Mischief* was called Azania. The ANC rejected the name.

A wave of strikes swept Natal and broke out in mines and industries in the Transvaal during the early seventies. There was a new militancy in the air and, a significant development, workers had learned how vulnerable organizers were to arrest. There were no identifiable leaders of these strikes.

The collapse of Portuguese colonialism after five centuries gave a tremendous boost to black South Africans. When Mozambique became independent on 25 June 1975 President Samora Machel, leader of FRELIMO, welcomed Oliver Tambo as his comrade and brother-in-arms. The struggle for the liberation of Zimbabwe also received great impetus with Mozambique providing a base for Robert Mugabe's Zimbabwe African National Union (ZANU) guerrillas.

But in South Africa black exuberance was rapidly clamped down on with the detention of seventy-seven people under Section 6 of the Terrorism Act. They included Black Consciousness leaders who had been planning celebrations to express solidarity with FRELIMO, as well as men and women suspected of recruiting for the ANC.

Unexpectedly, when Winnie Mandela's bans ran out, they were not renewed. For the first time in twelve years she was free to leave Johannesburg and to attend and address gatherings. She joined in the demands for the release of the seventy-seven, describing her own experience a few years earlier under Section 6 of the Terrorism Act which, she said, was 'meant to destroy completely every form of opposition to this totalitarian state, a method of traumatization so as to destroy all personal autonomy, a savage and psychological process of dehumanizing those who dare to identify themselves with this struggle'.

She visited Durban where an old friend, Fatima Meer, was lecturer in sociology at Natal University. There the Black Women's Federation, formed by African, Indian and Coloured organizations, was gathering strength. 'I don't think that there is a country where women are as exploited as in this country,' Winnie said in a speech to the Federation. 'The black woman has to put up with the laws. She is faced with this and she has no status at all. . . The death of her husband means the automatic loss of her home. She has no rights whatsoever, just the same as a child.'

Women had played an outstanding role in fighting the cause of all black people; they were supposed to build the nation, yet they were in 'the most hopeless situation to try and bring up children in a society riddled with racial hatred'.

In the course of a series of speeches and interviews with the press, Winnie turned to the subject of the rising anger of young blacks. She warned that subjecting them to the brutal experience of detention and solitary confinement would result in 'painful consequences' for the country and that the Bantu Education Act, with its insistence on teaching Afrikaans to black children, would fail in its intention 'to instil the master-servant relationship'. 'There's an African saying,' she added, 'to the effect that a dying horse kicks. The country will suffer from the last kicks of the dying Afrikaner Nationalist horse.'

On 16 June 1976 from early in the morning huge crowds of excited black schoolchildren gathered in Soweto to march in protest against being forced to study in the Afrikaans language. Police moved in to block them and shot dead Hector Petersen, aged thirteen, and other boys and girls. As the children retaliated with sticks and stones, wanton police shooting multiplied the casualties. Two white men were stoned to death. Police and army, equipped for war, poured into the townships.

Police massacres of blacks had punctuated South Africa's history but nothing so terrible had been known: a modern armed force moving against schoolchildren. As the toll of death and injuries mounted, riots swept the country in massive destruction of buildings representing white domination. The young blacks who recklessly confronted the police and taunted the military were the products of Bantu Education: the system which Dr Verwoerd had conceived in order to condition them to servitude.

Students turned to the Black Parents' Association for urgent help for bereaved families. Winnie Mandela was one of its leaders, as were Dr Manas Buthelezi, respected theologian, Mrs Phakathi, President of the YMCA, and Dr Nthato Motlana, a Soweto community leader. They found doctors to assist Motlana in identifying the corpses, undertakers to donate coffins, and taxis to transport people to the funerals. The BPA became spokesman not only for Soweto's distraught parents but for the rebellious students who, though quite capable of speaking for themselves, had no wish to meet the authorities.

'We know what we want,' Winnie Mandela told a public protest meeting. 'Our aspirations are dear to us. We are not *asking* for majority rule; it is our right, we shall have it at any cost. We are aware that the road before us is uphill, but we shall fight to the bitter end for justice.' Within weeks she was among women, men and students detained under the Internal Security Act, the re-titled Suppression of Communism Act. They were held in the Johannesburg Fort for five months.

While tens of thousands of black pupils boycotted schools, with teachers resigning and parents joining protest stay-at-home strikes, the uprising continued – a 'baptism of fire' in which the youth lost their fear of violence, as the government Commission of Inquiry put it. The thousand-page report amounted to a severe indictment of apartheid for causing 'hatred' of the whites, and recorded witnesses' bitter condemnation of separate development, group areas and, above all, influx control and the pass laws.

During sixteen months, recorded deaths numbered some six hundred but were thought to be nearer a thousand – all but two of them black, and most of them school pupils shot by police. Nearly four thousand injured; thousands more vanished into detention, some to spend five years in solitary confinement, some never to be seen by their parents again. Hundreds managed to cross the borders and head north, seeking military training or hoping to acquire a genuine education.

On Robben Island, 16 June had been wretchedly wet and cold. Mandela and the others on the sea-weed *span* strongly objected to working under such conditions. They were forced to go out. Warders accused them of not working properly and that afternoon when they returned, frozen and filthy from the sea-weed, they found the hot water in the showers had been cut off. They guessed that there had been some important event but only later did they learn that the children of Soweto had, as Winnie Mandela put it, 'risen and fought battles on behalf of their elders'.

Students convicted for their part in the uprising soon occupied a communal section on the Island; like the Namibians and men sentenced under the Terrorism Act, they must be segregated from the influence of Mandela, Sisulu and other long-established leaders. At least nine of the students were under eighteen years old.

Among themselves the men could discuss these events but there remained a total prohibition on referring to them during visits or in letters. However, at this time Mandela wrote to his wife telling about a tomato plant he had inadvertently damaged in the garden he now tended in the special section. He described the plant's beauty, how it had grown and grown, how he had cared for it and how, when it died, he pulled it from the soil, washed the roots and thought of the life that might have been. Winnie understood that this was a metaphor for a child growing up in the South African situation – as a parent you gave it whatever you could, nursing that life to a young age, and then it was mowed down – his feelings were the feelings of the parents at the mowing down of those hundreds of children. 'If he had written to me about that, I wouldn't have got the letter,' she has explained.★

Memories of friendships, and of events which had happened before their capture, were a vital part of everyday life. The men reminisced and reminded each other; they shared the news in their letters and, on occasion, they mourned. Several friends from the 1940s had died: Yusuf Dadoo and Michael Scott, Bram Fischer and Lilian Ngoyi. Fischer, serving the tenth year of his life sentence in Pretoria Central, died of cancer in May 1975; after the funeral the authorities demanded the return of his ashes to the jail. And Robert Sobukwe, leader of the rival PAC, who

★ *Part of My Soul*, Penguin Books, 1985.

had been reconciled to Mandela through the years of imprisonment, and who since his release from the Island had lived under bans in Kimberley, also died of cancer; he was in his early fifties.

That torture and murder had become endemic in the interrogation of detainees was most blatantly revealed by the last days in the life of Steve Biko: after three weeks' interrogation at police headquarters in Port Elizabeth he was taken, naked and nearly comatose, on a 700-mile drive in the back of a Land-Rover to the Pretoria prison where he died the next day, 12 September 1977. His close friend, Mapetla Mohapi, had also died in detention and a young Indian, Ahmed Timol, was killed in a drop from the tenth floor of security police headquarters in Johannesburg. The South African police and Bureau of State Security (BOSS) were forces to be reckoned with outside the country as well: a SASO leader, Abraham Tiro, was but the first of several activists killed by a parcel bomb; he was in Botswana at the time.

In October 1977 virtually every leader and organizer of the Black Consciousness movement still at large was detained. All organizations including cultural, trade union and self-help were banned, along with two black newspapers and such sympathetic whites as the Reverend Beyers Naude, Afrikaner head of the Christian Institute.

The detention of Dr Motlana, Chairman of the Committee of Ten in Soweto, was further evidence that the government would not tolerate authentic African organizations or leadership. This Committee represented the most positive effort yet made by urban blacks to propose alternatives to government policies and to the government-appointed hirelings who were contemptuously regarded as stooges and puppets, whether in urban areas or in Bantustans. Motlana, first active in the ANC Youth League at Fort Hare and the Defiance Campaign of 1952, had become a respected community spokesman, and his reputation must have been considerably enhanced by the government crediting him and Winnie Mandela with incitement of the June 1976 uprising.

In the subsequent trial, he and Winnie not only rebutted state evidence but won a R6,000 defamation case.

But the state had a further and very special form of punishment for Winnie Mandela. Early on the morning of 16 May 1977, twenty policemen in camouflage uniform arrived at her house in Soweto and ordered her to pack her possessions. She was to be banished for seven years. The government feared her influence on the students; besides, this crude and arbitrary uprooting from the only home she and Mandela knew came just a week before Andrew Young – American Ambassador to the United Nations – was due to visit Soweto.

Police drove her, with seventeen-year-old Zindzi, three hundred miles to the south-west, to a village called Brandfort in the flatlands of the Orange Free State, where they dumped mother and daughter at house No. 802 in the dusty location. It was the most alien environment the state could have chosen: politically and culturally the essence of Afrikanerdom; indeed it was there that Hendrik Verwoerd had spent formative years as his father hawked Bibles and religious tracts for the Dutch Reformed Church. The Mandelas spoke neither of the local languages, Afrikaans and Sotho.

Voortrekker Straat, as the main road was called, connected the *dorp*'s amenities for the two thousand whites: churches, a Standard Bank, a Barclays Bank, a Post Office, two hotels, a supermarket, newsagent and filling station, a railway station and an Afrikaans school. A rough track, watched over by the Bantu Administration office, led to the location, Phathakahle (Handle with Care), which, a journalist remarked, was singularly appropriate to the new arrival. Here the amenities for nearly three thousand blacks were a Bantu store and a beerhall – sufficient for the subsistence of blacks considered mere 'labour units'.

'My cells', Winnie called the three-roomed concrete house: no ceilings, no running water, no electricity, an outside bucket lavatory. It was a dwelling like all the others, except that hers was filled with rubble, and the furniture which she had been ordered to bring from home could not be fitted through the small doors and had to be sent back to Orlando.

Not only was she restricted to Brandfort, but she was placed under house arrest each night, through weekends and on public holidays; visitors were forbidden and whenever she left the house, she was prohibited from being with more than one person at a time. Sergeant Prinsloo, a gloomy man, kept guard outside, watching from his car, following her whenever she went out: 'doing his duty', as he put it; 'dedicated to messing up her life', as an American observer put it.

If the state intended that Mandela's wife should be subdued, if not broken, by this exile among particularly hostile whites and illiterate blacks, it was a laughable miscalculation. Brandfort was set by the ears when this sophisticated, beautiful black woman strode into supermarket and Post Office and bank: white preserves which blacks dared not enter; there were queues for service at small windows outside. And when she and Zindzi not only entered the one 'fashion' shop but proceeded to try on dresses, the police were sent for in the ensuing fracas. For Winnie the behaviour of the whites revealed the psychological nature of their fear: the Afrikaner had retreated into his laager and he had trapped himself there. She thought it sad.

Her neighbours in the location had been warned against consorting with this 'dangerous communist' but gradually they plucked up courage; they could not long resist her warmth and generosity. She was appalled by the deprivation – the poverty, hunger and subservience – and began thinking out ways of helping them.

But the ubiquitous Sergeant Prinsloo soon brought her to court in Bloemfontein. Winnie had gone to see a neighbour to find out where to buy coal and, while she was there, a man had come by, carrying a chicken he had just bought. Winnie had asked the price. The prosecutor, in submitting that this constituted a 'gathering' of three people and therefore a contravention of her banning orders, went on to chide her for 'flaunting ANC colours': she was wearing a dress in black, green and yellow.

'Among the limited rights still left to me,' Winnie retorted, 'is the choice of a wardrobe.' The magistrate found her guilty, and gave her a suspended sentence. Outside the court, people cheered her.

The South African press was prohibited from quoting a banned person, but a correspondent from *The New York Times* elicited her opinion. 'The rulers of this country have really gone insane,' she said. 'I mean in what other country would the price of chickens be entered as evidence?' On appeal the sentence was quashed and Winnie was acquitted.

Before long she was back in court, charged with receiving visitors. 'I will be thinking of you,' Mandela wrote on one of these occasions, 'especially as you are ordered to the dock, and as you listen to the expected and unexpected turns in the state evidence. I am solidly behind you and know too well that you suffer because of your love of and loyalty to the children and me, as well as to our large family. It is an evergrowing love and loyalty . . .'*

It amused Winnie that so much effort and money should be spent by the state on such cases, and it amazed her that people could be so petty and insensitive. But what deeply angered her, and her husband when she was able to share her anxiety with him, was the effect on Zindzi. Prinsloo's constant spying, his arrest of Zindzi's friends who had come from Soweto to visit her, the stress and hardship of life in Brandfort, had brought on serious depression and she had to abandon her studies at a crucial time while she saw a psychiatrist. Only after her father had brought the matter before the Supreme Court was her right to have visitors established. Winnie could not bring the application because, under South African law, black women were minors.

To Mandela's delight, Zindzi was becoming a writer and had had an article published. 'You have already received your first cheque. That's no small achievement at your age,' he complimented her. He added words of advice: 'Writing is a prestigious

---

* Letter of 1 March 1981.

profession which puts one right into the centre of the world and, to remain on top, one has to work really hard, the aim being a good and original theme, simplicity in expression and the use of the irreplaceable word.'

Zindzi had written to reassure him that Brandfort was 'a nice place after all' and he replied:

I can't believe it. Mum has lost almost everything; she'll never get any job there except perhaps as domestic or farm hand or washer-woman; she'll spend all her days in poverty. She's described the sort of structure in which you must now live and the type of toilet and water facilities that you have to use . . .

Nonetheless, darling, I'm glad to note that you're adjusting your-self and trying to be happy all the same. I felt tremendous when I read the line 'a nice place after all'. As long as you have an iron will, you can turn misfortune into advantage, as you yourself say. Were it not so, Mum would have been a complete wreck by now.*

Zindzi had found an outlet in writing poetry, at which she had excelled while at Waterford School. Usually she crumpled up what she had written and tossed it in the waste-paper basket. Her mother became adept at retrieving such poems and in 1978 a collection was published, together with photographs by an old friend of the family, Peter Magubane. Zindzi dedicated the book to her parents and, in the opening poem, wrote of her father:

A tree was chopped down
and the fruit was scattered
I cried
because I had lost a family
the trunk, my father
the branches, his support
so much
the fruit, the wife and children
who meant so much to him
tasty
loving as they should be

* Letter of 4 September 1977.

all on the ground
some out of his reach
in the ground
the roots, happiness
cut off from him.*

Zindzi's book won a $1,000 prize in the first annual Janusz Korczak Literary Competition, an award for books about children that exemplified selflessness and human dignity. She was denied a passport and in New York Magubane accepted the award on her behalf. It honoured a Jewish Polish paediatrician who had refused to leave children in the Warsaw ghetto, perishing with them in the Nazi gas chambers of Treblinka.

'The centre and cornerstone of the struggle for freedom and democracy in South Africa lies inside South Africa itself,' Mandela had said in 1962. During 1977 the armed struggle began in earnest as guerrillas and saboteurs filtered back across the borders. These were young men who had been educated on the battlefields of the townships from Soweto to New Brighton to Langa; now their readiness for self-sacrifice was seen as the measure of their determination totally to reject what they called 'the system'.

Among ANC recruits to be captured soon after re-entry, to be detained under the Terrorism Act and brought to trial, was Solomon Mahlangu. He himself had not shot anyone but he was sentenced to death. Despite appeals or protests from western governments and from the East, and even from the widow of one of the whites killed in the incident in which he had been involved, he was hanged. Another recruit in his early twenties, Mosima Tokyo Sexwale, was tried alongside veterans who had already served sentences on Robben Island. Sentenced to eighteen years imprisonment, he said he was willing to make the sacrifice for his ideals and he had no doubt those ideals would triumph.

The political prisoners could not know that Umkhonto had

* From *Black As I Am,* Guild of Tutors Press of International College, Los Angeles, California, 1978.

clashed with police and army, but bit by bit they pieced together the fact that the struggle was moving forward. During 1977 there were ninety-five trials under security laws, an index both of escalation and of mistakes made: the charges concerned recruiting for military training, forming cells, smuggling arms and explosives or engaging in sabotage or guerrilla activity.

Zindzi Mandela attended the trial of the Soweto Students' Representative Council, accused of masterminding the continuing protests after the June 1976 uprising. It was the beginning of her role as deputy for her imprisoned father and exiled mother.

Zeni, meanwhile, had married Prince Thumbumuzi Dlamini, son of King Sobhuza of Swaziland. They had diplomatic privilege which allowed them to have a 'contact' visit to Mandela: it would be his first experience of normal human contact with his family since his imprisonment. In June 1978, with their year-old baby, they went from Mbabane to Robben Island and, as they all came together in the visitors' room, Zeni thought her father would break down. She nearly dropped the child as she ran to him, but her husband took the little girl and Zeni and her father held each other. Then Mandela took the baby and as they sat talking Zeni saw that he knew just what to do, although he had not held a child since she herself was small. 'He noticed when the baby needed her nappies changed and even knew to make her burp, then he played with her and she went to sleep.'*

Mandela already had four grandchildren: Thembi's two daughters and Makgatho's sons. Now he chose the baby's name, Zaziwe (Hope), and two weeks later the christening took place in the Anglican cathedral in Bloemfontein. Winnie was permitted to travel the thirty miles from Brandfort provided she returned home by noon. The godparents were the 91-year-old Dr Moroka, who had been President-General of the ANC during the Defiance Campaign, and Helen Joseph, a close and muchloved friend of the Mandelas. 'Sacred to us', Winnie has said of this woman whose long record of triumphantly resisting every

* *Part of My Soul*, Penguin Books, 1985.

kind of police persecution was 'our history in its real form'. Grandmother and godmother were prevented by bans from doing more than smile at each other. At the age of seventy-three Mrs Joseph had just spent two weeks in prison for refusing to give information to the police about a visit she had paid to Winnie in Brandfort.

Mandela's sixtieth birthday in July 1978 was an occasion to celebrate internationally the man *The New York Times* said would probably head a black government in South Africa. In the House of Commons in London, a meeting honoured him and, since Mandela himself was not allowed to receive the mass of greetings cards from all parts of the world, these had been addressed to No. 802, the Location, Brandfort. There the family gathered to pray for all political prisoners.

'Had it not been for your visits, wonderful letters and your love,' Mandela was to write to Winnie, 'I would have fallen apart many years ago.' Every morning, he had told her in an earlier letter, he dusted her photo carefully; now he went on: 'I paused here and drank some coffee, after which I dusted the photo on my bookcase. I start with that of Zeni, which is on the outer side, then Zindzi's and lastly, yours . . .'*

* Letter of 6 May 1979.

14

'RELEASE MANDELA!'

1978–81

The forced inactivity of prison life obliged Mandela and his comrades to 'sit back and look at the whole scene', as Mac Maharaj, serving a twelve-year sentence, put it. Pulled out from the rush of everyday life, in which they saw only one corner of their world, they had an opportunity to see the general direction of developments and changes. Mandela's approach, as he pieced together news from the outside world, was to look for contradictions in the regime's behaviour, to see how these could be widened by the liberation movement, thereby narrowing the government's base of operations.

He was to find plenty of contradictions as P. W. Botha, the new Prime Minister, embarked on a haphazard course by which he sought to disarm intensified international condemnation with reformist rhetoric, while reinforcing not simply white control, but Afrikaner Nationalist domination. Whatever the cost, Afrikanerdom must survive.

Botha had come to power in September 1978 after a corruption scandal had brought down J. B. Vorster. He had been succeeded as Minister of Defence by General Magnus Malan.

Since South Africa's invasion of Angola in 1975 and the escalation of the war in Namibia, the Defence Force had almost doubled in size to an estimated five hundred thousand in 1979. Blacks were recruited into combat units. And on 22 September 1979, according to the US Naval Research Laboratory, South Africa detonated a nuclear device in the southern ocean.

While police continued to uncover caches of weapons in widely separated areas from Soweto to Cape Town, during May 1979 Umkhonto guerrillas embarked on new action, attacking police stations in black townships. Three policemen were killed.

General Malan's advice to the country was that you could not fight effectively with 85 per cent of the population sympathetic to the guerrillas; defences against an ultimate 'onslaught' must therefore be built not just by military but by economic and political initiatives.

'Total onslaught' was the government's new catch-phrase to replace the previous bogeys, which had ranged from *swart gevaar* (black danger) to 'communism', 'sickly humanism' and 'liberalism'.

The Botha/Malan strategy for the retention of white power was based on the need to co-opt middle-class blacks by giving them a stake in the system, and this objective had the backing of big business. The 'changes' that were vaunted included electricity for some townships, an easing of restrictions on black businesses, and the opening of certain hotels, restaurants and theatres to the black bourgeoisie. Increased educational facilities, especially in the technical field, were somewhat undermined by the fact that the gap in expenditure for the various races was as wide as ever: R621 for each white student and R72 for each African student (according to parliamentary figures for 1978–9).

Certainly the government was now prepared to grant 99-year leases to blacks on homes in urban townships; however, should the lease-holder lose his or her job or transgress a law, the right to the lease was lost. In Soweto alone twenty-five thousand families were on the waiting-list for houses.

The talk of 'change', as one American correspondent perceived, aimed 'to split prosperous urbanites from impoverished rural peasants', thus militating against 'a united front of black people dedicated to the overthrow of white rule'. Ironically, for an avowedly anti-communist government, 'class' was coming to replace 'race' as the dominant feature of segregation.

As part of the new propaganda, apartheid must be camouflaged: the Department of Bantu Administration was called Plural Relations and then Cooperation and Development. A new Minister, Piet Koornhof, told Americans in June 1979 that apartheid was 'dying and dead'; a claim quickly contradicted by Prime Minister Botha, who said he preferred the term 'good neighbourliness' to 'apartheid'.

Black spokesmen gave their opinions: Percy Qoboza (who had been detained in 1977 when the *World* had been banned), as editor of the *Sunday Post*, remarked that if apartheid was dead, urgent funeral arrangements needed to be made because 'the body is still around and is making a terrible smell'. Dr Nthato Motlana said he could not believe the black people would fall for this kind of 'confidence trick'. Headlines in the western press were little consolation to the South African government: THE NIGHTMARE AHEAD FOR SOUTH AFRICA, TIME RUNS OUT FOR SOUTH AFRICA, PRETORIA SAYS NO TO HOPE, PASS SYSTEM: DAILY AFFRONT TO BLACK SOUTH AFRICANS.

An essential factor in government policy which aimed at dividing urban blacks into privileged and destitute was the removal of the latter (except when they were required as labour units on short-term contracts) from the 87 per cent of the country claimed as 'white'. Since the inception of apartheid two million Africans had been forcibly 'resettled' in the ten home-lands: 'dumped like sacks of potatoes', said Bishop Desmond Tutu, General-Secretary of the South African Council of Churches. In 1979 under two new laws millions more were to be moved.

The Black Sash, an organization of white women who for six-teen years had dedicated themselves to assisting Africans caught in the web of the pass laws, had never before experienced such anger or such a sense of 'impending catastrophe'. The anger would not be confined to the homelands, they warned. 'People are not going to sit and watch their sons and daughters die of hunger. They will remain in the towns and, as they are hounded from their places of illegal accommodation . . . their rage will be fuelled, to fuel again the rage of those who are legally in town and to whom so many promises have been made but not fulfilled.'

A warning to the leaders of the business community was given not only by the Black Sash in their journal but by Allister

Sparks, editor of the *Rand Daily Mail*. *Sash* pointed out that a 'visible alliance between government and big business in the "total strategy"' was causing personal disaster to thousands of individuals and could only result in 'the black–white political conflict becoming irrevocably identified with the Marxist–capitalist economic conflict'. Sparks, in September 1979, wrote that 'More and more blacks – especially young blacks – are beginning to identify apartheid with the capitalist system, and to see their struggle to overthrow apartheid in terms of a struggle to overthrow the capitalist system as a whole.'

After four years of economic recession following the 1976 Soweto massacre, with the price of gold rocketing, South Africa was into a boom. The surplus revenue from gold of more than 40 per cent above the 1978 total came at a critical time, and more than offset the rise in prices of oil and of armaments. To the casual white observer the country appeared prosperous and stable. But at the giant Anglo-American Corporation the four hundred thousand black miners were earning less than a fifth of white miners' pay and when the price of gold had risen to $400 an ounce, their request for a Christmas bonus had been turned down. Mandela had called the gold mines 'the most vicious system of exploitation'.

Throughout the country black unemployment was one in four and rising. This meant nearly two million workers queueing for jobs, joined each year by hundreds of thousands of rebellious school leavers. For whites thousands of jobs lay vacant and white immigrants were welcomed by the State President and invited to become citizens, with the promise for themselves and their descendants of 'peace, happiness and prosperity'.

'In 1976,' said Bishop Tutu, 'the anger came from people's heads. Now it is coming from their guts and that is much more serious.'

'The gunpowder is there,' said the Chairman of the Soweto Teachers' Action Committee, 'all it is waiting for is a spark.'

All the while news of events in Rhodesia was followed by both blacks and whites in the south. At last, in 1979, the guerrilla war, combined with economic and diplomatic pressures, achieved a breakthrough: with the support of the Frontline States and the Commonwealth, and also the unlikely cooperation of the South African government spurred on by Henry Kissinger, the British convened a conference at Lancaster House at which all sides to the conflict were brought together and a ceasefire agreed. After seven years of armed struggle Zimbabwe was independent, with Robert Mugabe its Prime Minister. Ian Smith, who only a few years earlier had sworn that not in his lifetime would there be black majority rule, now said that 'living and working with our enemies has never been a problem'.

For South Africa the question presented itself with greater urgency than ever before: must there be a yet more terrible sacrifice in lives and human resources before the white government recognized the elementary facts so clearly spelled out to the north?

From exile the ANC declared 1980 the 'Year of Action' and celebrated the twenty-fifth anniversary of the Freedom Charter. Oliver Tambo circulated a message from political prisoners on Robben Island; issued in the name of Mandela, this had been drafted by Maharaj and smuggled out of the jail:

> The gun has played an important part in our history. The resistance of the black man to white colonial intrusion was crushed by the gun. Our struggle to liberate ourselves from white domination is held in check by force of arms ... The toll of dead and injured since the 1976 uprising has surpassed that of all previous massacres.
>
> What lies ahead? From our rulers, we can expect nothing. They are the ones who give orders to the soldier crouching over his rifle, theirs is the spirit that moves the finger that caresses the trigger. Vague promises, tinkerings with the machinery of apartheid, constitutional juggling, massive arrests and detentions, side by side with renewed overtures aimed at weakening and forestalling the unity of us blacks and dividing the forces of change – these are the fixed paths along which they will move. For they are neither capable nor willing to heed the verdict of the masses of our people.

That verdict was: apartheid had failed. And the prisoners went on to call for 'black unity'. That was the first condition for victory: 'This is not the time for the luxury of division and disunity. At all levels and in every walk of life, we must close ranks ... differences must be submerged to the achievement of a single goal – the complete overthrow of apartheid and race domination.' Confidently the men declared, 'The world is on our side ... victory is certain.'

One of Mandela's strengths as a leader was his determination to seek unifying points among people of differing views. It was vital, he said, to work against divisiveness, not just in theory but in daily practice. On the Island, according to Fikile Bam, a member of the Unity Movement, he showed great tolerance, was always ready to listen, slow to express an opinion, slower to criticize positions of others unless he was sure he fully understood. Where he personally came in for criticism was from younger men or those with a rigid ideological view who felt his politeness to warders was a sign of moderation, of 'softness'. This, said Bam, was unjust. He was always firm with prison officials, having complete confidence in himself and control over his emotions. Nor had he any need to rely on slogans and rhetoric. Along with Sisulu, he remained the most respected and, indeed, revered leader.

As for unity on the mainland, Black Consciousness followers and Chief Gatsha Buthelezi, chief minister of the KwaZulu homeland and head of Inkatha, the Zulu nationalist movement which he had founded, engaged in mutual recrimination; a dispute which had its parallel abroad, where Buthelezi was at loggerheads with the ANC. He used the ANC colours and claimed to lead the largest black nationalist organization, but Inkatha showed no sign of actively confronting the government.

The ANC's reputation among the 'masses' was clearly boosted by new forms of action: early in 1980 Umkhonto guerrillas for the first time attacked a white police station; heavily guarded oil installations near Johannesburg were sabotaged; and, outside Pretoria, three young Umkhonto men who had left the country after June 1976 took hostages at a bank, demanding Mandela's release. All three were killed, as well as two women hostages, when police stormed the bank. Some twenty thousand people lined the streets of Soweto and crowded the cemetery for their funeral. Most blacks, reported a survey, regarded them as 'heroes, brave men desperate to bring about change'.

Pressure for change to come about peaceably was exerted not only by English-language newspapers but by two influential Afrikaner Nationalist newspapers. The editor of *Die Vaderland* warned that the country must learn to negotiate with radical as well as 'traditional' black leaders. 'The more radical they are the more support they have,' he conceded. *Die Beeld* said that such leaders 'are not just agitators and instigators. They are fighting for their rights just as the Afrikaners were fighting for theirs' – the same argument Mandela and his comrades had put in their petition some ten years earlier. And the call for a National Convention which he had made nearly twenty years earlier was now widely renewed. A banner headline FREE MANDELA! announced the start of a campaign initiated by the black newspaper *Sunday Post* on 9 March 1980.

Black community leaders insisted that before they themselves would participate in a National Convention, all political prisoners must be freed, exiles allowed to return, bans lifted from ANC, PAC and other black organizations, and apartheid scrapped. 'We believe that Alice-in-Wonderland solutions presently being pursued in this country are leading us slowly and painfully to a crisis,' said the *Post*'s editor, Percy Qoboza.

As the campaign gathered force, the *Post*'s headline the following week was LET MY FATHER GO. Pictures of Zindzi and her niece, Zaziwe, and of Winnie Mandela giving the *Amandla!* salute, surrounded an article about Mandela's life.

On the eve of the twentieth anniversary of Sharpeville, white students organized a crowded meeting in the Great Hall of the University of the Witwatersrand. 'Why shouldn't we be the first people in history to surrender from a position of power?' asked Sheen a Duncan, Black Sash leader. Qoboza addressed his statement to white South Africa: 'We believe the most visible act of faith by the government would be to release Nelson Mandela.'

Zindzi Mandela told the huge gathering: 'I have not joined you as a daughter calling for the release of her father. I have joined as part of my generation who have never known what a normal life is.' She spoke of what it was like for all those without a father and sometimes without a mother. Her generation had seen grave crimes of oppression committed against the people. Childhood conversations had been about the latest pass raids, whose father or mother had been detained, in which prison, when last they were visited and when the most recent police raid on the home took place.

> As years went by the reality of our grim situation dawned, as we not only watched trial after trial of our parents, our brothers and sisters, but saw more losing their lives in the hands of those who have the liberty to seize them any time from their loved ones. Without suggesting that I have suffered personally more than any black child, I have known the horrors of harassments. I've known the horrors of seeing my parents sacrifice all the material things, to fight for justice, honour and human dignity. I've seen them give up everything for the cause. I've seen millions of parents do this, but I've also seen these sacrifices achieve more and more of a loss of the very freedom they fought for ... I've seen the suffering of my people escalating to boiling point. I've seen the thunderous eruption of the Soweto volcano when my generation could take it no longer.

What horrified her, she added, was that throughout her father's active political career he had offered solutions for the country's problems, and had said that unless they were listened to, violence would escalate in an uncontrollable form. And Zindzi concluded: 'The call therefore for Mandela's release is merely to say there is an alternative to the inevitable bloodbath.'

Three days later on 23 March 1980 in the Regina Mundi Catholic church in Soweto, five thousand people commemorating Sharpeville responded to Dr Motlana's call for the release of Mandela and other political prisoners. Bishop Tutu, whose passport had just been withdrawn as punishment for his outspokenness, endorsed the *Post*'s 'Free Mandela' petition on behalf of the Executive of the SA Council of Churches. 'Needless suffering and bloodshed such as have been endured by the people of Zimbabwe,' stated the Council, 'can only he avoided if Mandela and other leaders in prison or in exile are enabled to share in the reshaping of a unitary South African society.'

As many thousands added their signatures to the petition, among them Winnie Mandela, the campaign gained international support. On 13 June 1980 the Security Council of the UN called on the government to release Mandela and the other political prisoners; only thus could 'meaningful discussion of the future of the country' be achieved.

The Afrikaner Nationalist press, whose call for a National Convention in the wake of Mugabe's victory in Zimbabwe had helped to precipitate the campaign, now denounced it as 'a bald propaganda trick'. But an important voice spoke up from the conservative business community: the senior researcher to the SA Foundation, which sought to improve South Africa's image abroad, said Mandela's release would be 'symbolic of the government's determination to effect a reconciliation between the races'.

In parliament on 15 April 1980 the Minister of Police and Prisons castigated all those campaigning for Mandela's release. He quoted an editorial in the *Cape Times* of 12 March which said that with the end of the war in Rhodesia and the election of a black government there, 'the lessons to be learnt from Rhodesia's mistakes are obvious. The release of Mandela would be an excellent starting-point . . .'

'If this is not an outrageous influencing of the public of South Africa,' said the Minister, 'then I do not know what is. This call was taken up by just about every other English-language newspaper in South Africa. But this is nothing new. This campaign for the release of Mandela is nothing new . . .' And he proceeded to give what he called a 'factual' account of Mandela's record, which claimed that he had travelled through Africa on documents supplied 'by the Russian KGB', and that he had visited countries behind the Iron Curtain in order to coordinate sabotage and terrorist campaigns (a unique event for Britain to be labelled 'countries behind the Iron Curtain'). Mandela, he concluded in the same vein, 'remains just as staunch a communist and just as staunch a member of the SA ANC as he had been all his life'.

In short, the government refused to set Mandela free. The Prime Minister exploded in anger when dissident students at the Afrikaner University of Stellenbosch booed and hissed his declaration that he would not release the 'arch-Marxist'. A court of law had sentenced Mandela and he must serve his sentence for life.

A singular protest came from General van den Bergh, the former head of BOSS, who had fallen into disfavour with the government. He said that Mandela was not a 'communist' but 'stood for black nationalism just as Afrikaners still stand for Afrikaner nationalism'.

By the end of May it was clear that the government had swept aside the opportunity for peaceful negotiation. The Afrikaner *volk* were inexorably concerned with survival on their own terms and, with immense military and economic power, they had chosen to go down fighting in face of the black revolution. The struggle threatened to be prolonged, with appalling consequences.

The 'Free Mandela' campaign had come to stand for the demand for release of all political prisoners. They themselves could now read about its progress. Their sixteen-year struggle for access to news was at last successful: on 13 May 1980 the Minister of Prisons, Louis le Grange, announced that they could receive one English-language daily and one Afrikaans newspaper. And they could buy groceries and toiletries from a prison commissary, using money they had earned by gardening. The days of hard labour were over, at least for Mandela and the others in the special section.

Each time Winnie returned from visiting Mandela, she spoke of his 'fantastic spirits', 'our PM on holiday'. She said, 'Don't believe those stories in the Nationalist press about a tottering old man. He's as upright and proud as the day he was arrested.' And he was much more confident, she added.

As for herself: 'I look forward to the visits so much,' she told Allister Sparks, 'but the trip back is awful. I feel so empty. Look, I'm confident he will come off the Island one day. I have no doubt about that. But I can't help thinking of all these years of our lives that have gone down the drain, our best years. Nelson is sixty-three now, and I am like a young girl, still longing for the experience of married life.'*

Winnie had just been served with a new order restricting her to a further five years in Brandfort. Three years earlier, in May 1979, shortly after Zindzi had left her to return to Johannesburg, she had written to me in London:

> Well since miracles don't stop happening, the first thing I'll do when I'm unbanned (if I ever am) is to go to church to thank God for letting your letter reach me at a time when I was thinking of all our dear friends and taking stock of myself, a common feature of exile. Being with Zindzi in the past two years sort of cushioned the impact of the pain; now she is gone to prepare for e ams and is with Helen.
>
> It is the first time that I truly feel what my little Siberia is all about. The empty long days drag on, one like the other, no matter how hard I try to study. The solitude is deadly, the grey matchbox shacks, so desolate, simply stare at you as lifeless as the occupants, who form a human chain of frustration as they pass next to my window. From the moment the bar opens until it closes at eight p.m., they are paralytic drunk; schoolchildren who find nothing to eat at home when they return from pseudo-schools simply join their parents there.
>
> They haven't even the 'honour' of being sojourners in this ghetto, they are spare labour units of the fat farmers who threw them out of their farms in the first place. The highest wage is R5 a month for the lucky mothers. Social life is the nightly raids and funerals!

* *Observer*, January 1982.

How grim that must sound, yet there's something so purifying about exile. Each minute is a reminder that blackness alone is a commitment in our sick society; it is so strengthening too. I have no doubt how sacrosanct our cause is and how near we are to our goal in terms of historical periods. What could be greater than being part of such a cause no matter how infinitesimal our contribution is.

In those three years Winnie Mandela had transformed her life in Brandfort as foreign and local correspondents discovered when, one by one, they came to interview her about the effects of the new order of exile. There was never a flicker of self-pity, only bright peals of laughter, particularly when she told of Prinsloo's continuing dedication: one evening she had emerged from the house at 9.30 p.m. to throw out her bath water and there he was, watching from his car. As for the *dorp*'s white community, three people had become friendly but to most, she explained, it was as if she 'symbolized some terrible threat: the deep fear the Afrikaner has of his extinction'. The mayor, owner of a hotel and liquor store, confided to one correspondent, 'Yes, people were unhappy when she came here, but we have got used to her. We accept her now. She is clean and well-behaved. She comes in here to buy things: champagne, Cinzano, stuff like that. I've spoken to her, and she's well-educated.'★

The transformation had begun through her being accepted by her neighbours, so that she could say, 'I live with the people; we love each other. Bringing me here conscientized them in a manner no organization could; the ANC should be grateful, I don't need to stand on platforms or shout.' Children started greeting her by raising their fists in the *Amandla!* sign. Blacks, who saw whites waiting while Winnie used 'their' public telephone outside the Post Office, began themselves to use the phone. In 1981 there had been small strikes by workers in a

★ Allister Sparks, *Observer*, January 1982.

bakery and by night-soil removers for higher wages. In Brand-fort, these were political strides.

A crèche and meals for children, soup for the aged, a clinic, a sewing group which enabled women to make money by selling school uniforms – these were the practical endeavours in which western embassies competed to provide assistance: if Winnie could not go to the outside world, its representatives came to her.

The most visible effect however was brought about by her years of hard work in creating an oasis in the arid location; and as her garden with its lawn, flowers, vegetables and fruit trees flourished, her neighbours were encouraged to follow the exam-ple, with the SA Christian Council providing seeds for vegetables.

As for the house, there was still no bathroom but a tap had been installed, and friends had provided a paraffin fridge and battery television. There were stacks of books, fine African pots and bright patches of colour from neighbours' gifts of embroi-dery. Visitors could now come to the house and have tea under the willow tree beside the clinic.

A correspondent of the *Christian Science Monitor* visited Winnie early in 1981 and elicited her views of President Reagan's policy of constructive engagement. The United States government, she replied, was increasingly being viewed as a defender, even a promoter, of white minority rule in South Africa and the President had shown himself to be 'no friend of the black people'. Winnie declared that the South African government's policies were stoking black resentment to the point where a violent revolution was now 'inevitable' and she strongly criti-cized western investors, arguing that their involvement in South Africa contributed to the continued enslavement of black workers.

'We have one goal,' she said, 'to overthrow a minority government, a settler government.' And she pointed out that the government was bringing about its own destruction: 'If you strip men of each and every right, you can only organize them into a force to be reckoned with. The government is actually organizing the masses for us.' The South African government was responsible for the escalation of violence. 'They have created a revolution, and they blame it on us.' She defended the right of blacks to accept aid from any quarter, including the Soviet bloc, in order to bring about their own liberation. If America would not provide support for the struggle to end minority rule, it should at least drop all trade, sporting and diplomatic links with Pretoria.

In twenty years she had become a leader in her own right; and she had become more beautiful. 'I think it's because of the kids,' said Zeni when this was remarked on. 'They really keep her happy and busy, and when they play you see that glow in her eyes.' She had four grandchildren: Zeni and Thumbumuzi's two girls, Zaziwe born in 1977 and Zamaswazi in 1978, their boy, Zinhle, born in 1980, and Zindzi's baby girl, Zoleka, born in 1980, whose father Johannes 'Oupa' Seakamela had helped them settle into Brandfort.

Meanwhile Winnie had acquired a companion, a Rastafarian artist. To her husband she explained that this 'lodger' was a necessary precaution and Mandela, reassured, hoped she would look after him well.

Mandela's letters* expressed the feelings and thoughts of a husband and father for the family from whom he was forcibly separated, and whose happiness, security and educational progress profoundly concerned him.

'Doesn't your mother ever get depressed?' Zeni was asked. 'If she does, she hides it well,' was the answer. Oliver Tambo had once said of Nelson Mandela that he had never known him to be depressed. When it came to physical ailments, he touched on them lightly in his letters: 'On 16 August I saw an orthopaedic surgeon,' he wrote to Winnie in September 1979, 'and he examined my right heel which worries me now and again.'

* Those written between 1978 and 1980 are quoted in Fatima Meer's *Higher than Hope*, Penguin Books, 1990.

He went on to describe the voyage to Cape Town where he had seen the surgeon:

> The sea was rough and though I occupied a sheltered spot on the deck, it seemed that rain was falling. The boat rocked on endlessly, taking every wave on its prows. Midway between the Island and Cape Town an army of demons seemed to be on the rampage and, as the Dias was tossed about, it looked as if a thousand irons were falling apart. I kept my eyes glued on a lifebelt a few paces away. There were about five officials in between me and the belt, two young enough to be my grandsons. I said to myself, 'If something happens and this boat goes under, I will commit my last sin on earth and tender my humble apologies when I reach heaven. I will run over them all and be the first on that belt.' Fortunately no disaster overtook us.

In March 1981 he was entertained by the thought of competing with Princess Anne and Jack Jones for the Chancellorship of the University of London:

> The support of 7,199 against such prominent candidates must have inspired the children and all our friends inside and outside the country. To you in particular it must have been even more inspiring, turning that miserable shack into a castle, making its narrow rooms as spacious as those of Windsor. I want all our supporters to know that I did not expect to poll even a hundred, to say nothing of 7,199, against a British princess and against so distinguished an English reformer as Mr Jack Jones.

He had hoped that Winnie could represent him in Delhi in August 1980 – he was to be given the Nehru Award for International Understanding – but the South African government had denied her a passport. Oliver Tambo therefore read the statement which Mandela had to smuggle out of Robben Island after the prison authorities refused to forward it to India.

Recalling his student days in Johannesburg, when he had first become familiar with Pandit Nehru's book *The Unity of India*, Mandela referred to the Youth League's 'intense but narrow form of nationalism':

However, with experience, coupled with the unfurling of events at home and abroad, we acquired new perspectives and, as the horizon broadened, we began to appreciate the inadequacy of some youthful ideas. Time was to teach us, as Panditji says, that: 'Nationalism is good in its place but is an unreliable friend and an unsafe historian. It blinds us to many happenings and sometimes distorts the truth, especially when it concerns us and our country.'

In a world in which breathtaking advances in technology and communication have shortened the space between the erstwhile prohibitively distant lands; where outdated beliefs and imaginary differences among the people were being rapidly eradicated, where exclusiveness was giving way to cooperation and interdependence, we too found ourselves obliged to shed our narrow outlook and adjust to fresh realities.

Like the All-India Congress, one of the premier national liberation movements of the colonial world, we too began to assess our situation in a global context. We quickly learned the admonition of a great political thinker and teacher that no people in one part of the world could really be free while their brothers in other parts were still under foreign rule . . .

Mahatma Gandhi, he added, 'had exerted an incalculable influence' on the history of the peoples of both India and South Africa; 'indeed, it was on South African soil that Mahatmaji founded and embraced the philosophy of *Satyagraha*'. Mandela paid tribute to Nehru's sister, Madame Pandit, who as India's Ambassador to the United Nations during the 1950s had spoken for the people of South Africa and of Namibia.

The knowledge of shared suffering, though formidable in dimension, at the same time keeps alive in us our oneness with mankind and our own global responsibilities that accrue therefrom. It also helps to strengthen our faith and belief in our future. [He invoked Nehru's words:] 'In a world which is full of conflict and hatred and violence, it becomes more necessary than at any other time to have faith in human destiny. If the future we work for is full of hope for humanity, then the ills of the present do not matter much and we have justification for working for that future.'

In this knowledge we forge ahead firm in our beliefs, strengthened by the devotion and solidarity of our friends; above all by an underlying faith in our own resources and determination and in the invincibility of our cause.

15

'AN IDEA WHOSE TIME HAS COME'

1982–5

Winnie Mandela's confident expectation that her husband would 'come off the Island one day' was fulfilled, but not in the manner she had meant – not to freedom. One night in April 1982 Mandela and Sisulu, with three other Rivonia men – Kathrada, Mhlaba and Mlangeni – were ordered to pack their belongings and were abruptly transported to the mainland. Next morning when their comrades on the Island awoke, they found the five cells empty: Sisulu had been their confidant; Mandela, their father.

Winnie read of the move in a newspaper, then heard about it on television. Eventually she received a letter from the Prisons Department informing her that her husband had been transferred to Pollsmoor Maximum Security prison. No reason was given; she surmised that it could have been to put a stop to the administrative work he had been doing: funds had been sent to him to enable young prisoners to study. Or had the government hoped to dispel the concept 'Mandela on Robben Island' which had reached almost mythic proportions?

From Cape Town harbour the five men were driven in a closed-in army truck – standing all the way – nearly an hour's journey to Pollsmoor in the white suburb of Tokai. They could see nothing of the scenery – the valley between Table Mountain and the hills beyond the prison – one of South Africa's glories, with its wide-spreading vineyards and pine groves. It was the beginning of a cruel deprivation, to be cut off entirely from landscape, to be confined within high walls so that, as Mandela later told a visitor, he came to know what Oscar Wilde meant by 'the little tent of blue that prisoners call the sky'.

Pollsmoor, a modern complex of long, yellow-brick buildings, housed thousands of prisoners of all races in segregated sections. On the third floor of an 'isolation' building Mandela and his four companions were locked in a large dormitory cell with access to an L-shaped high-walled yard. Imprisoned with them was a young man, Patrick Maqubela, serving a twenty-year sentence.

Mandela continued with his routine, rising at 3.30 a.m. for two hours of exercises – what he called 'working up a good sweat' – reading and studying during the day.

The men found that certain conditions were an improvement on those of the Island: better food and, occasionally, meals from friends in Cape Town; they could now receive a range of newspapers, including the *Guardian Weekly* and *Time* magazine, as well as a radio: 'VHF only, unfortunately,' said Mandela, 'so that we can get South African stations, not the BBC.'

As Winnie found on her first visit there, the waiting-room was pleasant and in the cubicle a larger glass partition enabled her to see her husband from the waist upwards; instead of the phone, the sound was transmitted by special microphones and she could for the first time in twenty years hear his voice clearly. He looked and sounded very well. No longer was there a sharp warder's announcement of 'Time up!' Sergeant Gregory remarked, 'Mrs Mandela, you still have five minutes.' 'A really nice man', Zeni has said of this prison officer, who had changed as he grew to know Mandela and his comrades on the Island and who had accompanied the group to Pollsmoor. These modest improvements were valued by a couple who through the years had endured so much coarse treatment, such privation.

In a subsequent visit a year later in March 1983, Mandela broke the restriction on discussing prison conditions. He had opened the discussion, Winnie said afterwards, by telling the prison officers who were overseeing the visit that he was allowed to discuss the question of his health with his family: 'I have to discuss it as a result of the conditions here. It is a right.' It was the first time he had sounded a note of desperation, she wrote to me, as he told her that conditions were deteriorating terribly and his cell-mates had decided that he should inform her, with the object of conveying the facts to 'relevant people and the press'.

Most painful was the loss of the community life the men had enjoyed over the years in the special section on Robben Island and, whereas previously each had had his own cell, in Pollsmoor they were confined together and were completely isolated from all other prisoners. On the Island they had moved freely in their section and spent most of the day out of doors. Now they had no walks; they had not seen a blade of grass since leaving the Island. Those who wanted to study could not expect the others to remain silent, and other small 'privileges' which had helped make life bearable had been withdrawn. More serious was the hazard to health from water seeping through the cell wall when it rained; the men wanted an urgent medical inspection. Mandela, forced to wear a shoe that was too small, had to have an operation on a toe. It was a bitter irony that Robben Island should now seem an agreeable environment.

Winnie's report on her husband's protest about conditions was widely publicized abroad, with certain embellishments, since he and his comrades were the subject of growing international concern. No news of conditions in Pollsmoor had filtered out since the men's transfer. In July 1983 Helen Suzman was permitted to visit them and told a correspondent from *The New York Times* that she found Mandela fit and in good spirits. The cell, she said, was spacious and it was the yard, so she had been informed, and not the cell which sometimes flooded. As for Mandela's injured foot, when she'd inquired about it he had been surprised. 'That is his nature,' commented Winnie. 'He minimized it when talking to Helen. In fact, during my visit he took his shoe off and showed it through the window' – a recollection which made her laugh – 'I saw his foot for the first time in twenty-one years.'

Walter Sisulu celebrated his seventieth birthday in the cell; a packed meeting in the Great Hall of the University of the Witwatersrand had given a standing ovation in his honour.

The newcomer who had been imprisoned with the five Rivo-nia men, Patrick Maqubela, was a young lawyer found guilty of ANC offences and sentenced to twenty years for high treason; offences which previously had come under the Suppression of Communism Act as 'furthering the aims of an unlawful organiza-tion' were now charged as treason, enabling the state to call for a far higher sentence. Maqubela had been articled to Griffiths Mxenge, an attorney who had appeared for the families of men who had died in detention and in a SA Defence Force raid on ANC houses in Mozambique. Highly respected both in the Eastern Cape and in Durban, Mxenge had been treasurer of the Release Mandela Committee. On 20 November 1981 his badly mutilated body was found in a cycling stadium near Durban.

Mxenge's death was but one example of the violent deaths meted out to activists who effectively opposed the state. The Mandelas were deeply grieved by the death of their friend, Ruth First, killed by a letter bomb while at work in the University of Mozambique, in August 1982. 'Such waste, such beauty, a bundle of energy,' wrote Winnie. 'How could anyone be so cruel as to cut short such a fruitful life?'

Among the other men and women assassinated was Joe Gqabi, ANC representative in Zimbabwe and well known to Mandela and Sisulu; he had served a long sentence on Robben Island. The massive build-up in South Africa's Defence Force from 500,000 to 626,000 was accompanied by attacks on what it claimed were ANC bases in neighbouring countries. In 1981 ANC offices in Maputo were raided; thirteen men and women were killed. A year later houses in Maseru were the target; in the small hours of the morning people were massacred in their beds – among the forty-two killed were five women and children and twelve Basotho. In retaliation, ten days later Umkhonto blew up a section of the Koeberg nuclear power station near Cape Town, their most dramatic act of sabotage since an attack on the Sasol oil-from-coal plant two years earlier. And sabotage of railway lines and of apartheid buildings, such as black community council offices, was stepped up.

But, as Oliver Tambo told Anthony Sampson, British commentator on international affairs, people were wondering to what end the ANC was persisting in its policy of hitting pylons – objects which were repaired the next day – 'when, as a result of even trying, you are sentenced to life imprisonment or hanged, if you are caught'. The massacre in Maputo had been 'a very ugly thing'; the Maseru massacre was 'uglier still'. An opinion poll taken among whites after this raid had recorded that 68 per cent were happy about it. He was sure that 100 per cent of blacks were mourning, and were impatient with ANC policy. That was the background to Umkhonto's first car-bomb attack in May 1983, when the Air Force headquarters in Pretoria was the target. 'The idea,' said Tambo, 'was not to hit civilians but something had to be done about this succession of massacres.' Nineteen people were killed and two hundred injured, among them civilians and blacks.

Reading of the deaths, Mandela felt deep regret. As he later put it to a visitor: 'It was a tragic accident ... We aim for buildings and property. It may be that someone gets killed in a fight, in the heat of battle, but we do not believe in assassinations.'*

Tambo understood Mandela's feelings: the South African press had highlighted the civilian casualties, obscuring the fact that the target had been a military one. As for people in the townships, according to a report in *The New York Times*, they felt that at last the ANC had learned to hit a real instead of a symbolic target.

In July 1984 Tambo strongly criticized men responsible for a car bomb intended for a military convoy which instead had killed five black civilians; 'intolerable', the cadre's failure to take precautions. But, he said, the starting-point was not the bomb, 'it is what made it necessary to bomb anybody at all, including the military. The apartheid system is to blame.' An opinion in which Mandela would surely concur: he regarded an incident in

---

* Interview with Nicholas Bethell, 27 January 1985.

which a South African officer was killed in Natal as 'quite justified'. Umkhonto men, approached by security forces whose policy was now to shoot to kill rather than to arrest, had opened fire in self-defence; the lieutenant was killed, as were several Umkhonto men.*

South African attempts to destabilize neighbouring states, particularly its invasions of Angola, where SWAPO had established bases, and its support for the rebel RENAMO force fighting to overthrow Samora Machel's government in Mozambique, were causing immense suffering for countries already denuded by long years of war against Portugal. Suddenly, in March 1984, President Botha initiated a 'good-neighbours' treaty with President Machel: he promised to withdraw all support for RENAMO if Machel would expel the ANC who were operating from Mozambique. Machel promptly carried out his part of the agreement – a heavy blow for the ANC – but the South African government continued clandestinely to support RENAMO, a betrayal of trust not exposed until 1985.

None of these events could be mentioned by the Mandelas during Winnie's monthly visits to Pollsmoor, nor could they directly discuss the founding of the United Democratic Front. However when Mandela was elected a patron, he managed to convey his appreciation; a standing ovation greeted his message at the UDF's first national conference in August 1983. Some six hundred organizations had come together – community groups, trade unions, churches, student bodies, cultural and political associations – from all races and from all parts of the country, including villages hitherto untouched by political action. The elected leaders were members of the Indian Congress, Albertina Sisulu, Helen Joseph and Archie Gumede, whose father had been a President-General of the ANC during the late 1920s and who himself had been a defendant in the Treason Trial. Dr Allan Boesak, President of the World Alliance of Reformed Churches and a dynamic spokesman, was a patron. Among the members

---

* Interview with Nicholas Bethell, 27 January 1985.

were many 'Charterists' (people who supported the Freedom Charter), and one person, one vote in a united South Africa was the aim. The 'Release Mandela' campaign was re-activated.

On 11 May 1984 when Winnie Mandela arrived at Pollsmoor, with Zeni and her youngest child, she was called to the office by Sergeant Gregory. She at once assumed that her husband was ill, but Gregory had a message from the prison authorities: Mandela was henceforward to be allowed 'contact' visits. Zeni has described the moment when, after twenty-two years, her father and mother kissed and held each other, for a long time.

Mandela and Sisulu and their four companions, locked away in their dormitory cell on the third floor, remained isolated from the other prisoners and from their people. Day after day they studied newspapers and listened to the state-controlled radio, discussing each new development in the world beyond the confines of Pollsmoor.

Triumphant weeks for P. W. Botha, that winter of 1984, or so it seemed: in the West the Nkomati Pact had been hailed as a further sign of his reformist policies. And he had won overwhelming endorsement from the white electorate for a new constitution, defeating the Afrikaner right-wing opposition. Under his presidency a tricameral parliament was to be set up in which the three and a half million Coloured people and Indians would have representation along with the 4,600,000 whites; their powers, however, would be subject to white veto. The 'rights' of the twenty-one million Africans would be confined to Bantustans and to urban councils.

A storm of protest erupted: blacks, as well as many Coloureds and Indians, saw compliant Coloureds and Indians being co-opted to reinforce Afrikaner oppression while the world was encouraged to believe that apartheid was being abandoned. Less sophisticated critics in the West were disarmed: Margaret Thatcher received President Botha despite vehement criticism and protest marches. He was the first South African leader to pay an official visit to a British Prime Minister since General Smuts's day and went on to be received by the Pope. After the

French government had refused to meet Botha, Mandela found an opportunity to 'salute' the French people, as he put it, when his daughter Zeni received an award from the Bordeaux Bar Association on his behalf.

White South Africans gave the returning Botha a hero's welcome, but the elections to the tricameral parliament sparked off yet angrier demonstrations. More than 80 per cent of eligible voters boycotted the election. By the time the new parliament was ceremoniously opened in September, the country was racked by racial unrest.

Extreme poverty, economic recession and prolonged drought drove people in arid Bantustans and townships to despair. A large increase in rents in the Vaal Triangle (an area from Johannesburg to Vereeniging) was met with the refusal to pay; people simply could not pay. One township, Sebokeng, found itself surrounded by seven thousand troops while police went from house to house, searching and arresting the outraged residents. 'We are at war,' was a statement frequently made by blacks. Winnie Mandela made this declaration when speaking about Sebokeng; she added: 'When the army has to be called in to surround a township because people are demonstrating against the increase in rents – because people are protesting as they do in every democratic country – then that political situation must have deteriorated to zero.'

So intense had the pressure become that two major federations of the emerging trade unions, previously cautious about political demonstrations – FOSATU (Federation of SA Trade Unions) and CUSA (Council of SA Unions) – joined with the UDF and COSAS (the Council of SA Students) to organize a stay-away in the Vaal Triangle: the largest strike in living memory, bringing industry to a halt.

Bishop Tutu was in America at that time: the announcement had come from Oslo that he was to be awarded the Nobel Prize for Peace. Twenty-three years earlier Chief Lutuli had been a Nobel Laureate and he had called for international sanctions against the South African government and its policy of apartheid.

Through the years persistent lobbying of Congress in support of Lutuli's initiative had made little apparent progress. 'Greater than the tread of mighty armies is an idea whose time has come,' wrote Victor Hugo. This, said Tutu, was such a time; not simply in the United States but, surely, in the world at large.

Tutu's role and prestige, the power and passion and wit of his appeals, coincided with other significant factors to transform American policy towards South Africa. President Reagan's 'constructive engagement' had proved a fiasco, only emboldening the South African government. Jesse Jackson's campaign during the Presidential elections had helped to put South Africa on the map of public consciousness, while in Congress the black caucus and liberal members had worked steadily, with important assistance from Randall Robinson's 'Trans-Africa' organization. Each day television reports revealed Afrikaner intransigence, the brutality of South Africa's police and defence forces, and the reckless courage, the resolve of the blacks.

On Thanksgiving Eve 'Free South Africa' demonstrators sat-in at the South African Embassy in Washington, precipitating an ongoing countrywide campaign in which Democrats and some Republicans, black and white, celebrities and so-called 'nonentities' courted arrest. A slow-burning movement to disinvest from South Africa suddenly took fire.

A leading figure in these movements and in Congressional pressure for sanctions was Senator Edward Kennedy. During a tour of South Africa in January 1985, after visiting Winnie Mandela at her house in Brandfort, he applied to visit Mandela and was firmly rebuffed. Instead, a few days later, a British Conservative, Lord Bethell, Member of the European Parliament, was permitted to enter Pollsmoor. Throughout twenty-two years Mandela had been forbidden to discuss prison conditions and political subjects with his family; now with a sequence of strangers he was allowed to do so.

Then Minister of Justice, Kobie Coetsee, was frank in telling Lord Bethell that the visit had been authorized so that he could confirm that Mandela was well treated and in good health.

Clearly the authorities had not forgotten the international publicity given to Winnie Mandela's report in 1983.

Nicholas Bethell has described the scene:

> I waited for Nelson Mandela in the Governor's office in the maximum security block ... Senior officers in yellow-khaki uniforms with gold stars on their epaulettes, some with peaked caps pulled over their eyes like Guards' sergeant-majors, scurried in and out talking excitedly in Afrikaans. At last three men entered the room and one came towards me. 'How do you do,' he said. I greeted him in return. 'You must be related to Winston Churchill,' he went on, hinting presumably at my need to lose a few pounds in weight. 'Anyway, I'm very pleased and honoured to receive you.'
>
> He was anxious to put me at my ease and he invited me to sit down at the desk where I was ready to make my notes. It was a second or two before I realized that this was the man I had come to see.
>
> A tall lean figure with silvering hair, an impeccable olive-green shirt and well-creased navy-blue trousers, he could almost have seemed like another general in the South African prison service. Indeed his manner was the most self-assured of them all and he stood out as obviously the senior man in the room. He was, however, black. And he was a prisoner, perhaps the most famous in the world, the man they write songs about in Europe and name streets after in London, the leader of the African National Congress, a body dedicated to the destruction of the apartheid system, if necessary by force.

Mandela told Bethell about the 'really very bad years' on Robben Island, the assaults and psychological persecution, and of the dramatic improvements around 1974. 'Things can now only be made significantly better by dismantling the whole South African system,' he added.

He confirmed that he was in good health: it was not true, as had been rumoured, that he had cancer, nor that he had had a toe amputated. But, he said, he still had complaints about conditions in the cell: 'There is a damp patch on the wall. There must have been a fault in the way it was built. And it is wrong for the six of us to be segregated from all the other prisoners.

We would like more companions.' He also wanted greater privacy for studies. 'In fact, our basic demand which we made in 1969 is for political status: for instance, the right to keep a diary and to be visited by the family. I mean the African family, not just wives, brothers and children, which is the family in the European sense.'

The problem, Bethell later commented, was not therefore one of brutal prison conditions. 'It is that Mandela and his friends are in prison at all. Mandela, Sisulu and Kathrada have spent eighteen years on Robben Island and three in Pollsmoor all for no worse a crime than conniving at the destruction of property. It is a punishment that far exceeds the offence even if one ignores the argument that they had every right to use force against apartheid, deprived as they were of the right to vote, to stand for election or to reside where they wish in their own country.' Mandela had said: 'The armed struggle was forced on us by the government. And if they want us now to give it up, the ball is in their court. They must legalize us, treat us like a political party and negotiate with us. Until they do, we will have to live with the armed struggle. It is useless simply to carry on talking. The government has tightened the screws too far.'

'Of course,' he added, 'if there were to be talks along these lines, we in the ANC would declare a truce ... But meanwhile we are forced to continue, though within certain limits.' The aim was to attack military installations and the symbols of apartheid, not to assassinate people. 'I would not want our men to assassinate, for instance, the major here!' The major, Fritz van Sittert, who guarded Mandela and his five comrades, was supervising the visit, not censoring but ensuring that no document or other object passed between Bethell and Mandela. Mandela continued, 'I would only justify such a death in the case of an informer who was a danger to our lives.'

Bethell had been asked to obtain Mandela's signature on a document authorizing his name to go forward in the election of rector of Edinburgh University. The prison authorities would not allow this. Mandela could only express delight that a section of students and faculty had wanted him as rector: 'I am a politician,' he remarked, 'and of course I like to win elections, but in this case it is such a kind gesture that I really don't mind if I win or lose.'

He had kind words, Bethell reported, for the governor of the prison, Brigadier Munro: 'The Brigadier does his best to solve our little problems. But, poor man, he has very little authority. Everything concerning the six of us he has to refer to Pretoria.' And Mandela spoke of prisoners' mail being interfered with: his letter to Bishop Tutu, congratulating him on winning the Nobel Prize, had been blocked, and one of his companions had received a letter, cut to ribbons. Not the Brigadier's fault, but the politicians'. There were no problems with the staff, racial or otherwise.

The Brigadier invited Bethell to visit Mandela's cell in the isolated wing of the long, low building. They set off along corridors and up flights of stairs, a procession of warders and visitor with sergeants unlocking doors with heavy keys. 'Always, though,' said Bethell, 'Mandela was the one who showed the way, inviting me to go first through every door and plying me with questions on Britain and the world: did I think that the Gorbachev visit [to Britain] would relax East–West tension? What were my hopes for the Shultz–Gromyko talks? Would the Liberals at last make a breakthrough in British politics? What was Mrs Thatcher's secret of success? Who was now leader of the Labour Party?'

The last door to be unlocked revealed the 'Mandela enclosure' on the third floor, a large room with six beds, plenty of books, and washing and toilet facilities. As the main door was locked behind them, Mandela led Bethell through an open inner door to a long L-shaped yard which was surrounded by high white walls. There, in several oil drums, Mandela cultivated his 'garden' of tomatoes, broccoli, beans, cucumbers and strawberries. His pride in showing the vegetables reminded Bethell of a landowner showing his farm; as a countryman, he said, he longed for green. After introducing the visitor to his comrades, he pointed out the damp patch in the cell wall. And then, as a sergeant unlocked the heavy steel outer door, he shook hands with Bethell, saying, 'This is my frontier, this is where I must leave you.'*

Soon after that visit, an American professor, Samuel Dash, with his wife, had a similar two-hour talk with Mandela. Looking far younger than his sixty-six years, he was, reported Dash, calm, confident and dignified, and the Americans felt they were in the presence not of a guerrilla fighter or radical ideologue, but of a head of state. To Professor Dash's further surprise, Mandela was aware that he had been counsel to the Senate Watergate Committee, and was well-informed about the conference in South Africa on the sentencing of criminal offenders, at which the professor had been speaking.

Dash asked Mandela's opinion of the government's plan to abolish the Immorality Act and the Prohibition of Mixed Marriages law. Such reforms affected 'pinpricks', said Mandela. It was not his ambition to marry a white woman; the central issue was political equality. As for the fear of many whites that such equality would mean subjugation to an embittered black majority, he declared: 'Whites in South Africa belong here, this is their home. We want them to live here with us and to share power with us.' It was a reiteration of ANC policy affirmed in the Freedom Charter. Again he led the procession up to the cell and, as one after another of the steel doors was unlocked, he joked that his prospects for escape were not good.†

The next American visitors to be approved by the South African authorities gave a very different slant to their report. From the 'far-right', one was a columnist from a 'Moonie' newspaper, the *Washington Times*, and the other an associate of the Reverend Jerry Falwell, leader of the so-called Moral Majority. Under the headline MANDELA URGES 'VIOLENT' REVOLUTION, they described him as a 'terrorist and revolutionary' who 'sees "no alternative" to violent revolution and "no room for

---

* Interview with Nicholas Bethell, 27 January 1985.
† Interview in *The New York Times* Magazine, 7 July 1985.

peaceful struggle" in South Africa'. This was followed by a report of what Mandela actually said during their brief interview: since conditions in the country were the same, if not worse, than when he had been jailed there was no alternative to taking up arms.

To Lord Bethell he had spoken of being a socialist and a believer in a classless society, adding: 'I see no reason to belong to any political party at the moment. Businessmen and farmers, white or black, can also join our movement to fight against racial discrimination. It would be a blunder to narrow it.' He appreciated the Soviet Union because it was the one country which had long ago condemned racialism and supported liberation movements; that did not mean he approved of their internal policy. He had also been grateful to Emperor Haile Selassie, who had received him in Ethiopia in 1962: a feudal ruler, but he had supported the ANC.

He was 'definitely not' a communist, he told the *Washington Times* columnist, but an African nationalist who had been influenced by the idea of a classless society. And he was a Christian, a member of the Methodist church. Questioned about the use of violence, he pointed out that Christian countries had gone to war to fight against various forms of injustice. When reminded that Martin Luther King's strategy had been one of non-violence, he replied that conditions in South Africa were totally different: in the United States democracy was entrenched in the constitution; the white community there was more liberal and public authorities were restrained by law. In South Africa, he added, there were two worlds: for whites, democracy, and, for blacks, 'a colonial power crawling on crutches out of the Middle Ages'.

Disinvestment, economic sanctions: this strategy won his enthusiastic support; it had already 'agitated the powers-that-be'. As for the argument that blacks would be most hurt, 'We have to tighten our belts,' he declared. 'There must be sacrifice for liberation.'*

* *Washington Times*, 22 August 1985.

The impact Mandela made on these visitors, the opportunity given him to address the outside world, could not have been quite what the Minister of Justice had intended. In the European Parliament Lord Bethell, as Vice-Chairman of the Human Rights Sub-Committee, initiated a move urging Foreign Ministers to put pressure on the South African government to set Mandela free, and an article in the conservative *Mail on Sunday*, reporting on his visit to Pollsmoor, was accompanied by a powerful editorial which began: 'The *Mail on Sunday* is proud to publish today the words of Mr Nelson Mandela, the undisputed leader of the black population of South Africa . . .' It conceded that he believed it was only through violence that the 'vile policy of apartheid' could be overthrown, and added: 'A great violence is, however, being done to this man by keeping him in prison . . . A great violence is being done to his people when they are denied their undoubted political rights.'

'This newspaper,' the editorial concluded, 'unhesitatingly joins all those, throughout the world, of whatever political persuasion, who cry the slogan, Release Mandela Now!'*

* *Mail on Sunday*, 27 January 1985.

16

'YOUR FREEDOM AND MINE
CANNOT BE SEPARATED'

1985–90

On 31 January 1985 President Botha announced to the South African House of Assembly:

> The government is willing to consider Mr Mandela's release in the Republic of South Africa on condition that Mr Mandela gives a commitment that he will not make himself guilty of planning, instigating or committing acts of violence for the furtherance of political objectives, but will conduct himself in such a way that he will not again have to be arrested . . . It is therefore not the South African government which now stands in the way of Mr Mandela's freedom. It is he himself. The choice is his. All that is required of him now is that he should unconditionally reject violence as a political instrument. This is, after all, a norm which is respected in all civilized countries of the world.

On 8 February Winnie Mandela, accompanied by the family's attorney, Ismail Ayob, visited her husband to obtain his reply to the President's 'offer'. Mandela wanted to address his people. He had begun to dictate the statement when one of the prison officers monitoring the visit protested that he could not do this. Mandela declared that he had every right to reply to the President in whatever manner he chose, and as the officer left the room he continued with his work. A senior officer then appeared and ordered him to desist. Firmly Mandela advised that the prison authorities should telephone the President, and he went on to complete his dictation.

On Sunday 10 February Zindzi read her father's statement 'to the people' gathered at Jabulani amphitheatre in Soweto. The occasion had been planned by the UDF to celebrate Tutu's

Peace Prize and, through Zindzi, Mandela and his comrades were able to thank the organization and to send warm greetings to the Bishop. Winnie Mandela, defying restrictions, was present to witness the vast crowd's exultant response as her daughter read the address:

My father and his comrades wish to make this statement to you, the people, first. They are clear that they are accountable to you and to you alone. And that you should hear their views directly and not through others.

My father speaks not only for himself and for his comrades at Pollsmoor prison but he hopes he also speaks for all those in gaol for their opposition to apartheid, for all those who are banished, for all those who are in exile, for all those who suffer under apartheid, for all those who are opponents of apartheid and for all those who are oppressed and exploited.

Throughout our struggle there have been puppets who have claimed to speak for you. They have made this claim, both here and abroad. They are of no consequence. My father and his colleagues will not be like them.

My father says, 'I am a member of the African National Congress. I have always been a member of the African National Congress and I will remain a member of the African National Congress until the day I die. Oliver Tambo is much more than a brother to me. He is my greatest friend and comrade for nearly fifty years. If there is any one among you who cherishes my freedom, Oliver Tambo cherishes it more, and I know that he would give his life to see me free. There is no difference between his views and mine.'

My father says, 'I am surprised at the conditions that the government wants to impose on me. I am not a violent man. My colleagues and I wrote in 1952 to Malan asking for a round table conference to find a solution to the problems of our country but that was ignored.

'When Strijdom was in power, we made the same offer. Again it was ignored.

'When Verwoerd was in power we asked for a National Convention for all the people in South Africa to decide on their future. This, too, was in vain.

'It was only then when all other forms of resistance were no longer open to us that we turned to armed struggle.

'Let Botha show that he is different to Malan, Strijdom and Verwoerd. Let him renounce violence. Let him say that he will dismantle apartheid.

'Let him unban the people's organization, the African National Congress. Let him free all who have been imprisoned, banished or exiled for their opposition to apartheid. Let him guarantee free political activity so that the people may decide who will govern them.

'I cherish my own freedom dearly but I care even more for *your* freedom. Too many have died since I went to prison. Too many have suffered for the love of freedom. I owe it to their widows, to their orphans, to their mothers and to their fathers who have grieved and wept for them. Not only I have suffered during these long lonely wasted years. I am not less life-loving than you are. But I cannot sell my birthright nor am I prepared to sell the birthright of the people to be free. I am in prison as the representative of the people and of your organization, the African National Congress, which was banned. What freedom am I being offered while the organization of the people remains banned? What freedom am I being offered when I may be arrested on a pass offence? What freedom am I being offered to live my life as a family with my dear wife who remains in banishment in Brandfort? What freedom am I being offered when I must ask for permission to live in an urban area? What freedom am I being offered when I need a stamp in my pass to seek work? What freedom am I being offered when my very South African citizenship is not respected?

'Only free men can negotiate. Prisoners cannot enter into contracts. Herman Toivo Ja Toivo, when freed, never gave any undertaking, nor was he called upon to do so.'

My father says, 'I cannot and will not give any undertaking at a time when I and you, the people, are not free. Your freedom and mine cannot be separated. I will return.'

While drafting the statement – his first opportunity to address his people since the early sixties – Mandela had learned of the death of Winnie's sister Nikiwe Xaba, in an accident. His shock and sorrow were intensified by a sense of Winnie's anguish and the knowledge that three of her family had died recently. He wrote to her:

On occasions like this I often wonder just how far more difficult it would have been for me to take the decision to leave you behind if I had been able to see clearly the countless perils and hardships to which you would be exposed in my absence. I sincerely think that my decision would, nonetheless, have been easily the same, but it would certainly have been preceded by far more heart-searching and hesitation than was the case twenty-four years ago.

As I see it, the true significance of marriage lies not only in the mutual love which unites the parties concerned, although that is undoubtedly one of the cornerstones, but also in the faithful support which the parties guarantee – that it will always be there in full measure at critical moments.

Your love and support . . . the charming children you have given the family, the many friends you have won, the hope of enjoying that love and warmth again, is what life and happiness mean to me . . .

Yet there have been moments when that love and happiness, that trust and hope, have turned into pure agony, when conscience and a sense of guilt have ravaged every part of my being, when I have wondered whether any kind of commitment can ever be sufficient excuse for abandoning a young and inexperienced woman in a pitiless desert, literally throwing her into the hands of highwaymen; a wonderful woman without her pillar and support at times of need.*

Winnie had come through 'the most emotional storms' in their life of separation, she told him in her reply. His letter had reconstructed her shattered soul. And she told him how proud she had been of his message to the people. 'I've often wondered,' she added, 'how I would have reacted if I met you, Uncle Walter and others on the Pollsmoor steps and was told to take you home . . .'†

Walter Sisulu, Kathrada, Mbeki and the other Rivonia men in Pollsmoor and on Robben Island had all rejected President

---

* Letter of 4 February 1985.
† *Part of My Soul*, Penguin Books, 1985.

Botha's terms of conditional release. Kathrada wrote to a friend in London:

> It may have seemed as if we were a hairsbreadth away from 'Freedom'. But in fact from the very moment the announcement was made, it was a non-starter. I don't want to indulge in any false modesty when I say I have not got that stuff that heroes are made of. But really I did not have to go through any sleepless nights to arrive at a decision. It was so patently designed to humiliate us that there just could be no other decision for me but to reject it.

For Albertina Sisulu the inevitable rejection was one more episode in a long story of triumphing over hardship and harassment. She had brought up and educated five children on her modest nurse's pay; there had been days when they went hungry and days when neighbours had helped. Her second son, Zwelakhe, a journalist and leader of the Media Workers' Union, had been detained for many months and her elder daughter had been badly tortured. She herself had been banned and put under partial house arrest since the 1960s. Recently she had been sentenced to four years' imprisonment for singing ANC songs at a funeral and, while on bail pending an appeal, had again been arrested, this time to be charged with treason as one of the UDF leaders. Her husband could read about the trial, as from their cell the prisoners followed each day's events.

'Render South Africa ungovernable!' Oliver Tambo urged the people in February and indeed, spontaneously, in the townships they were well on their way to doing so. After years of rhetoric and unrealistic prophecies the ANC confidently declared: 'The future is within our grasp ... The conditions of a revolutionary leap forward are beginning to mature.'

Only a few months earlier Botha had ridden the crest of a wave; now, at a time of severe drought and serious economic recession, he and his policies were engulfed. The effect of the 1984 Nkomati agreement depriving the ANC of its bases in Mozambique had been to internalize the struggle in South Africa; and inadequate though his promises of reform had been, they added up to an admission that apartheid was obsolete.

His police force accentuated the hollowness of those promises. In the Eastern Cape they were, notoriously, a law unto themselves: a further example happened on the twenty-fifth anniversary of the shootings at Sharpeville and Langa. Once again, on 21 March, police shot into a crowd of unarmed Africans. Once again it was in a township called Langa, but this time not near Cape Town, near Uitenhage. Twenty men and women were shot dead, seventeen of them in the back.

In a storm of outrage, protesters grew more violent, more purposeful – from stone-throwing to arson – destroying the symbols of apartheid. The government's declaration of a State of Emergency on 22 July, sealing off many townships and giving its agents licence to kill with impunity, only exacerbated anger at home and abroad.

In Pollsmoor, Mandela and his companions, having no television, could only read about and surmise what the rest of the world was watching day after day: police and army invading townships and from their armoured vehicles shooting down people, children as well, as if they were big game; police – black as well as white – whipping protesters, white as well as black; and police rounding up thousands – community leaders, churchmen, trade unionists, students – to be held incommunicado. Leaderless mobs swung from stoning police to burning 'collaborators': the black policemen, mayors, councillors and suspected informers who were more accessible than the white oppressors they represented. Whites appeared to remain immune, heavily protected in their segregated suburbs, not only physically but mentally, as their censored television showed no scenes of police sjamboking white students but extensive coverage of black burning black.*

Funerals were attended by three thousand mourners, twenty

---

* Thirteen million handguns were legally held by the 4,600,000 whites: *Financial Times*, 6 September 1985.

thousand, thirty thousand, in dusty townships and small villages up and down the country: each a celebration of the dead martyrs and a provocation to rebellion. 'We will never be the same again,' said a woman in one rural backwater, a place of abject poverty where the villagers were mourning a thirteen-year-old boy and a twenty-year-old youth, both shot by police. 'These killings have changed our lives for evermore. They have forced us, a non-violent community, into a situation of violence.'

Funerals at which Bishop Tutu attempted to calm the rage of reckless youths and uttered a prayer Trevor Huddleston had once written: 'God bless Africa. Guard her children. Guide her leaders. And give her peace.'

Funerals where ANC flags fluttered above the graves and freedom songs were sung: songs composed by Canon James Calata, the ANC leader of the thirties and forties, who had been a minister in Cradock in the Eastern Cape. Now it was at a funeral in Cradock that people stamped their defiance as they praised Mandela and Tambo, and warned Botha to heed the tide of history before it was too late: the funeral of Calata's grandson, Fort, of Matthew Goniwe – a quiet young headmaster of the school – and of two other community leaders who, returning from a UDF meeting in Port Elizabeth, had been killed – atrociously mutilated – by a 'death squad'. At the heart of the huge throng of mourners who had travelled to Cradock from Cape Town and Johannesburg and Port Elizabeth were Allan Boesak and Beyers Naude, head of the SA Council of Churches. The latter, an Afrikaner, had moved a long way intellectually, politically and spiritually since he had been a fervent Afrikaner Nationalist, member of the secret Broederbond. And Molly Blackburn was there, member of the Black Sash, of the Progressive Federal Party and of the Cape Provincial Council, a friend of the four young men and a symbol of those whites who identified themselves with the black community.

Funeral after funeral: on Sunday 11 August, Victoria Mxenge was buried beside her husband in Rayi township near King

William's Town in the Ciskei. Like him, she had been murdered. At the time she had been one of the lawyers defending Albertina Sisulu and other UDF leaders on trial for high treason. Speakers at the funeral referred to Mandela by his prison number, D220, or spoke of 'Uncle Nelson'. He had sent a message: Victoria Mxenge's murder was 'an atrocity we shall never forget or forgive'.

Not even mourners at funerals were safe from attack by police and military. All the while the death toll mounted: nearly nine hundred killed in twenty-one months. Seemingly random killings spread through townships and squatter camps such as Cape Town's KTC where black vigilantes burnt shacks and killed scores of inhabitants. These vigilantes were named *witdoeke* for the white headcloths they sported and witnesses noticed that plain-clothed police were urging them on. A similar pattern emerged in Natal where Buthelezi's Inkatha, sporting red headcloths, were in conflict with the UDF and were seldom checked by the security forces. 'Black on black' violence, the Government proclaimed it and many in the media accepted that distortion of the truth. Perceptive observers were convinced that a sinister third force was involved, a conviction strengthened when, in 1989, Dr David Webster, an academic who was investigating murders by vigilantes, was assassinated.

Botha's failure to curb the violence and his inflexible refusal to lift the State of Emergency gave tremendous impetus to the campaign for international sanctions. A 'capital boycott' brought the rand to the point of collapse. South Africa's business community stepped up calls for the government to start negotiating with black leaders 'even if some were in detention'. Business leaders led one of a series of several delegations which conferred with Oliver Tambo, Thabo Mbeki and others in exile. Tambo impressed influential businessmen in London and in the States, and officials of the Reagan administration conceded that no solution could be found without the involvement of the ANC. In Britain, however, Prime Minister Thatcher was impressed by Chief Buthelezi who, during visits to London and Washington, argued that blacks would suffer most from the effects of sanctions.

'Release Mandela, talk to him', Botha was urged by critics at home and abroad. Only in this way might the cycle of violence be halted and defused, the economy revived. And, overriding Mrs Thatcher's objections, Commonwealth countries threatened to impose sanctions if the Pretoria government did not dismantle apartheid, release Mandela and other political prisoners, and establish political freedom. President Botha's response was to urge South Africans to 'stand together against forces of darkness calling on foreign aid to destroy the fatherland'.

Despite desperate frustration at their imprisonment, Mandela and his companions were able to give deep consideration to each development in the crisis. Mandela had grown into a reflective man, looking back on his life, evaluating the work and learning from mistakes. But he did not deviate from statements made during the Treason Trial in 1960. The demand for universal franchise would never be abandoned and, if the government were to say 'Let's talk' he would reply, 'Yes, let us talk.' Now, in November 1985, he was convinced the time had come to try yet again to make contact with the government. But at this moment he was forced to undergo surgery for an enlarged prostate gland. What seemed a setback unexpectedly provided the opportunity he needed.

Kobie Coetsee, Minister of Justice, Police and Prisons, had become intrigued by this man who could command worldwide attention. During a flight to Cape Town he encountered Winnie Mandela and, after telling her of the government's concern for her husband's health, went on to visit Mandela in Cape Town's Volk's Hospital. Nothing of substance was discussed but Coetsee was to tell Allister Sparks★ that Mandela had impressed him as a man with the qualities of a Roman citizen: *dignitas, gravitas, honestas* and *simplicitas*.

Mandela, on his return to Pollsmoor, was disturbed to find himself separated from his close friends and moved into a comfortable cell in the prison hospital. What would they think

★ *New Yorker*, 11 April 1994.

of this special treatment? Would they suspect him of doing a deal? He felt he had a duty to see them before approaching the authorities but was sure, if he did, that they would reject the idea of his initiating talks with Botha's government. Besides, when in history had a minority which had held power for generations surrendered it peacefully? After 'agonizing soul-searching' he decided to continue in his attempts. Few would ever realize what courage that decision took.

Ironically, protests came from the outside world when it was assumed that his isolation was punitive. The Commonwealth Group of Eminent Persons – chaired by General Obasanjo of Nigeria and Malcolm Fraser of Australia – which toured South Africa early in 1986 in search of peaceful means to end apartheid had several meetings with Mandela in a prison guesthouse and described this 'living legend' as 'an isolated and lonely figure'. They found him 'unmarked by any trace of bitterness' and with a longing 'to be allowed to contribute to the process of reconciliation'. They also referred to his 'commanding presence', to the manner in which 'he exuded authority' and how he was respected by his gaolers. And they were impressed by his 'immaculate appearance', which must have delighted the prison tailor who had fitted Mandela with a pin-striped suit for their visit.

A surge of optimism greeted the Commonwealth Group's recommendations for government actions which could lead to all-party negotiations; these included the release of political prisoners and the unbanning of outlawed organizations. But, on the very day when the Group was to meet members of the Cabinet, Botha, swayed by right-wing securocrats, unleashed devastating raids on targets in Botswana, Zimbabwe and Zambia – the ANC's main external base. Such outrageous action, and the arrest or banning of prominent leaders of the UDF (but not of Inkatha), as well as the renewal each year of the State of Emergency,* only intensified Mandela's determination. His talks

---

* Between 1985 and 1989 about fifty thousand people were detained, a quarter of them children or teenagers, many of whom were tortured.

with Coetsee continued and officials were brought in for further secret discussions.

'FREE MANDELA!' Around the world the cry went up on his seventieth birthday in July 1988. At a festive concert in London Stevie Wonder expressed the mood with his song 'I Just Called to Say I Love You'. In South Africa police disrupted celebrations and Mandela's comrades were not allowed to join him. This was at the very time when it seemed that his formal request for a meeting with President Botha would be granted.

Another, far more serious, setback followed. Early in August when Sisulu and the other men from the big cell were permitted to visit him, they found that, although cheerful, he had a cough and spoke with difficulty. Tuberculosis was diagnosed; he needed an operation to remove fluid from his lungs. He underwent treatment in a hospital near Stellenbosch and told his attorney Ismail Ayob that he wanted no fuss. However, calls from western leaders for his release took on fresh urgency, only to be countered by threats from South Africa's far-right Conservative Party and neo-Nazi extremists.

Mandela's remarkably quick recovery owed much to long years of self-discipline in following a daily routine of exercises. By Christmas he had been installed in a warder's house in Victor Verster prison outside Paarl. The government issued pictures of the 'comfortable and secure' bungalow with a swimming-pool – but with no sign of Mandela himself. No photograph of him had been permitted since those taken on the Island in 1966 but, in any event, publication of pictures of political prisoners remained illegal. Not surprisingly then, he was not recognized when, in preparation for his possible release, he was driven at weekends into Cape Town or the countryside. Citizens of Paarl or joggers along a beach might have noticed a tall, distinguished African who, accompanied by a group of white men – warders in civvies – occasionally strolled among them.

The talks continued and the small house became an office. Since Botha was virtually controlled by his hawkish securocrats, Mandela had to respond patiently to reiterated queries as to the

ANC's attitude to violence, to its communist allies and to its stand on majority rule. Warrant Officer Gregory who, years before on Robben Island, had hated Mandela as a 'terrorist', an 'animal', was now an ardent admirer and in charge of his household where warders waited on the prisoner and his visitors. Friends were brought from the Island, as well as from Pollsmoor, and his family enjoyed visits. Maki, progressing well at Amherst College in Massachusetts, happily recalls days of relaxed conversations with her father and Mandla – Makgatho's son, studying at Waterford-Kamhlaba school in Swaziland – proudly demonstrated his swimming prowess to his grandfather. In a letter Mandela described one party to me: 'It was nice to have the family around – the children, a daughter-in-law, nine grandchildren, one great-grandson and Zami, of course. Maki's husband Isaac, Zeni and family, and a great grandson were unable to attend. Nevertheless, it was a memorable occasion.'

Zami – Mandela's name for his wife – had become embroiled in what some have compared to a Greek tragedy. Friends, not wanting to alarm her husband, had played down rumours of her increasingly irrational behaviour and her resort to alcohol. Besides, in Brandfort, she had suffered greatly, suffering which culminated in her house being petrol-bombed during 1986. Not only was the clinic burnt down but she lost personal possessions, including awards to her husband and her carefully preserved wedding cake, as well as the family's pet kitten. Winnie promptly defied banning orders and settled back in the house in Soweto. It was as if this successful challenge to the government imbued her with a sense of power and she became a law unto herself.

She formed a group of young men – some rescued off the streets – into what she named the Mandela United Football Club and they accompanied her as a toyi-toyiing bodyguard. At a time of intensifying police repression and township insurrection, she rallied young comrades, addressing a crowd with the brazen message that, in face of the state's sophisticated weapons, 'We have no guns, only stones, boxes of matches and petrol. Together hand in hand, with our boxes of matches and our necklaces, we shall liberate this country.' (In necklace killings a rubber tyre doused in petrol was slung round the victim's neck and set alight.) Years later Gregory was to tell of Mandela's anger and of Winnie obeying his order to visit him at once. However, his stern reprimand proved ineffectual.

Within months Winnie's 'bodyguard' was terrorizing the neighbourhood – several of them were involved in fatal shootings. Apartheid's culture of violence had bred kangaroo courts which punished suspected 'sell-outs' – and such a 'court' was set up in a house Winnie had recently acquired. Not only did she ignore her husband's continuing efforts to restrain her but a 'crisis committee' of community and church leaders who attempted to do so was treated with contempt.

The scandal finally hit the headlines in January 1989 when it was revealed that members of the 'team' had kidnapped four young men from a Methodist refuge and had taken them to Winnie's house where they were interrogated and assaulted with sjamboks, the rawhide whips police used. A week later the small corpse of one of the victims, fourteen-year-old Stompie Moeketsi Seipei, was discovered in a Soweto field. Accused of being an informer, he had been brutally beaten, then killed. Jerry Richardson, 'trainer' of the 'football team', was found guilty of the murder and also of the attempt to kill another youth with garden shears. (Sentenced to death, but with the sentence later commuted to life imprisonment, he remains on death row in Pretoria prison.)

From exile the ANC, with 'terrible sadness', questioned Winnie's 'judgement', and on 16 February 1989 leaders of the United Democratic Front and the Congress of South African Trade Unions, while praising her past contribution and acknowledging her suffering, expressed outrage at the team's 'reign of terror'. Mrs Mandela, they declared, had abused 'the trust and confidence' of the community.

Meanwhile Mandela was painstakingly preparing a statement to deal with issues raised by Coetsee's committee during their three years of discussions – years in which he had not once raised the question of his own release. He had been allowed to communicate with the ANC in Lusaka and now his visitors included young leaders from the UDF and from trade unions. He was well aware of the danger of straining the tolerance of those who believed that liberation could only be achieved through armed 'revolution'. During the years on the Island he had explained that there were two dimensions to the struggle, not simply militant confrontation but also talking and reasoning – a question of strategy. The meeting with President Botha had been postponed, as in January 1989 Botha had had a stroke. Two months later Mandela's ten-page memorandum was delivered to the President.

'The deepening political crisis in our country has been a matter of grave concern to me for quite some time,' Mandela declared, 'and I now consider it necessary in the national interest for the African National Congress and the government to meet urgently to negotiate an effective political settlement.'

The only reason he was acting on his own initiative, he remarked with a touch of irony, was his inability to consult freely with his organization; his task therefore was simply to bring the country's two major political bodies to the negotiating table. He emphasized that the question of his release was not an issue.

He dealt sharply with the Government's refusal to negotiate with the ANC because it had resorted to violence: ' . . . we consider the armed struggle a legitimate form of self-defence against a morally repugnant system of government which will not allow even peaceful forms of protest'. The truth was that the government was not yet ready to negotiate directly and in good faith with the acknowledged black leaders.

As for the charge that the ANC was dominated by the Communist Party, a party which had supported the ANC in the struggle against racism, he replied, 'Which man of honour will ever desert a lifelong friend at the insistence of a common opponent and still retain a measure of credibility among his people?' He quoted a report by the American State Department which concluded that although the party's influence was strong it was unlikely to dominate.

Majority rule, he pointed out, was a pillar of democracy worldwide. White South Africa had to accept there would never be peace and stability until the principle was fully applied. There should be two stages in the steps towards lasting peace: 'The first, where the organization and the government will work out together the preconditions for a proper climate for negotiations. The second would be the actual negotiations.'

He appealed to President Botha to seize this opportunity to overcome deadlock and to normalize the political situation. He believed that the overwhelming majority – black and white – hoped to see the ANC and the government working together to lay the foundations for a new era 'in which racial discrimination and prejudice, coercion and confrontation, death and destruction, will be forgotten'.

On the evening of 5 July 1989 Mandela at last set out for the Tuynhuys, the President's official residence in Cape Town. Later, he amusingly described the precautions taken before he was smuggled into the presence: his blood group was checked in case he was wounded in a shoot-out. His garments were carefully chosen: new suit, shirt, tie, socks and shoes. But the new shirt showed its folds and, never mind the delay, he must take it off, it must be rapidly ironed. And the shoes – he had not tied the laces! After twenty-five years of wearing prison sandals and then loafers, he had forgotten how. Outside the President's door the Director-General of the National Intelligence Service knelt to tie his laces.

Mandela later confessed that he'd gone into the meeting 'quite frightened' – Botha was notorious for his explosive temper. Then he'd been disarmed to discover that the 'Old Crocodile' could be warm and charming. But on the crucial question of negotiation Botha remained unforthcoming. None the less commentators thought that the tea party symbolically legitimized the ANC. 'You could say it is the outgoing President meeting someone who is going to succeed him,' quipped Tutu.

On 13 August 1989 Oliver Tambo, who had worked and travelled at a furious pace, suffered a stroke and was admitted to the London Clinic. Profoundly anxious, Mandela awaited Adelaide Tambo's daily reports. Tambo, he was to say, 'is the one man who was able to keep the organization together for the last three decades, and to help place the ANC in a strong position to win the struggle for freedom in our country'.

Within months Botha was furiously resisting calls to resign because of his failing health. Cabinet ministers, led by the Transvaal leader, F.W. de Klerk, were unmoved by his thundering protests. On 20 September 1989 De Klerk was inaugurated President. Conservative, but also a pragmatist, and with the knowledge that South Africa had lost its war in Namibia and Angola, De Klerk promised a 'new South Africa, a totally changed South Africa' . The first indication came when twenty thousand marchers led by Tutu – now an Archbishop – were allowed to demonstrate against police killings in Cape Town. The march went off peacefully. But if the legendary Mandela were to be released, would black emotions prove uncontrollable?

As a test Govan Mbeki had already been quietly freed from Robben Island to return to Port Elizabeth. Then Albertina Sisulu and other Rivonia wives met Mandela in the warder's house and were told that their husbands would soon be joining them. Throughout the country the mood was feverish with anticipation. Tens of thousands took to the streets waving illegal ANC flags and exploding with joy until, very early on Sunday, 15 October they were able to welcome home Walter Sisulu, Ahmed Kathrada, Andrew Mlangeni, Elias Motsoaledi and Raymond Mhlaba. In Soweto, watched by security forces from their armoured vehicles, the white-headed Sisulu, aged seventy-seven and looking remarkably spry, hugged an ecstatic Albertina. They had to fight their way through a wildly excited crowd surrounding their small house. For days, filmed by international television teams, Albertina and the family had been painting and cleaning in preparation for the marvellous moment.

Would there soon be a black government, Sisulu was asked. 'We don't judge persons in terms of colour,' he replied. 'We are talking in terms of a democratic movement where a black man can be a President and a white man can be President.'

Some eighty thousand people from throughout the country gathered in Johannesburg's football stadium to welcome back the Rivonia men. Helen Joseph, frail and approaching the end of her life, sat beside them. The ANC, after almost three decades underground, had surfaced and the massive crowd triumphantly sang the outlawed anthem, 'Nkosi Sikelel' iAfrika'.

Mandela, who had negotiated these releases, now awaited President De Klerk's response to the ten-page memorandum he had put to Botha. During December three meetings with De Klerk proved amicable.

With his own release in sight and the media daily speculating on the date, he was determined that, once freed, he would do all he could to protect his wife. Over the years he had never ceased to feel responsible for 'abandoning' Winnie as a young woman. In October 1979 he had written: '. . . every time I see you carrying visible signs of suffering, I am tortured by a sense of guilt and shame'. In a rare expression of intimate feeling, he spoke of the happiness of looking forward to joining his 'beloved wife', knowing 'that we would be able to handle problems together and that I would be able to give her the love and dignity and security which every woman desires'. He could not know that Winnie had fallen passionately in love with a young man – Dali Mpofu – who was articled to the firm of attorneys dealing with the cases of kidnapping and assault.

On 2 February 1990 President De Klerk announced to Parliament in Cape Town that the ANC, the PAC and other outlawed organizations were unbanned. Kobie Coetsee had reason to smile broadly. Foreign Minister Pik Botha remarked, 'I think we will return to international respect soon.' De Klerk's unbanning of the Communist Party was particularly courageous as, against fierce opposition, he and his supporters had argued that to leave any organization outlawed would provide grounds for protests, the government would lose its moral advantage and, besides, the South African Communist Party had surely been weakened by the fall of their friends among communist regimes in Europe.

Celebrations spread through townships and city centres, but after a thanksgiving service in St Mary's Cathedral in Johannesburg the members of the congregation who emerged singing into the streets were viciously attacked by baton-wielding police.

What of Mandela, the man perceived by millions as a Moses who would lead his people to the Promised Land? There was still no word of when, precisely, he would be released.

17

'ALL HUMANITY WILL BE PROUD . . .'

1990–94

Sunday, 11 February 1990: a hot summer's day in the Cape. For the crowd waiting outside Victor Verster prison, and for the world watching on television, the expectation was thrilling. What would he look like, the world's most famous political prisoner who had been kept invisible from the public gaze for more than a quarter of a century? The man labelled a 'terrorist' by the government which was about to release him?

For hour after hour the people waited. The delay added tension to the expectation as eyes strained in the glare and television cameras focused on the prison gates. And then a motorcade of cars approached and from the leading car stepped Nelson Mandela. A tall, very slim and distinguished, elegantly suited man beamed as, with his handsome wife, he walked through the gates into freedom.

Mandela felt he had entered 'a totally different South Africa'. He was amazed at the friendly crowd which jostled to draw close and by the whites, smiling and waving to identify themselves with what was happening, who lined the roads along the thirty-five-mile drive to Cape Town.

On his arrival there, Mandela was escorted to the balcony of the City Hall. He was overwhelmed by the sight of eager, upturned faces filling the Grand Parade below. Raising a fist, he cried out, *'Amandla! Amandla! Mayibuye iAfrika!'* (Power! Power! Let Africa return!) Those slogans echoed with a roar before – with Cyril Ramaphosa, the mineworkers' leader, holding the microphone – he could continue: 'Friends, comrades and fellow South Africans, I greet you all in the name of peace, democracy and freedom for all. I stand here before you not as a prophet but as a humble servant of you, the people.'

After stressing that he himself had at no time entered into negotiations about the future of the country except to insist on a meeting between the ANC and the Government, he paid tribute to De Klerk for going further than any other Nationalist President in taking real steps to normalize the situation. He declared that the ANC's resort to armed struggle was a purely defensive action against the violence of apartheid and, since apartheid still existed, there was no option but to continue. Sanctions should also be maintained until a climate conducive to a negotiated settlement was created.

'Your tireless and heroic sacrifices,' he told the people, 'have made it possible for me to be here ... I place the remaining years of my life in your hands.' Despite his much delayed arrival, the crowd had waited patiently but now the occasion was marred as, in darkness, a handful of rioters broke away from the departing thousands to loot shops and the police retaliated with gunfire. HANG MANDELA a banner proclaimed at a neo-Nazi demonstration in Pretoria.

Next day took on a dreamlike quality when the Mandelas emerged from Archbishop Tutu's residence, Winnie was beautiful in a caftan with a swathed head-scarf and her husband smiled happily as hand-in-hand they strolled through the garden and down steps to join the Sisulus and meet the press.

In this first encounter with Mandela representatives of the international media were utterly charmed. Hearing the names of writers whose columns he had read in jail, he greeted them like old friends. According to the correspondent of a London daily, 'It was a stunning performance for someone who had not held a press conference for thirty years.'

He was asked what he'd felt on release. 'I confess I am unable to describe my emotions,' he replied. 'The enthusiasm – it was something I did not expect ... Breathtaking is all I can say. I am also excited to have the opportunity of addressing you.'

What had he to say about the twenty-seven years in jail? 'I

have lost a great deal and my wife has been under all sorts of pressures. It is not a nice feeling for a man to see his family struggling without security, without the dignity of having the head of the family around, but despite the hard time we have also had the opportunity to think about our problems.' Winnie listened impassively.

Notwithstanding the high morale of the political prisoners, Mandela added, there were moments when they doubted whether the day of freedom would ever come. But the calibre of men on the Island was fantastic: 'Men with whom you could sit down and at the end of a conversation you would be enriched, your horizons would be widened.'

He emphasized the ANC's concern to reassure white South Africans and the other minorities, saying, 'We understand their fears.' It was a theme he would repeatedly return to. Mandela's 'lack of bitterness, inner calm and certainty, were so unexpected, it was quite overpowering', said one foreign journalist.

A flight to Johannesburg and Mandela came 'home'. Crowds, singing and dancing their welcome awaited him and Winnie outside his small brick house, 8115 Vilakazi Street in Orlando West. He was astounded by the vast sprawl of Soweto, stretching far beyond the townships of his youth, where untold millions now lived.

With Sisulu beside him, he told the crowd: 'We have reached seventy years. We can't have many years left before we close our lives. But because of the support and inspiration you have given us, we will all sleep permanently with a smile on our faces.'

'Never ever such an event in South Africa's history!' enthused a television presenter as Mandela, accompanied by Winnie, Zindzi with her baby son, and a retinue of ANC members, made his 'Olympian progress' round the running track of Soweto's football stadium, to cheers and freedom songs from the 85,000 in the stands and some 120,000 outside. 'Ninety per cent of them were not born when Mandela was jailed,' the commentator pointed out. Mounting the rostrum the Mandelas joined the Sisulus, the Mlangenis, UDF leaders and old friends, among them Arthur Chaskalson and George Bizos, defence advocates in the Rivonia trial.

'My return fills my heart with joy,' Mandela began. 'At the same time I feel a deep sense of sadness – sadness to learn that you are still suffering under an inhuman system. We must convince our white compatriots by our conduct and arguments that a new South Africa without apartheid will be a better home for all.' Unemployment, the housing shortage, the schools crisis, the crime rate and the fighting in Natal were his deepest concerns. Only the achievement of one person one vote could address such conditions.

He was not a rousing orator. His measured speech was that of a schoolmaster as he called on the youth who had been enticed by the slogan LIBERATION BEFORE EDUCATION to return to school. And when he enjoined a crowd estimated at a hundred thousand – most of them Zulus – in Durban on 25 February to 'Take your guns, your knives, your pangas and throw them into the sea!' many turned away in boredom.

Hopes of 'talks about talks' between the ANC and the government were dashed when in March – thirty years since Sharpeville – in nearby Sebokeng police massacred eleven protesters and wounded some four hundred. Two days later in Natal Inkatha attacked ANC strongholds; within a week eighty were killed and hundreds wounded.

After Mandela had conferred in Lusaka with exiled ANC leaders, among them Chris Hani, the young Umkhonto and communist leader, and comrades from the Treason Trial, he was at last reunited with the ailing Oliver Tambo on 12 March in a small palace outside Stockholm. During this most moving occasion Tambo asked him to take over the leadership of the ANC. 'But,' Mandela later explained, 'I said it would be misunderstood for someone who had just left prison. So I became Deputy-President.'

Immediately the ANC had to transform itself from liberation movement to political party. The modern offices rented in Johannesburg – soon to be replaced by the entire block of Shell

House — couldn't disguise the organization's administrative inefficiency.

During six weeks Mandela travelled to fourteen countries. He wanted to thank the international community for their support of the ANC, and to urge them to continue the pressure of sanctions. Equally important was the need to raise funds for the return to the community of thousands of political prisoners and exiles. In Harlem he spoke of the kinship the ANC felt for that community, the kinship of a shared historical experience and, during a moving address to the American Congress on 16 June, said, 'We shall need your support to achieve post-apartheid economic objectives.' In the United States, however, attempts to raise funds were undermined by his loyal, if somewhat tactless, expressions of friendship for Fidel Castro, Gaddafi and Arafat. Interrogated by critics there, Mandela retorted that *they* had backed Umkhonto's armed struggle when the West had turned away and, 'No freedom fighter of integrity would now abandon his friends who helped him in hard times.'

Wherever he journeyed, in Africa, Asia or the West, he was fêted. Winnie accompanied him to London's celebratory rock concert and rode beside him in New York's tickertape parade. In Africa he wore dashikis, in Detroit he sported a baseball cap. Paris surpassed all cities with a floodlit Eiffel Tower in the background as the Mitterands and Mandelas regally approached each other across the vast expanse of the *terrasse* of the Trocadéro to embrace, while cheering citizens watched.

In Victor Verster prison Mandela had had time for thought, for study, and he particularly enjoyed literature. In 1976 he wrote in metaphoric mood to Winnie, saying that he'd felt 'dry like a desert' until a letter from her brought 'summer rains that livened [his] life'.* He also spoke of 'putting on a mask behind which [he] pined for the family'. Now, returning home, he had again to resort to that mask as he struggled to come to terms with the knowledge of Winnie's infidelity. At the same time he

* Fatima Meer, *Higher than Hope*, Penguin Books, 1990.

was concerned about the violence and the delay to negotiations. Publicly he was charming and courteous, bringing a festive mood to occasions. At Helen Joseph's birthday party he greeted each domestic worker who hurried there as word of his presence spread.

Back in Soweto, at the ANC's insistence that his house was too small and a security risk, he moved into a mansion Winnie had designed, but he felt ill at ease. It was in Qunu, his birthplace, that he wanted to build the home he had long dreamed of. He decided that it should be a replica of the warder's house at Victor Verster prison. On his return there, Qunu's huts and houses showed little sign of change, but the acute poverty shocked him. He felt moved at being reunited with his family and friends, and visited the graves of his parents. Searching for the spirit of his childhood, he remembered romantic days, the most pleasant and carefree of his life, when he herded cattle and goats in country which seemed a paradise.

Reminiscing about those days to a writer from *Vogue*,★ he described his experience of the Xhosa ceremony of initiation, a ritual which transformed youths into responsible adults. He was seventeen at the time and, with elders of the tribe watching as the blade cut the foreskin, he had remained stoical, inspired by the prospect of becoming a man, although almost crying with pain. And the elders, he was asked, what had they thought of his reaction? With evident pride Mandela recounted their comment: 'Here is a man!', such a compliment to him. He believed that the psychological effect of not giving in to that terrible pain had for ever after strengthened him.

Throughout the arduous months which followed the groundwork so patiently and quietly achieved in gaol, he remained remarkably fit. If forced to withdraw briefly from public life – once when struck down by pneumonia – he sometimes rested at a friend's game farm. He seemed to draw energy from the affection of those who gathered to honour him – energy and

★ Colombe Pringle, *Vogue*, Paris, December 1993.

pleasure – yet he remained an intensely private man. Questioned about his religious beliefs, he explained that he had never missed a service on the Island where he'd often read the scripture lesson. 'I am not particularly spiritual,' he added, 'I am just an ordinary person interested in trying to make sense of the mysteries of life.'

Official talks between ANC and government were eventually held between 2 and 4 May 1990 at Groote Schuur. Built for Cecil Rhodes, it had been the Cape Town residence for a succession of Governor-Generals and Presidents who had unrelentingly maintained the structures of white domination. In those august surroundings, Thabo Mbeki was to remark, 'within a matter of minutes, everyone understood there was no one in the room who had horns and that, in fact, discussions ought to have taken place years ago.'

Pictured on television screens and on the front pages of newspapers, the sight of De Klerk and Mandela shaking hands, backed by delegates who included Joe Slovo – once regarded as a dreaded communist hard-liner and now an influence for moderation – sent a wave of euphoria through the country.

This mood was rudely dissipated and the ANC began reconsidering the wisdom of talking with the government as more sinister violence erupted. Zulus – recruited from Natal's killing fields where thousands were dying – were transported by bus to occupy migrant workers' hostels in townships along the Witwatersrand. They organized attacks on residents and ANC-supporting young comrades fought back. Men in balaclavas rampaged through commuter trains, slaughtering innocent passengers. There were random shootings at blacks in combi taxis, in bars and homes. Police stood by or, as in the Cape, urged the killers on. 'A time for weeping', Rich Mkhondo, Reuters' correspondent, called his chapter* on the atrocities. He pointed out that they had started immediately after the ANC, meeting the government on 6 August 1990, had agreed to suspend the armed struggle.

* In *Reporting South Africa*, James Currey and Heinemann, 1993.

'Black on black' violence, 'Xhosas versus Zulus' – the cries went up. Commentators questioned whether apartheid's culture of violence had spawned this barbarism. Appalling conditions in the hostels and in squatter camps, unemployment, poverty, landlessness, bitterly frustrated youths lacking education – all contributed to the dangerous climate. But Mandela was not alone in claiming that a 'third force' from within the security forces was attempting to destabilize the black community and the ANC.

Despite opposition from ANC leaders in Natal, Mandela met Buthelezi in January 1991. Buthelezi warned that the ANC's demands for an elected assembly and interim government could only lead to disaster. Mandela attempted to bridge the gulf and thanked Buthelezi for helping to obtain his release from prison, but there was no genuine will on either side to implement the peace agreement they signed. Within weeks Inkatha had seized a hostel housing thousands in Alexandra township, near Johannesburg's luxurious northern suburbs. In three days of fighting forty-five people died. Police again took no action here but promptly killed ANC demonstrators in another township.

Enraged at the government's failure to deal with the violence, Mandela, addressing members of the American Congress at a symposium in Cape Town, launched a tirade against President De Klerk whom he had once commended as 'a man of integrity'.

However he realized that it was self-defeating for the ANC to postpone talks because of the violence. This was precisely what forces in De Klerk's camp wanted. He decided to risk advocating the ANC's abandonment of preconditions for talks with the government. During July 1991 in Durban, close to the heartland of the Zulus, the ANC held its first national conference inside South Africa after nearly thirty years. On this important occasion Mandela argued successfully that negotiations were another 'theatre of struggle' for the movement and further delay was playing into the hands of the enemy.

Oliver Tambo, who had returned to a tumultuous welcome in December 1990, took part in the formalities and political prisoners released from gaol, together with exiles back after long years abroad, joined in the celebrations. Mandela was elected President and despite a reputation for stubbornness and an authoritarian streak – possibly emphasized by his aristocratic roots and years of solitude – he was defeated when it came to the election of a secretary-general. He had wanted Alfred Nzo, an old-timer returned from exile, to remain in the role but younger members, who had led the internal UDF, voted in the popular and respected Cyril Ramaphosa.

Less than two weeks later, on 19 July, the *Weekly Mail* published a series of articles revealing that the security forces had for years been secretly funding Inkatha rallies and other anti-ANC activities. Yet President De Klerk rejected the implications of what became known as the Inkathagate scandal. Before Mandela's release De Klerk had tried to create an alliance with Buthelezi and leaders of the puppet regimes in the homelands. Now it was as though, having had the courage to launch Mandela, he was still intent on trying to weaken him. Inkatha violence and ANC counter-attacks continued.

It seemed that talks about talks would finally bear fruit when, almost two years after Mandela's release, on 20 December 1991 the Convention for a Democratic South Africa (CODESA) opened at Johannesburg's World Trade Centre – a white barn of a building left empty through years of sanctions. The Pan-Africanist Congress had dropped out and Buthelezi was playing hard to get, sending observers but not negotiators. The day ended sourly after De Klerk had lashed out at the ANC and Mandela retaliated.

During the resulting hiatus President De Klerk, who had failed to deal forcefully with the neo-Nazi AWB (Afrikaner Weerstand Beweging), was stunned by the National Party's loss to the far right in a by-election. To test what support he had among whites for his policy of negotiating with the ANC, a referendum was held. Liberals, despite their discomfort at supporting the Nationalists, contributed to his resounding victory: 68.6 per cent of the electorate approved his policy.

Meanwhile the ANC had been damaged by the continuing scandal surrounding Winnie Mandela. Sections of the organization held the media responsible for 'unfounded allegations' against her when, early in 1991, she was charged with kidnapping and for being an accessory to assault. Prosecution witnesses disappeared, among them a key witness whom ANC members smuggled to Lusaka where he was imprisoned by the Zambian authorities. Mandela, who still maintained his wife's innocence, accompanied Winnie to court. George Bizos led the defence. In the past he had successfully defended Winnie in cases of breaking her banning orders. In the course of his judgement Mr Justice Michael Stegmann said that Mrs Mandela 'showed herself on a number of occasions to be a calm, composed, deliberate, unblushing liar'. On 14 May 1991 he pronounced sentence: five years on kidnapping charges and one year as an accessory to assault. Bizos would appeal against the judgement.

Mandela, against all expectations, supported his wife's appointment as head of the ANC's Social Welfare department. She chose her lover, Mpofu, as deputy and in October they flew by Concorde to the States 'to raise funds for charity'. On their return Mpofu was sacked and Winnie promptly resigned. Yet, a month later, both were reinstated by the ANC's National Executive, a decision all the more startling when it was known that they had allegedly been involved in the disappearance of funds from the Welfare department account. This was referred to in a letter Winnie wrote Mpofu on 17 March 1992 which was leaked to the press. Clearly written in a jealous rage at Mpofu's affair with another woman, the letter also revealed that Mandela had not been speaking to her for the past five months. (Some time before he had moved to a house in Johannesburg's northern suburbs.)

On 13 April 1992 Mandela called a press conference and, flanked by his oldest friends, Tambo and Sisulu, and by Ramaphosa, announced his separation from 'Comrade Nomzamo Winnie Mandela'. He paid tribute to her as 'an indispensable pillar of support and comfort' through his years on Robben Island, for 'accepting the onerous burden' of raising their children on her own, and for enduring 'the persecutions heaped on her by the government with exemplary fortitude'. 'However,' he added, 'in view of the tensions that have arisen owing to differences between ourselves on a number of issues in recent months, we have mutually agreed that a separation would be best for each of us.' He would never regret the life they had tried to share together.

'I part from my wife with no recriminations,' he concluded. 'I embrace her with all the love and affection I have nursed for her inside and outside prison from the moment I first met her.'

Then, rising from his seat, with great dignity and barely disguised anguish, he appealed to the press, 'Ladies and gentlemen, I am sure you will appreciate how painful this is for me. The conference is now over.' Not one reporter broke the silence as he walked stiffly from the room.

For two years Mandela had lived with the hope that he and the woman he loved might yet find happiness together. An intensely proud man, he had survived political martyrdom only to face personal betrayal and unimaginable humiliations. He could well have been destroyed by the perversity of his wife's behaviour; instead – as in his political life – he fought and won a very private battle. It was one of the most heroic episodes in his life.

Winnie, in her statement to the media, spoke tearfully of her continuing love for her husband and of her 'commitment' to him, to the ANC and 'to the oppressed and impoverished people of South Africa'.

In speaking to the press Mandela urged that the issue of Winnie's guilt or innocence be left to the judicial system to determine. A year later, on 1 June 1993, in the Appeal Court Chief Justice Michael Corbett dismissed her appeal and found her guilty of kidnapping but not of being an accessory to assault. The sentence was reduced to a fine of 15,000 rand and a payment of 5,000 rand to each of three victims.

Mandela had constantly to coax the radical wing of the ANC to accept that talks would lead to a constitutional settlement, but no sooner had he met with De Klerk to discuss a fresh start in what was called CODESA II than, on 12 June 1992, Inkatha men from a hostel massacred forty-nine residents of Boipatong township. De Klerk, to express condolence, attempted to visit Boipatong – the first such gesture any white leader had made – and was driven away by a distraught community waving placards: GO AWAY MURDERER, KILL APARTHEID NOT US. Next day Mandela toured the township and was met with frantic demands for guns.

The outraged ANC withdrew from talks to organize mass rallies and strikes. The symbolic march Mandela led on 6 August, thirty years to the day since his capture, to the seat of government in Pretoria, attracted eighty thousand supporters, the largest political rally ever seen at the Union Buildings. To the astonishment of security forces ranged along the roads, the crowd had a cheerful encounter with a relaxed Mandela. He praised the four million who had taken part in that week's protest strike and reiterated calls for the government to control political violence and to accede to the ANC's demands for elections for a constituent assembly.

A month later radicals headed a march of fifty thousand into the tin-pot dictatorship of the Ciskei. They had been given permission to gather in a stadium but Ronald Kasrils, formerly an MK leader, recklessly led a dash through a broken fence and on towards Bisho, the capital. Ciskei troops opened fire. Twenty-eight people were killed and more than two hundred wounded. It was another bloodbath.

The government was involved in a series of scandals. Widespread corruption was exposed in the 'independent' homelands and the Department of Development Aid. The Catholic-funded *New Nation* published the photocopy of a signal sent on the instructions of Brigadier Christoffel van der Westhuizen (later a general and head of Military Intelligence) which, in 1985, directed that Matthew Goniwe and his companions should be 'permanently removed from society'.* Former members of Intel-

---

* In the subsequent inquest the judge also found that the actual murderers were members of the security forces.

ligence were already going public about 'dirty tricks' aimed at destabilizing southern Africa – including Namibia which had recently achieved independence. According to a colonel, this 'headless force out of control' had been created in the early 1980s by former President Botha's State Security Council. Police inaction was part of the agenda: between July 1990 and August 1992 fewer than eighty arrests were made in connection with more than six thousand deaths in the Johannesburg area while thousands more continued to die in Natal. Despite this corroboration of Mandela's claim that a third force had long been active in undermining the moves toward democracy, De Klerk adamantly refused to acknowledge its existence. However, after an investigating commission under Judge Richard Goldstone had raided a secret Military Intelligence operations centre, De Klerk suspended or retired twenty-three senior officers – but not the most notorious, among them Van der Westhuizen.

The ANC faced a separate commission which inquired into Umkhonto's violation of human rights while in exile. Suspected informers and dissidents had been tortured and even executed. Certain leaders from the exiled movement accepted collective responsibility, arguing that in war such punishments, though deeply regretted, were inevitable. Mandela criticized the leadership for not adequately monitoring and eradicating abuses, but no action was taken against individuals alleged to be responsible.

For months Ramaphosa and the government's chief negotiator, Roelf Meyer, with small groups of assistants, had been quietly meeting behind the scenes to advance the process towards negotiations. Joe Slovo had persuaded the radicals to accept what became known as a 'sunset clause': since the movement had not won the war, it should go for a fixed period of 'compulsory power-sharing'. Breakthrough was on 12 February 1993: ANC and government agreed in principle on a five-year transition during which a multi-party cabinet and parliament would share power after a general election, probably early in 1994.

No sooner had CODESA resumed with twenty-five parties, including white Conservatives and the PAC, now in discussion with the government, than a fresh atrocity, a shocking tragedy, rocked the country. Chris Hani was assassinated. The killer was a Polish immigrant member of the AWB; conspiring with him was a British-born parliamentarian from South Africa's Conservative Party. (Both were later sentenced to death.) Hani would undoubtedly have played a key role in the future government and would probably have inherited Mandela's mantle.

In fury and hopeless anguish young militants went on the rampage through city centres. Over seventy people died. More than two million attended eighty-five rallies to mourn Hani's death. At the funeral Mandela movingly described Hani's birthplace: 'Sabalele, in Cofimvaba district, is a place well known to me. Not for its beauty, but for its harshness. No running water. No electricity. No decent housing. Inadequate health care. Little formal education. Yet this small, virtually unknown village produced a Chris Hani whose life shook the whole country.'

Hani, he said, had a passion for justice. The murder was no aberration, and he referred to Hani's insistence that weapons missing from an Air Force base had not been stolen but taken for use in covert operations: one of those weapons was the gun used to kill Hani. Angrily Mandela accused President De Klerk: 'It is you who have allowed the bully-boy tactics of the AWB to go unchallenged ... you treat the far-right with kid gloves ... Black lives are cheap and will remain so as long as apartheid continues to exist. And let there be no mistake: there have been many changes, and negotiations have started, but for the ordinary black person apartheid is alive and well.' Clearly he spelled out the root cause of much of the violence: 'It is precisely because negotiations will force them to relinquish power that certain elements are resorting to the cowardly tactics of assassination.'

His attack on De Klerk's impotence in the face of the far-right was promptly vindicated. The AWB, infuriated by resumption of CODESA's talks, invaded the Trade Centre; their armoured vehicle crashed through glass walls to lead assaults on those gathered in conference. Police watched and made no attempt to intervene. As Mkhondo, who was present, pointed out,* had the invaders been black the police would have opened fire and probably hundreds would have been killed.

On 3 June CODESA took the historic decision: a general election with universal franchise would be held on 27 April 1994. By 17 November the country's first democratic constitution had been ratified. In Johannesburg's World Trade Centre, after two years of patient work, often interrupted by fractious disputes, the negotiating teams led by Ramaphosa and Meyer celebrated with President De Klerk and delegates from twenty-one parties. 'We are at the end of an era. We are at the beginning of a new era,' Mandela declared. 'Millions of those who were not allowed to vote will do so. I, too,' he added jovially, 'for the first time in my short life will vote.'

On visits to Europe and America he appealed for his country's most immediate need, the voter-education programme required for twenty million potential black voters. At the UN he endorsed the lifting of sanctions. He and De Klerk might still on occasion clash at home but they were courteously in accord when President Clinton presented them with replicas of the Liberty Bell in Philadelphia.

Five months later in Oslo on 10 December they together received the Nobel Prize for Peace. Mandela praised De Klerk's courage and foresight, and De Klerk congratulated Mandela on his great contribution to peace. Once again, as it had been for Albert Lutuli and Desmond Tutu, 'Nkosi Sikelel' iAfrika' was sung.

Back in South Africa it seemed that every lamp post carried election posters portraying De Klerk or Mandela or the Democratic Party candidate Tony Leon or – in *dorps* demanding an Afrikaner Volkstaat – General Constand Viljoen. Viljoen, after conciliatory discussions with Mandela and Thabo Mbeki, had broken from the far-right who themselves were becoming embarrassed by AWB bombings in Afrikaner strongholds.

---

* In *Reporting South Africa*.

Inkatha, under Chief Buthelezi, had long before withdrawn from CODESA.* The Zulu king Goodwill Zwelithini was increasingly brought into the dispute. Following a march of some ten thousand Zulus to the Union Buildings, he met President De Klerk who agreed that a joint working group should find ways to recognize and assure the positions of the monarchy and the kingdom.

The electioneering atmosphere of conflicting hopes and anxieties reached fever pitch. The imposition of a State of Emergency in Natal had only a limited effect on the killings there. Frightening rumours continued to spread that violence would put paid to the election, rumours which escalated when the AWB invaded 'independent' Bophuthatswana on 12 March to give backing to President Lucas Mangope's tyrannical regime. In the ensuing fracas they shot bystanders, provoking a local black policeman to execute three of them. Mobs, sensing the imminent downfall of Mangope, ran amok in a paroxysm of looting. The AWB retreated in disarray. Then, a demonstration in the centre of Johannesburg, organized by notorious Inkatha leaders, was attacked by anonymous snipers; Zulus who simultaneously marched on Shell House were fired at by ANC security guards – in both instances innocent bystanders again were among those killed.

Supermarkets profited from a wave of panic-buying and news programmes quoted scaremongering articles from Britain's Tory press: the *Sunday Times* forecast electoral chaos and the *Mail* announced that the British government was providing a fleet of planes to rescue its endangered citizens.

The violence in Natal diminished substantially after Chief Buthelezi, influenced among others by King Goodwill, agreed to take part in the election. And police rounded up AWB terrorists – though not before they had tragically killed twenty-one people in car-bombings.

---

* David Ottaway, correspondent for the *Washington Post*, details the background in *Chained Together*, Times Books, 1993.

Mandela campaigned from coast to coast for the ANC' addressing huge rallies as though, wrote Allister Sparks,* he was 'trying to make up for the wasted years' and seemed 'to revel in the action and the adulation as he waved to the crowds'. For their part, the humblest of supporters felt they could approach, even speak, to their leader who, as John Carlin,† writing of the impact the 'Mandela phenomenon' had on society, said, had given them 'new pride and dignity'.

Observers poured in from the United Nations, the Commonwealth, Europe and Africa. It became the most carefully watched election in history. Complaints of foul-ups in the process were soon forgotten. Mandela chose to vote in Inanda, once the home of the ANC's first president, Dr John Dube, lately in the heart of Natal's killings. Exactly thirty years and one week after he made his declaration to the court in the Rivonia trial, he repeated the historic words: 'I have fought against white domination and I have fought against black domination. I have cherished the ideal of a democratic and free society in which all persons live together in harmony and with equal opportunities. It is an ideal which I hope to live for and to achieve but, if need be, it is an ideal for which I am prepared to die.'

'Together in harmony' was how black and white eagerly lined up to vote on 27 April, sometimes standing throughout the day and on into subsequent days. Queues, one four miles long, snaked through townships, rural areas and posh white suburbs. Abroad, as well, South African citizens voted in this first democratic election. The mood was magical. Whites as well as blacks felt an extraordinary, deeply moving sense of personal liberation – as if a burden of guilt had suddenly lifted. Many blacks agreed with the woman who, asked if she was not exhausted after standing for eight hours, remarked, 'I've been waiting for forty-six years. I don't mind waiting a little longer.' For Elias Motsoaledi, the modest man of the people who, with his wife Caroline,

* *New Yorker*, 11 April 1994.
† *Independent on Sunday*, 10 April 1994.

241

had suffered greatly during the Rivonia trial, it was a last act before his death, a few days later, from cancer. Albert Lutuli's wife Nokukhanya, aged ninety, beamed as she recognized Mandela's picture on the voting form and drew her X beside it. Men and women wept. To queue together and chat with total strangers who shared in the joy was a delight.

On Monday 2 May 1994 F.W. de Klerk conceded victory to Nelson Mandela and the ANC. 'After so many centuries,' he said, 'we will finally have a government which represents all South Africans.' He praised Mandela for playing 'a leading and honourable' role during the past four years.

At a victory celebration in Johannesburg Mandela thanked those who had worked so hard and the hundreds of thousands who had patiently queued. 'South Africa's heroes are legend across the generations. But,' he emphasized, 'it is you, the people, who are our true heroes . . . I stand before you humbled, with a heart full of love.' He paid tribute to Oliver Tambo who had died shortly after Chris Hani's death, and to Hani himself, as well as others from the past. He went on to commend the security forces for 'sterling work'. A band was playing township music and, smilingly moving to the rhythm, Mandela urged South Africans 'to join together to celebrate the birth of democracy'.

At a minute after midnight on 4 May crowds in the nine new provincial capitals did just that, cheering the raising of the new flag which boldly combined the ANC colours of black for the people, green for the land and yellow for the gold, with red, white and blue. The homelands were no more; South Africa was one country.

Parliament had once consisted almost entirely of dour, ageing dark-suited white men, and Nationalist governments resembled a herd of bulls challenged by the tough and witty Helen Suzman, waving a red cape of devastating truths. For years Mrs Suzman was the sole woman MP but now, at the swearing in of MPs, the assembly was transformed, not only by the preponderance of black faces but by the presence of 106 women in a striking assortment of garments and colours – from gorgeous saris and exotic tribal attire to outfits straight from *Dynasty*. Under the negotiated settlement parliament represented 'national unity' and all parties unanimously supported Frene Ginwala, who had been among the ANC's ablest representatives abroad, as Speaker. Tambo's widow, Adelaide, and three of the Sisulus were sworn in: Albertina, her son Max and daughter Lindiwe. The ceremony reached its climax when Albertina rose to propose Nelson Rolihlahla Mandela as President. Cyril Ramaphosa seconded the proposal.

Mandela was intent on reconciliation. With Angola, Rwanda, Bosnia and Northern Ireland in continual horrifying conflict, and with a determination to heal the wounds of South Africa's past, he often referred to the need for forgiveness and was generous in offers of amnesty. But what of the families of those who had been murdered by members of the security forces? Would the promise of a Truth Commission at last bring justice?

Mandela's cabinet united ANC with previously hostile forces. He wanted to empower ordinary people yet soothe the fears of elements such as civil servants and the security forces, and, of course, the business community. The ANC must fulfil its electoral promises to provide houses, education and jobs and, most urgently, electricity, running water and flush toilets for those millions who lived in shacks. And then there was also the daunting problem of escalating crime.

Overall, Mandela's cabinet choices were praised: Mbeki and De Klerk, the Deputy-Presidents, Steve Tshwete Minister for Sport, Joe Slovo for Housing, and the retention of the previous government's Minister of Finance, Derek Keys. Kobie Coetsee was elected President of the Senate. But, for a 'new' South Africa, Mandela was disconcertingly loyal to old-timers. However, from the former UDF came impressive younger men to head provincial parliaments. And no doubt Cyril Ramaphosa, disappointed in his aspiration to become a Deputy-President, would again play a significant role. 'Reconciliation' meant Chief

Buthelezi as Minister of Home Affairs and, in parliament, unconvicted Inkatha warlords.

Winnie Mandela, Deputy Minister of Science, Technology, Arts and Culture, and Bantu Holomisa, former president of the Transkei, now Deputy Minister for the Environment, were not sworn in with their colleagues but appeared together for the ceremony and before the media. It was a formidable alliance for Winnie who, apart from retaining the loyalty of many in the Women's and Youth Leagues, was winning support among squatter communities neglected by the ANC.

In preparation for the presidential inauguration members of Mandela's family were invited to sit on the podium. Evelyn, his first wife, would not be there. (She, alone and dignified, was running a small shop in Cofimvaba.) Nor would Makgatho, busy with law exams in Durban, but his sons would be present, along with Thembi's daughters. Makaziwe, Mandela's eldest, independent-minded and distinguished daughter – recently appointed head of Affirmative Action at Wits University – would be accompanied by her husband, Isaac Amuah, a physicist. As his escort Mandela chose Zenani, who had returned to Johannesburg with Prince Thumbumuzi, now a banker. And Zindzi would be there with her husband, a young businessman, Zweli Tshongane, and with her mother, Winnie.

At Zindzi's wedding in 1992 Mandela had frankly and movingly reflected on his failures as a family man – failures which have been likened to those of Winston Churchill. He spoke of children growing up without his guidance and, when he did come out of prison, children who said: 'We thought we had a father and one day he'd come back. But, to our dismay, our father came back and he leaves us alone almost daily because he has now become the father of the nation.' His own frugal lifestyle – apart from that delight in elegant suits – did not influence his daughter's wedding which displayed the extravagant vulgarity of certain members of the ANC befriended by tycoons, among them the creator of gambling resorts throughout the former Bantustans, Sol Kerzner. Mandela himself, concerned about the threat of creeping corruption, was to be an unwilling and lonely occupant of vast presidential edifices.

As leaders from all parts of the globe arrived in Pretoria, Mandela was able to bring President Weizmann of Israel together with Yasser Arafat, but did not realize his hope that Hillary Clinton would talk to Fidel Castro.

Tuesday, 10 May 1994: a hot autumn day in Pretoria. In celebratory mood were the crowd of foreign dignitaries from 182 delegations, local parliamentarians and guests in the amphi-theatre of the Union Buildings, and the swarms of people on the vast lawn below. A bemused world watched on television: when before had such a happy event monopolized the media? For two hours all waited, entertained by choirs and the band of the South African Navy. This time, how familiar was the sight of the very tall, erect man who emerged from his bullet-proof car, how heart-warming the broad smile as, accompanied by Zenani, he approached the presidential podium to a roar of welcome from the crowds: 'Madiba' to old friends and staff waiting there, 'Tata' to children and grandchildren, 'Mr President' to the generals heading army, airforce, navy and the former Umkhonto.

First came the traditional praise singer with dramatic gestures emphasizing his guttural poetry, impressing and amusing Xhosa speakers, perplexing others. Then the new flag was slowly raised to the two national anthems: the Afrikaans 'Die Stem van Suid Afrika' (The Voice of South Africa) and the Xhosa 'Nkosi Sikelel' iAfrika' (God Bless Africa), fortunately accompanied by choirs as few in the crowd could sing in the other's language. ('We must make it a habit to sing both,' Mandela was to insist to football fans later that day.)

Chief Justice Michael Corbett swore in the first deputy-president, Thabo Mbeki, and next the second, Frederik Willem de Klerk. Then Mandela himself 'solemnly and sincerely' prom-ised to devote himself to the 'well-being of the Republic of South Africa and all its people'.

Nelson Rolihlahla Mandela, President of South Africa. When

the Chief Rabbi read from Isaiah, God's words could have been addressed to him and his people who had endured long years of hardship: 'For a small moment have I forsaken thee . . .' But now there was a promise: 'With everlasting kindness will I have compassion on thee . . . violence shall no more be heard in the land . . . justice shall make its home even in the wilderness . . . cities will live at peace. Happy shalt thou be.'

Mandela listened intently. There was a Hindu prayer for peace, a Muslim reading from the Koran and Archbishop Tutu added: 'Before our eyes we see a miracle unfolding . . .' His prayer of gratitude was spoken in Afrikaans, Sotho, Xhosa and English before he concluded, 'Let this land be one of laughter and joy.'

A host of white doves wheeled and swooped to rise again and fly away as Mandela began to speak: 'Out of the experience of an extraordinary human disaster that lasted too, too long, must be born a society of which all humanity will be proud.' Generals from the armed forces stood immediately behind him as he spoke of the pain of seeing 'our country tear itself apart in a terrible conflict . . . outlawed and isolated by the peoples of the world', because it had become 'the universal base of the pernicious ideology and practice of racism and racial oppression'.

Applause from the international guests greeted his expression of South Africa's gratitude at being given 'the rare privilege to be host to the nations of the world on our own soil'. 'Stand by us,' he appealed and entered into a covenant with the people. Looking around, he declared: 'Let there be justice for all. Let there be peace for all. Let there be work, bread, water and salt for all.'

The national anthems again were sung and, to a 21-gun salute, planes in precisely orchestrated formations roared towards the Union Buildings, once the symbol of Boer uniting with Briton, now of black with white. Trainers, spotters, and strike aircraft were followed by Impalas of the Silver Falcon unit which spewed smoke trails of red, white, green, gold, black and blue high above wildly cheering, ululating and waving crowds, stirred to tears at this spectacular sign of transformation by planes which had bombed targets in Angola and Namibia, tears which turned to laughter at Puma helicopters flying the National flag in a final witty gesture.

'Never, never and never again shall it be that this beautiful land will again experience the oppression of one by another,' Mandela concluded his speech. As he did so, a greatly moved Walter Sisulu reached out to take his hand. Sisulu, now honourably retired, had first influenced Mandela and Tambo to join the ANC. Fifty years ago they had led the Youth League and it was thirty years since they had been imprisoned and exiled, a unique trio of comrades who had never deviated in their loyalty to each other and to the cause.

Nelson Mandela fulfilled the promise made to the people on his release from prison: 'I place the remaining years of my life in your hands.'

Index

Note: Nelson Mandela is referred to as NM, Winnie Mandela as WM.

Visit Penguin on the Internet
and browse at your leisure

- ◆ preview sample extracts of our forthcoming books
- ◆ read about your favourite authors
- ◆ investigate over 10,000 titles
- ◆ enter one of our literary quizzes
- ◆ win some fantastic prizes in our competitions
- ◆ e-mail us with your comments and book reviews
- ◆ instantly order any Penguin book

and masses more!

'To be recommended without reservation ... a rich and rewarding on-line experience' – Internet Magazine

www.penguin.co.uk

READ MORE IN PENGUIN

In every corner of the world, on every subject under the sun, Penguin represents quality and variety – the very best in publishing today.

For complete information about books available from Penguin – including Puffins, Penguin Classics and Arkana – and how to order them, write to us at the appropriate address below. Please note that for copyright reasons the selection of books varies from country to country.

In the United Kingdom: Please write to *Dept. EP, Penguin Books Ltd, Bath Road, Harmondsworth, West Drayton, Middlesex UB7 0DA*

In the United States: Please write to *Consumer Sales, Penguin USA, P.O. Box 999, Dept. 17109, Bergenfield, New Jersey 07621-0120*. VISA and MasterCard holders call 1-800-253-6476 to order Penguin titles

In Canada: Please write to *Penguin Books Canada Ltd, 10 Alcorn Avenue, Suite 300, Toronto, Ontario M4V 3B2*

In Australia: Please write to *Penguin Books Australia Ltd, P.O. Box 257, Ringwood, Victoria 3134*

In New Zealand: Please write to *Penguin Books (NZ) Ltd, Private Bag 102902, North Shore Mail Centre, Auckland 10*

In India: Please write to *Penguin Books India Pvt Ltd, 706 Eros Apartments, 56 Nehru Place, New Delhi 110 019*

In the Netherlands: Please write to *Penguin Books Netherlands bv, Postbus 3507, NL-1001 AH Amsterdam*

In Germany: Please write to *Penguin Books Deutschland GmbH, Metzlerstrasse 26, 60594 Frankfurt am Main*

In Spain: Please write to *Penguin Books S. A., Bravo Murillo 19, 1° B, 28015 Madrid*

In Italy: Please write to *Penguin Italia s.r.l., Via Felice Casati 20, I–20124 Milano*

In France: Please write to *Penguin France S. A., 17 rue Lejeune, F–31000 Toulouse*

In Japan: Please write to *Penguin Books Japan, Ishikiribashi Building, 2–5–4, Suido, Bunkyo-ku, Tokyo 112*

In South Africa: Please write to *Longman Penguin Southern Africa (Pty) Ltd, Private Bag X08, Bertsham 2013*

READ MORE IN PENGUIN

A CHOICE OF NON-FICTION

Citizens Simon Schama

'The most marvellous book I have read about the French Revolution in the last fifty years' – *The Times*. 'He has chronicled the vicissitudes of that world with matchless understanding, wisdom, pity and truth, in the pages of this huge and marvellous book' – *Sunday Times*

Heisenberg's War Thomas Powers

'Heisenberg was one of the few distinguished German scientists who, rather than accepting the chance to emigrate to the US, elected to stay and work for Hitler. How concertedly he helped the Nazi war effort is the subject of Thomas Powers's brilliantly researched and compellingly narrated *Heisenberg's War'* – *Independent on Sunday*

A Short Walk from Harrods Dirk Bogarde

In this volume of memoirs, Dirk Bogarde pays tribute to the corner of Provence that was his home for over two decades, and to Forwood, his manager and friend of fifty years, whose long and wretched illness brought an end to a paradise. 'A brave and moving book' – *Daily Telegraph*

Murder in the Heart Alexandra Artley
Winner of the CWA Gold Dagger Award for Non-Fiction

'A terrible and moving account of domestic violence leading to murder . . . a profound indictment of the world we live in' – Beryl Bainbridge. 'A grim account of human savagery, but it enlightens as much as it horrifies' – *The Times Literary Supplement*

Water Logic Edward de Bono

Edward de Bono has always sought to provide practical thinking tools that are simple to use but powerful in action. In this book he turns his attention to providing a simple way of thinking about practical problems based on a visual 'flowscape'.

READ MORE IN PENGUIN

A CHOICE OF NON-FICTION

Bernard Shaw Michael Holroyd
Volume 3 1918–1950 The Lure of Fantasy

'An achievement of the highest order that no one interested in the dramatic, social and cultural history of the time can afford to neglect' – *Financial Times*

In the Fascist Bathroom Greil Marcus

'More than seventy short pieces on "punk", its fall-out and its falling-outs. They are mostly brilliant . . . much of this book is hate as love, spite as well as delight. But when the professor does fall in love . . . he is a joy to behold' – *Sunday Times*

Visiting Mrs Nabokov Martin Amis

'From the wahooing triumphalism of the 1988 Republican Convention to darting drama in a Bishopsgate pub, from toplessness in Cannes to hopelessness in the snooker-room, Amis is a fantastically fluent decoder of the modern age . . . he is also one of its funniest' – *Independent*

Eating Children Jill Tweedie

'Jill Tweedie re-creates in fascinating detail the scenes and conditions that shaped her, scarred her, broke her up or put her back together . . . a remarkable story' – Glyn Maxwell in *Vogue*. 'A beautiful and courageous book' – Maya Angelou

Journey into Cyprus Colin Thubron

This is the account of a unique journey – a six-hundred-mile trek on foot around Cyprus in the last year of the island's peace. 'Purchased by blistered and bleeding feet, this picture is extraordinarily detailed and vivid . . . An accomplished linguist and historian, his passionate concern for antiquity in all its aspects lends weight and warmth to every chapter' – *Financial Times*

READ MORE IN PENGUIN

A CHOICE OF NON-FICTION

My Secret Planet   Denis Healey

'This is an anthology of the prose and poetry that has provided pleasure and inspiration to Denis Healey throughout his life ... pleasurable on account of the literature selected and also for the insight it provides of Denis Healey outside the world of politics ... a thoroughly good read' – *The Times*

The Sun King   Nancy Mitford

Nancy Mitford's magnificent biography of Louis XIV is also an illuminating examination of France in the late seventeenth and early eighteenth centuries. It covers the intrigues of the court and the love affairs of the king, with extensive illustrations, many in full colour.

This Time Next Week   Leslie Thomas

'Mr Thomas's book is all humanity, to which is added a Welshman's mastery of words ... Some of his episodes are hilarious, some unbearably touching, but everyone, staff and children, is looked upon with compassion' – *Observer*. 'Admirably written, with clarity, realism, poignancy and humour' – *Daily Telegraph*

Against the Stranger   Janine di Giovanni

'In her powerfully written book Janine di Giovanni evokes the atmosphere of the Palestinian refugee camps in the Gaza Strip ... The effect of the Palestinians' sufferings on the next generation of children is powerfully documented' – *Sunday Express*

Native Stranger   Eddy L. Harris

Native Stranger is a startling chronicle of the author's search for himself in Africa, the land of his ancestors. 'Since Richard Wright's *Black Power*, there has been a dearth of travel narratives on Africa by black Americans. *Native Stranger* picks up where Wright left off, and does so with both courage and honesty' – Caryl Phillips in the *Washington Post*